CW00688853

THE LIFE OF JESUS OF NAZARETH, A STUDY

THE LIFE OF JESUS OF NAZARETH, A STUDY

Rhees, Rush

www.General-Books.net

Publication Data:

Title: The Life of Jesus of Nazareth, a Study
Author: Rhees, Rush
Publisher: London, Smith
Publication date: 1906
Subjects: Jesus Christ

How We Made This Book for You
We made this book exclusively for you using patented Print on Demand technology.
First we scanned the original rare book using a robot which automatically flipped and photographed each page.
We automated the typing, proof reading and design of this book using Optical Character Recognition (OCR) software on the scanned copy. That let us keep your cost as low as possible.
If a book is very old, worn and the type is faded, this can result in typos or missing text. This is also why our books don't have illustrations; the OCR software can't distinguish between an illustration and a smudge.
We understand how annoying typos, missing text or illustrations or an index that doesn't work, can be. That's why we provide a free digital copy of most books exactly as they were originally published. Simply go to our website (www.general-books.net) to check availability. And we provide a free trial membership in our book club so you can get free copies of other editions or related books.
OCR is not a perfect solution but we feel it's more important to make books available for a low price than not at all. So we warn readers on our website and in the descriptions we provide to book sellers that our books don't have illustrations and may have typos or missing text. We also provide excerpts from each book to book sellers and on our website so you can preview the quality of the book before buying it.
If you would prefer that we manually type, proof read and design your book so that it's perfect, we are happy to do that. Simply contact us for the cost.

Limit of Liability/Disclaimer of Warranty:
The publisher and author make no representations or warranties with respect to the accuracy or completeness of the book. The advice and strategies in the book may not be suitable for your situation. You should consult with a professional where appropriate. The publisher is not liable for any damages resulting from the book.
Please keep in mind that the book was written long ago; the information is not current. Furthermore, there may be typos, missing text or illustration and explained above.

THE LIFE OF JESUS OF NAZARETH, A STUDY

C. W. Mcc.

IN RECOGNITION OP WISE COUNSEL, GENEROUS HELP AND LOVING APPRECIATION

"I would preach. the need to the world of the faith in a Christ, the claim that Jesus is the Christ, and the demand for an intelligent faith, which indeed shall transcend but shall not despise knowledge, or neglect to have a knowledge to transcend." â JOHN PATTBBSON COYLB

PEEFACE

THE aim of this book is to help thoughtful readers of the gospels to discern more clearly the features of him whom those writings inimitably portray. It is avowedly a study rather than a story, and as a companion to the reading of the gospels it seeks to answer some of the questions which are raised by a sympathetic consideration of those narratives. These answers are offered in an un argumentative way, even where the questions are still in debate among scholars. This method has been adopted because technical discussion would be of interest to but few of those whom the book hopes to serve. On some of the questions a non-committal attitude is taken in the belief that for the understanding of the life of Jesus it is of little importance which way the decision finally goes. Less attention has been given to questions of geography and archaeology than to those which have a more vital biographical significance.

A word concerning the point of view adopted. The church has inherited a rich treasure of doctrine concerning its Lord, the result of patient study and, frequently, of heated controversy. It is customary to approach the gospels with this interpretation of Christ as a premise, and such a study has some mvie tionable advantages.

With the apostles and evangelists, however, the recognition of the divine nature of Jesus was a conclusion from their acquaintance with him. The Man of Nazareth was for them primarily a man, and they so regarded him until he showed them that he was more. Their knowledge of him progressed in the natural way from the human to the divine. The gospels, particularly the first three, are marvels of simplicity and objectivity. Their authors clearly regarded Jesus as the Man from heaven; yet in their thinking they were dominated by the influence of a personal Lord rather than by the force of an accepted doctrine. It is with no lack of reverence for the importance and truth of the divinity of Christ that this book essays to bring the Man Jesus before the mind in the reading of the gospels. The incarnation means that God chose to reveal the divine through a human life, rather than through a series of propositions which formulate truth (Heb. i. 1-4). The most perennially refreshing influence for Christian life and thought is personal discipleship to that Eevealer who is able today as of old to exhibit in his humanity those qualities which compel the recognition of God manifest in the flesh.

An Appendix is added to furnish references to the wide literature of the subject for the aid of those who wish to study it more extensively and technically; also to discuss some questions of detail which could not be considered in the text. This appendix will indicate the extent of my indebtedness to others. I would acknowledge special obligation to Professor Ernest D. Burton, of the University of Chicago, for generous help and permission to use material found in his " Notes on the Life of Jesus;" to Professor Shailer Mathews, also of Chicago, for very valuable criticisms; to my colleague, Professor Charles Kufus Brown, for most serviceable assistance; and to the editors of this series for helpful suggestions and criticism during the making of the book. An unmeasured debt is due to another who has sat at my side during the writing of these pages, and has given constant inspiration, most discerning criticism, and practical aid.

THE NEWTON THEOLOGICAL INSTITUTION, April, 1900.

CONTENTS PART I

PREPARATORY

26-30. The synoptic problem. 31-32. The Johannine problem. 34. The two narrative sources. 35. Agrapha and Apocrypha.

xil CONTENTS

THE HARMONY OF THE GOSPELS SECTIONS 36-44. PAGES 38-44

SECTION 36. The value of four gospels. 37. Tatian's Diatessa-ron. 38. Agreement of the gospels concerning the chief events. 39. The principal problems. 40. Relation of Mark and John. 41, 42. Matthew and Luke. 43. Doublets. 44. The degree of certainty attainable.

THE CHRONOLOGY SECTIONS 45-57. PAGES 45-56

SECTIONS 45-48. The length of Jesus' public ministry. 49. Date of the first Passover. 50. Date of the crucifixion. 51-56. Date of the nativity. 57. Summary.

THE EABLY YEARS OF JESUS SECTIONS 58-71. PAGES 57-69

SECTION 58. Apocryphal stories. 59. Silence of the New Testament outside the gospels. 60-62. The miraculous birth. 63. The childhood of Jesus. 64. Home. 65. Religion, Education. 66. Growth. 67. Religious development. 68. The view from Nazareth. 69. The first visit to Jerusalem. 70-71. The carpenter of Nazareth.

JOHN THE BAPTIST SECTIONS 72-84. PAGES 70-81

SECTION 72. The gospel picture. 73. Notice by Josephus. 74. Characteristics of the prophet. 75-78. John's relation to the Essenes; the Pharisees; the Zealots; the Apocalyptists. 79. John and the Prophets. 80-82. Origin of his baptism. 83. His greatness. 84. His limitations and self-effacement.

CONTENTS XIII

THE MESSIANIC CALL SECTIONS 85-96. PAGES 82-91

SECTIONS 85, 86. John and Jesus. 87. The baptism of Jesus. 88, 89. The Messianic call. 90. The gift of the Spirit. 91-94. The temptation. 95. Source of the narrative. 96. The issue.

VIII

THE FIRST DISCIPLES SECTIONS 97-105. PAGES 92-97

SECTION 97. John at Bethany beyond Jordan. 98. The deputation from the priests. 99. John's first testimony. 100. The first disciples. 101. The early Messianic confessions. 102. The visit to Cana. 103. The miracles as disclosures of the character of Jesus. 104. Jesus and his mother. 105. Removal to Capernaum.

PAET II

THE MINISTRY

GENERAL SURVEY OF THE MINISTRY SECTIONS 106-112. PAGES 101-105

SECTION 106. The early Judean ministry. 107. Withdrawal to Galilee; a new beginning. 108. The ministry in Galilee a unit. 109. Best studied topically. 110. The last journey to Jerusalem. 111. The last week. 112. The resurrection and ascension.

THE EARLY JUDEAN MINISTRY SECTIONS 113-124. PAGES 106-114

Outline of events in the Early Judean ministry. SECTION 113. The opening ministry at Jerusalem. 114. The record incomplete. 115. The cleansing of the temple. 116. Relation to synoptic account. 117. Jesus' reply to the challenge of his authority. 118. The reserve of Jesus. 119. Discourse with Nicodemus. 120. Measure of success in Jerusalem. 121. The Baptist's last testimony. 122. The arrest of John. 123. The second sign at Cana. 124. Summary.

1. WHEN Tacitus, the Roman historian, records the attempt of Nero to charge the Christians with the burning of Rome, he has patience for no more than the cursory remark that the sect originated with a Jew who had been put to death in Judea during the reign of Tiberius. This province was small and despised, and Tacitus could account for the influence of the sect which sprang thence only by the fact that all that was infamous and abominable flowed into Rome. The Roman's scornful judgment failed to grasp the nature and power of the movement whose unpopularity invited Nero's lying accusation, yet it emphasizes the significance of him who did " not strive, nor cry, nor cause his voice to be heard in the street," whose influence, nevertheless, was working as leaven throughout the empire.

2. Palestine was not under immediate Roman rule when Jesus was born. Herod the Great was drawing near the close of the long reign during which, owing to his skill in securing Roman favor, he had tyrannized over his unwilling people. His claim was that of an adventurer who had power to succeed, even as his method had been that of a suspicious tyrant, who murdered right and left, lest one of the many with better right than he should rise to dispute with him his throne. When Herod died, his kingdom was

divided into three parts, and Rome asserted a fuller sovereignty, allowing none of his sons to take his royal title. Herod's successors ruled with a measure of independence, however, and followed many of their father's ways, though none of them had his ability. The best of them was Philip, who had the territory farthest from Jerusalem, and least related to Jewish life. He ruled over Iturea and Trachonitis, the country to the north and east of the Sea of Galilee, having his capital at Csesarea Philippi, a city built and named by him on the site of an older town near the sources of the Jordan. He also rebuilt the city of Bethsaida, at the point where the Jordan flows into the Sea of Galilee, calling it Julias, after the daughter of Augustus. Philip enters the story of the life of Jesus only as the ruler of these towns and the intervening region, and as husband of Salome, the daughter of Herodias. Living far from Jerusalem and the Jewish people, he abandoned even the show of Judaism which characterized his father, and lived as a frank heathen in his heathen capital.

3. The other two who inherited Herod's dominion were brothers, Archelaus and Antipas, sons of Mal-thace, one of Herod's many wives. Archelaus had been designated king by Herod, with Judea, Samaria, and Idumea as his kingdom; but the emperor allowed him only the territory, with the title ethnarch. Antipas was named a tetrarch by Herod, and his territory was Galilee and the land east of the Jordan to the southward of the Sea of Galilee, called Perea. Antipas was the Herod under whose sway Jesus lived in Galilee, and who executed John the Baptist. He was a man of pas- sionate temper, with the pride and love of luxury of his father. Having Jews to govern, he held, as his father had done, to a show of Judaism, though at heart he was as much of a pagan as Philip. He, too, loved building, and Tiberias on the Sea of Galilee was built by him for his capital. His unscrupulous tyranny and his gross disregard of common righteousness appear in his relations with John the Baptist and with Herodias, his paramour. Jesus described him well as " that fox " (Luke xiii. 32), for he was sly, and worked often by indirection. While his father had energy and ability which command a sort of admiration, Antipas was not only bad but weak.

4. Both Philip and Antipas reigned until after the death of Jesus, Philip dying in A. D. 34, and Antipas being deposed several years later, probably in 39. Archelaus had a much shorter rule, for he was deposed in A. D. 6, having been accused by the Jews of unbearable barbarity and tyranny, â a charge hi which Antipas and Philip joined. The territory of Archelaus was then made an imperial province of the second grade, ruled by a procurator appointed from among the Roman knights. In provinces under an imperial legate (propraetor) the procurator was an officer for the administration of the revenues; in provinces of the rank of Judea he was, however, the representative of the emperor in all the prerogatives of government, having command of the army, and being the final resort in legal procedure, as well as supervising the collection of the customs and taxes. Very little is known of the procurators appointed after the deposition of Archelaus, until Tiberius sent Pontius Pilate in A. D. 26. He held office until he was deposed in 36.

Josephus gives several examples of his wanton disre gard of Jewish prejudice, and of his extreme cruelty. His conduct at the trial of Jesus was remarkably gentle and judicial in comparison with other acts recorded of his government; yet the fear of trial at Rome, which finally induced him to give Jesus over to be crucified, was thoroughly characteristic; in fact, his downfall resulted from a complaint lodged against him by certain Samaritans whom he had cruelly punished for a Messianic uprising.

5. There were two sorts of Roman taxes in Judea: direct, which were collected by salaried officials; and customs, which were farmed out to the highest bidder. The direct taxes consisted of a land tax and a poll tax, in the collection of which the procurator made use of the local Jewish courts; the customs consisted of various duties assessed on exports, and they were gathered by representatives of men who had bought the right to collect these dues. The chiefs as well as their underlings are called publicans in our New Testament, although the name strictly applies only to the chiefs. These tax-gatherers, small and great, were everywhere despised and execrated, because, in addition to their subserviency to a hated government, they had a reputation, usually deserved, for all sorts of extortion. Because of this evil repute they were commonly drawn from the unscrupulous among the people, so that the frequent coupling of publicans and sinners in the gospels probably rested on fact as much as on prejudice.

6. In Samaria and Judea soldiers were under the command of the procurator; they took orders from the tetrarch, in Galilee and Perea. The garrison of Jeru- salem consisted of one Roman cohort â from five to six hundred men â which was reinforced at the time of the principal feasts. These and the other forces at the disposal of the procurator were probably recruited from the country itself, largely from among the Samaritans, The centurion of Capernaum (Matt. viii. 5; Luke vii. 2-5) was an officer in the army of Antipas, who, however, doubtless organized his army on the Roman pattern, with officers who had had their training with the imperial forces.

7. The administration of justice in Samaria and Judea was theoretically in the hands of the procurator; practically, however, it was left with the Jewish courts, either the local councils or the great sanhedrin at Jerusalem. This last body consisted of seventy-one " elders." Its president was the high-priest, and its members were drawn in large degree from the most prominent representatives of the priestly aristocracy. The scribes, however, had a controlling influence because of the reverence in which the mul" titude held them. The sanhedrin of Jerusalem had jurisdiction only within the province of Judea, where it tried all kinds of offences; its judgment was final, except in capital cases, when it had to yield to the procurator, who alone could sentence to death. It had great influence also in Galilee, and among Jews everywhere, but this was due to the regard all Jews had for the holy city. It was, in fact, a sort of Jewish senate, which took cognizance of everything that seemed to affect the Jewish interests. In Galilee and Perea, Antipas held in his hands the judicial as well as the military and financial administration.

8. To the majority of the priests religion had become chiefly a form. They represented the worldly party among the Jews. Since the days of the priest-princes who ruled in Jerusalem after the return from the exile, they had constituted the Jewish aristocracy, and held most of the wealth of the people. It was to their interest to maintain the ritual and the traditional customs, and they were proud of their Jewish heritage; of genuine interest in religion, however, they had little. This secular priestly party was called the Sadducees, probably from Zadok, the high-priest in Solomon's time. What theology the Sadducees had was for the most part reactionary and negative. They were opposed to the more earnest spirit and new thought of the scribes, and naturally

produced some champions who argued for their theological position; but the mass of them cared for other things.

9. The leaders of the popular thought, on the other hand, were chiefly noted for their religious zeal and theological acumen. They represented the outgrowth of that spirit which in the Maccabean time had risked all to defend the sanctity of the temple and the right of God's people to worship him according to his law. They were known as Pharisees, because, as the name (" separated ") indicates, they insisted on the separation of the people of God from all the defilements and snares of the heathen life round about them. The Pharisees constituted a fraternity devoted to the scrupulous observance of law and tradition in all the concerns of daily life. They were specialists in religion, and were the ideal representatives of Judaism. Their distinguishing characteristic was reverence for the law: their religion was the religion of a book. By punctilious obedience of the law man might hope to gain a record of merit which should stand to his credit and secure his reward when God should finally judge the world. Because life furnished many situations not dealt with in the written law, there was need of its authoritative interpretation, in order that ignorance might not cause a man to transgress. These interpretations constituted an oral law which practically superseded the written code, and they were handed down from generation to generation as " the traditions of the fathers." The existence of this oral law made necessary a company of scribes and lawyers whose business it was to know the traditions and transmit them to their pupils. These scribes were the teachers of Israel, the leaders of the Pharisees, and the most highly revered class in the community. Pharisaism at its beginning was intensely earnest, but in the time of Jesus the earnest spirit had died out in zealous formalism. This was the inevitable result of their virtual substitution of the written law for the living God. Their excessive reverence had banished God from practical relation to the daily life. They held that he had declared his will once for all in the law. His name was scrupulously revered, his worship was cultivated with minutest care, his judgment was anticipated with dread; but he himself, like an Oriental monarch, was kept far from common life in an isolation suitable to his awful holiness. By a natural consequence conscience gave place to scrupulous regard for tradition in the religion of the scribes. The chief question with them was not, Is this right? but, What say the elders? The soul's sensitiveness of response to God's will and God's truth was lost in a maze of traditions which awoke no spontaneous Amen in the moral nature, consequently there was frequent substitution of reputation for character. The Pharisees could make void the command, Honor thy father, by an ingenious application of the principle of dedication of property to God (Mark vii. 8-13), and thus under the guise of scrupulous regard for law discovered ways for legal disregard of law. Their theory of religion gave abundant room for a piety which made broad its phylacteries and lengthened its prayers, while neglecting judgment, mercy, and the love of God.

10. Yet the earnest and true development in Jewish thinking was found among the Pharisees. The early hope of Israel was almost exclusively national. In the later books of the Old Testament, in connection with an enlarged sense of the importance of the individual, the doctrine of a personal resurrection to share the blessings of the Messiah's kingdom began to appear. It had its clear development and definite adoption

as part of the faith of Judaism, however, under the influence of the Pharisees. Along with this increased emphasis on the worth of the individual came a large development of the doctrine of angels and spirits. Towards both of these doctrines the Sadducees took a reactionary position. Politically the Pharisees were theocratic in theory, but opportunists in practice, accommodating themselves to the existing state of things so long as the de facto government did not interfere with the religious life of the people. They looked for a kingdom in which God should be evidently the king of his people; but they believed that his sovereignty was to be realized through the law, hence their sole interest was in the obedi- ence of God's people to that law as interpreted by the traditions.

11. The theocratic spirit was more aggressive in a party which originated in the later years of Herod the Great, and found a reckless leader in Judas of Galilee, who started a revolt when the governor of Syria undertook to make a census of the Jews after the deposition of Archelaus. This party bore the name Cananeans or Zealots. They regarded with passionate resentment the subjection of God's people to a foreign power, and waited eagerly for an opportune time to take the sword and set up the kingdom of God; it was with them that the final war against Rome began. They were found in largest numbers in Galilee, where the scholasticism of the scribes was not so dominating an influence as in Judea. Dr. Edersheim has called them the nationalist party. In matters belonging strictly to the religious life they followed the Pharisees, only holding a more material conception of the hope of Israel.

12. Another development in Jewish religious life carried separatist doctrines to the extreme. Its representatives were called Essenes, though what the significance of the name was is no longer clear. Although they were allied with the Pharisees in doctrine, they show in some particulars the influence of Hellenistic Judaism. This is suggested not only by the attention which Philo and Josephus give to them, but also by certain of their views, which were very like the doctrines of the Pythagoreans. They carried the pharisaic demand for separateness to the extreme of asceticism. While they were found in nearly every town in Palestine, some of them even practising marriage, the largest group of them lived a celibate, monastic life near the shores of the Dead Sea. This community was recruited by the initiation of converts, who only after a novitiate of three years were admitted to full membership in the order. They were characterized by an extreme scrupulousness concerning ceremonial purity, their meals were regarded as sacrifices, and were prepared by members of the order, who were looked upon as priests, nor were any allowed to partake of the food until they had first bathed themselves. Their regular garments were all white, and were regarded as vestments for use at the sacrificial meals, â other clothing being assumed as they went out to their work. They were industrious agriculturists, their life was communistic, and they were renowned for their uprightness. They revered Moses as highly as did the scribes; yet they were opposed to animal sacrifices, and, although they sent gifts to the temple, were apparently excluded from its worship. Their kinship with the Pythagoreans appears in that they addressed an invocation to the sun at its rising, and conducted all their natural functions with scrupulous modesty, " that they might not offend the brightness of God " (Jos. Wars, ii. 8. 9). Their rejection of bloody sacrifices, and their view that the soul is imprisoned in the body and at death

is freed for a better life, besides many features of their life that are genuinely Jewish, such as their regard for ceremonial purity, also show similarity to the Pythagoreans. It has always been a matter of perplexity that these ascetics find no mention in the New Testament. They seem to have lived a life too much apart, and to have had little sympathy with the ideals of Jesus, or even of John the Baptist.

13. The common people followed the lead of the Pharisees, though afar off. They accepted the teaching concerning tradition, as well as that concerning the resurrection, conforming their lives to the prescriptions of the scribes more or less strictly, according as they were more or less ruled by religious considerations. It was in consequence of their hold on the people that the scribes in the sanhedrin were able often to dictate a policy to the Sadducean majority. Jesus voiced the popular opinion when he said that "the scribes sit in Moses' seat" (Matt, xxiii. 2). Their leaders despised " this multitude which knoweth not the law " (John vii. 49), yet delighted to legislate for them, binding heavy burdens and grievous to be borne. Many of the people were doubtless too intent on work and gain to be very regardful of the minutice of conduct as ordained by the scribes; many more were too simple-minded to follow the theories of the rabbis concerning the aloofness of God from the life of men. These last reverenced the scribes, followed their directions, in the main, for the conduct of life, yet lived in fellowship with God as their fathers had, trusting in his faithfulness, and hoping in his mercy. They are represented in the New Testament by such as Simeon and Anna, Zachariah and Elizabeth, Joseph and Mary, and the majority of those who heard and heeded John's call to repentance. They were Israel's remnant of pure and undefiled religion, and constituted what there was of good soil among the people for the reception of the seed sown by John's successor. They had no name, for they did not constitute a party; for convenience they may be called the Devout.

14. Two other classes among the people are mentioned in the gospels, â the Herodians and the Samaritans. The Herodians do not appear outside the New Testament, and seem to have been hardly more than a group of men in whom the secular spirit was dominant, who thought it best for their interests and for the people's to champion the claims of the Hero-dian family. They were probably more akin to the Pharisees than to the Sadducees, for the latter were hostile to the Herodian claims, from the first; yet in spirit they seem more like to the worldly aristocracy than to the pious scribes. The Samaritans lived in the land, a people despising and despised. Their territory separated Galilee from Judea, and they were a constant source of irritation to the Jews. The hatred was inherited from the days of Ezra, when the zealous Jews refused to allow any intercourse with the inhabitants of Samaria. These Samaritans were spurned as of impure blood and mixed religion (II. Kings xvii. 24-41). The severe attitude adopted towards them by Ezra and Nehemiah led to the building of a temple on Mount Gerizim, and the establishment of a worship which sought to rival that of Jerusalem in all particulars. Very little is known of the tenets of the Samaritans in the time of Jesus beyond their belief that Gerizim was the place which, according to the law, God chose for his temple, and that a Messiah should come to settle all questions of dispute (John iv. 25).

15. Although the religious life of the Jews centred ideally in the temple, it found its practical expression in the synagogue. This in itself is evidence of the relative

influence of priests and scribes. There was no confessed rivalry. The Pharisee was most insist- ent on the sanctity of the temple and the importance of its ritual. Yet with the growing sense of the religious significance of the individual as distinct from the nation, there arose of necessity a practical need for a system of worship possible for the great majority of the people, who could at best visit Jerusalem but once or twice a year. The synagogue seems to have been a development of the exile, when there was no temple and no sacrifice. It was the characteristic institution of Judaism as a religion of the law, furnishing in every place opportunity for prayer and study. The elders of each community seem ordinarily to have been in control of its synagogue, and to have had authority to exclude from its fellowship persons who had come under the ban. In addition to these officials there was a ruler of the synagogue, who had the direction of all that concerned the worship; a chazzan, or minister, who had the care of the sacred books, administered discipline, and instructed the children in reading the scripture; and two or more receivers of alms. The Sabbath services consisted of prayers, and reading of the scriptures â both law and prophets, â and an address or sermon. It was in the sermon that the people learned to know the "traditions of the elders," whether as applications of the law to the daily life, or as legendary embellishments of Hebrew history and prophecy. The preacher might be any one whom the ruler of the synagague recognized as worthy to address the congregation.

16. The religious life which centred in the synagogue found daily expression in the observance of the law and the traditions. In the measure of its control by the scribes it was, concerned chiefly with the Sab- bath, with the various ablutions needful to the maintenance of ceremonial purity, with the distinctions between clean and unclean food, with the times and ways of fasting, and with the wearing of fringes and phylacteries. These lifeless ceremonies seem to our day wearisome and petty in the extreme. It is probable, however, that the growth of the various traditions had been so gradual that, as has been aptly said, the whole usage seemed no more unreasonable to the Jews than the etiquette of polite society does to its devotees. The evil was not so much in the minuteness of the regulations as in the external and superficial notion of religion which they induced.

17. Optimism was the mood of Israel's prophets from the earliest times. Every generation looked for the dawning of a day which should banish all ill and realize the dreams inspired by the covenant in which God had chosen Israel for his own. In proportion as the rabbinic formalism held control of the hearts of the people, the Messianic hope lost its warmth and vigor. Yet the scribes did not abandon the prophetic optimism; they held to the letter of the hope, but as its fulfilment was for them dependent on perfect obedience to the law, oral and written, their interest was diverted to the traditions, and their strength was given to legal disputations. Of the rest of the people, the Sadducees naturally gave little thought to the promise of future deliverance, they were too absorbed with regard for present concerns. Nor is there any evidence that the Essenes, with all their reputed knowledge of the future, cherished the hope of a Messiah. The other elements among the people who owned the general leadership of the scribes looked eagerly for the coming time when God should bring to pass what he had promised through the prophets. While some expected God himself to come in judgment, and gave no thought to an Anointed one who should represent

the Most High to the people, the majority looked for a Son of David to sit upon his father's throne. Even so, however, there were wide differences in the nature of the hope which was set on the coming of this Son of David. The Zealots were looking for a victory, which should set Israel on high over all his foes. To the rest of the people, however, the method of the consummation was not so clear, and they were ready to leave God to work out his purpose in his own way, longing meanwhile for the fulfilment of his promise. One class in particular gave themselves to visionary representations of the promised redemption. They differed from the Zealots in that they saw with unwelcome clearness the futility of physical attack upon their enemies; but their faith was strong, and at the moment when outward conditions seemed most disheartening they looked for a revelation of God's power from heaven, destroying all sinners in his wrath, and delivering and comforting his people, giving them their lot in a veritable Canaan situated in a renewed earth. Such visions are recorded in the Book of Daniel and the Revelation of John. They are found in many other apocalypses not included in our Bible, and indicate how persistently the minds of the people turned towards the promises spoken by the prophets, and meditated on their fulfilment. The Devout were midway between the Zealots and the Apocalyptists. The songs of Zachariah and Mary and the thanksgiving of Simeon express their faith. They hoped for a kingdom as tangible as the Zealots sought, yet they preferred to wait for the consolation of Israel. They believed that God was still in his heaven, that he was not disregardful of his people, and that in his own time he would raise up unto them their king. They looked for a Son of David, yet his reign was to be as remarkable for its purification of his own people as for its victories over their foes. These victories indeed were to be largely spiritual, for their Messiah was to conquer in the strength of the Spirit of God and " by the word of his mouth." Such as these were ready for a ministry like John's, and not unready for the new ideal which Jesus was about to offer them, though their highest spiritualization of the Messianic hope was but a shadow of the reality which Jesus asked them to accept.

18. This last conception of the Messiah is found in a group of psalms written in the first century before Christ, during the early days of the Roman interference in Judea. These Psalms of Solomon, as they are called, are pharisaic in point of view, yet they are not rabbinic in their ideas. Their feeling is too deep, and their reliance on God too immediate; they fitly follow the psalms of the Old Testament, though afar off. Of another type of contemporary literature, Apocalypse, at least two representatives besides the Book of Daniel have come down to us from the time of Jesus or earlier, â the so-called Book of Enoch, and the fragment known as the Assumption of Moses. These writings have peculiar interest, because they are probably the source of quotations found in the Epistle of

Jude; moreover, some sayings of Jesus reported in the gospels, and in particular his chosen title, The Son of Man, are strikingly similar to expressions found in Enoch. Can Jesus have read these books? The psalms of the Devout were the kind of literature to pass rapidly from heart to heart, until all who sympathized with their hope and faith had heard or seen them. The case was different with the apocalypses. They are more elaborate and enigmatical, and may have been only slightly known. Yet, as Jesus was familiar with the canonical Book of Daniel, although it was not read in the synagogue service in his time, it is possible that he may also have read or heard other books which had not won recognition as canonical. If, however, he knew nothing of them, the similarity between the apocalypses and some of Jesus' ideas and expressions becomes all the more significant; for it shows that these writings gave utterance to thoughts and feelings shared by men who never read them, which were, therefore, no isolated fancies, but characteristic of the religion of many of the people. With these ideas Jesus was familiar; whether he ever read the books must remain a question.

19. This literature exists for us only in translations made in the days of the early church. Most of these books were originally written in Hebrew, the language of the Old Testament, or in Aramaic, the language of Palestine in the time of Jesus. Traces of this language as spoken by Jesus have been preserved in the gospels, â the name Rabbi; Abba, translated Father; Talitha cumi, addressed to the daughter of Jairus; Ephphctiha, to the deaf man of Bethsaida; and the cry from the cross, Eloi, Eloi, lama salachthani (John i. 38;. Mark xiv. 36; v. 41; vii. 34; xv. 34). It is altogether probable that in his common dealings with men and in his teachings Jesus used this language. Greek was the language of the government and of trade, and in a measure the Jews were a bilingual people. Jesus may thus have had some knowledge of Greek, but it is unlikely that he ever used it to any extent either in Galilee, or Judea, or in the regions of Tyre and Sidon.

SOURCES OF OUR KNOWLEDGE OF JESUS 20. THE earliest existing record of events in the life of Jesus is given to us in the epistles of Paul. His account of the appearances of the Lord after his death and resurrection (I. Cor. xv. 3-8) was written within thirty years of these events. The date of the testimony, however, is much earlier, since Paul refers to the experience which transformed his own life, and so carries us back to within a few years of the crucifixion. Other facts from Jesus' life may be gathered from Paul, as his descent from Abraham and David (Rom. i. 3; ix. 5); his life of obedience (Rom. v. 19; xv. 3; Phil. ii. 5-11); his poverty (II. Cor. viii. 9); his meekness and gentleness (II. Cor. x. 1); other New Testament writings outside of our gospels add somewhat to this restricted but very clear testimony.

21. Secular history knows little of the obscure Galilean. The testimony of Tacitus is that the Christians " derived their name and origin from one Christ, who in the reign of Tiberius had suffered death by the sentence of the procurator, Pontius Pilate " (Annals, xv. 44). Suetonius makes an obscure and seemingly ill-informed allusion to Christ in the reason he assigns for the edict of Claudius expelling the Jews from Rome (Vit. Claud. 25). The younger Pliny in the second century had learned that the numerous Christian community in Bithynia was accustomed to honor Christ as God; but he shows no knowledge of the life of Jesus beyond what must be inferred concerning one who caused men "to bind themselves with an oath not to enter into any wickedness, or commit thefts, robberies, or adulteries, or falsify their word, or repudiate trusts committed to them " (Epistles x. 96). This secular ignorance is not surprising; but the silence of Josephus is. He mentions Jesus in but one clearly genuine passage, when telling of the martyrdom of James, the "brother of Jesus, who is called the Christ" (Ant. xx. 9. 1). Of John the Baptist, however, he has a very appreciative notice (Ant. xviii. 5. 2), and it cannot be that he was ignorant of Jesus. His appreciation of John suggests that he could not have mentioned Jesus more fully

without some approval of his life and teaching. This would be a condemnation of his own people, whom he desired to commend to Gentile regard; and he seems to have taken the cowardly course of silence concerning a matter more noteworthy, even for that generation, than much else of which he writes very fully.

22. The reason for the lack of written Christian records of Jesus' life from the earliest time seems to be, not that the apostles had a small sense of the importance of his earthly ministry, but that the early generation preferred what at a later time was called the " living voice " (Papias in Euseb. Ch. Hist. iii. 39). The impression made by Jesus was supremely personal; he wrote nothing, did not command his disciples to write anything, preferring to influence men's minds by personal power, appointing them, in turn, to represent him to men as he had represented the Father to them (John xx. 21). But the time came when the first witnesses were passing away, and they were not many who could say, "I saw him." Our gospels are the result of the natural desire to preserve the apostolic testimony for a generation that could no longer hear the apostolic voice; and they are precisely what such a sense of need would produce, â vivid pictures of Jesus, agreeing in general features, differing more or less in details, reflecting individual feeling for the Master, and written not simply to inform men but to convince them of that Master's claims. One evidence of the reality of the gospel pictures is the fact that we so seldom feel the individual characteristics of each gospel. This is especially true of the first three, which, to the vividness of their picture, add a remarkable similarity of detail. Tatian, in the second century, felt it necessary to make a continuous narrative for the use of the church by interweaving the four gospels into one, and he has had many successors down to our day; but the fact that unity of impression has practically resulted from the four pictures without recourse to such an interweaving, invites consideration of the characteristics of these remarkable documents.

23. The first gospel impresses the careful reader with three things: (1) A clear sense of the development of Jesus' ministry. The author introduces his narrative by an account of the birth of Jesus, of the ministry of John the Baptist, and of Jesus' baptism and temptation and withdrawal into Galilee (i. 1 to iv. 17). He then depicts the public ministry by grouping together, first, teachings of Jesus concerning the law of the kingdom of heaven, then a series of great miracles confirming the new doctrine, then the expansion of the ministry and deepening hostility of the Pharisees, leading to the teaching by parables, and the final withdrawal from Galilee to the north. This ministry resulted in the chilling of popular enthusiasm which had been strong at the beginning, but in the winning of a few hearts to Jesus' own ideals of the kingdom of God (iv. 18 to xvi. 20). From this point the evangelist leads us to Jerusalem, where rejection culminates, the sterner teachings of Jesus are massed, and his victory in seeming defeat is exhibited (xvi. 21 to xxviii. 20). (2) The evangelist's interest is not satisfied by this clear, strong, picture; he wishes to convince men that Jesus is Israel's Messiah, hence, throughout, he indicates the fulfilment of prophecy. The things in which he sees the fulfilment are striking, for, with but one or two exceptions, they are features of the life of Jesus objectionable to Jewish feeling. This fact, taken in connection with the emphasis which the gospel gives to the death of Jesus at the hands of the Jews, and to the resurrection as God's seal of approval of him whom his people

rejected, forms a forcible argument to prove the Messiahship of Jesus, not simply in spite of his rejection by the Jews, but by appeal to that rejection as leading to God's signal vindication of the crucified one. (3) This evangelist, while proving that Jesus is the Messiah promised to Israel, recognizes clearly the freedom of the new faith from the exclusiveness of Jewish feeling. The choice of Galilee for the Messianic ministry (iv. 12-17), the comment of Jesus on the faith of the centurion (viii. 10-12), the rebuke of Israel in the parable of the Wicked Husbandmen (xxi. 33-46), and especially the last commission of the risen Lord (xxviii. 18-20), show that this gospel sought to convince men of Jewish feeling not only that Jesus is Messiah, but also that as Messiah he came to bring salvation to all the world.

24. The second gospel is much simpler in construction than the first, while presenting essentially the same picture of the ministry as is found in Matthew. To its simplicity it adds a vividness of narration which commends Mark's account as probably representing most nearly the actual course of the life of Jesus. While it reports fewer incidents and teachings than either of the others, a comparison with Matthew and Luke shows a preference in Mark for Jesus' deeds, though addresses are not wanting; and, while shorter as a whole, for matters which he reports Mark's record is most rich in detail, most dramatic in presentation, and actually longer than the parallel accounts in the other gospels. The whole narrative is animated in style (note the oft-repeated "immediately") and full of graphic traits. The story of Jesus seems to be reproduced from a memory which retains fresh personal impressions of events as they occurred. Hence the frequent comments on the effect of Jesus' ministry, such as " We never saw it on this fashion " (ii. 12), or "He hath done all things well" (vii. 37), and the introduction into the narrative of Aramaic words, â Boanerges (iii. 17), Talitha cumi (v. 41), and the like, which immediately have to be translated. The gospel discloses no artificial plan, the chief word of transition is "and." While some of the incidents recorded, such as the second Sabbath controversy (iii. 1-6) and the question about fasting (ii. 18-22), may owe their place to association in memory with an event of like character, the book impresses us as a collection of annals fresh from the living memory, which present the actual Jesus teaching and healing, and going on his way to the cross and resurrection. After the briefest possible reference to the ministry of John the Baptist and the baptism and temptation of Jesus (i. 1-13), this gospel proceeds to set forth the ministry in Galilee (i. 14 to ix. 50). The narrative then follows Jesus to Jerusalem, by way of Perea, and closes with his victory through death and resurrection (x. 1 to xvi. 8).

25. The third gospel is more nearly a biography than any of its companions. It opens with a preface stating that after a study of many earlier attempts to record the life of Jesus the author has undertaken to present as complete an account as possible of that life from the beginning. The book is addressed to one Theophilus, doubtless a Greek Christian, and its chief aim is practical, â to confirm conviction concerning matters of faith (i. 1-4). The author's interest in the completeness of his account appears in the fact that it begins with incidents antecedent to the birth of John the Baptist and Jesus. Moreover, to his desire for completeness we owe much of the story of Jesus, otherwise unrecorded for us. Like the first two gospels, Luke represents the ministry of Jesus as inaugurated in Galilee, and carried on there until the approach

of the tragedy at Jerusalem (iv. 14 to ix. 50). It is in connection with the journey to Jerusalem (ix. 51 to xix. 27) that he inserts most of that which is peculiar to his gospel. His account of the rejection at Jeru- salem, the crucifixion, and resurrection, follows in the main the same lines as Matthew and Mark; but he gained his knowledge of many particulars from different sources (xix. 28 to xxiv. 53). It is characteristic of Luke to name Jesus "Lord" more often than either of his predecessors. With this exalted conception is coupled a noticeable emphasis on Jesus' ministry of compassion; here more than in any other gospel he is pictured as the friend of sinners. Moreover, we owe chiefly to Luke our knowledge of him as a man of prayer and as subject to repeated temptation. An artificial exaltation of Christ, such as is often attributed to the later apostolic thought, would tend to reduce, not multiply, such evidences of human dependence on God. This fact increases our confidence in the accuracy of Luke's picture. The gospel is very full of comfort to those under the pressure of poverty, and of rebuke to unbelieving wealth, though the parable of the Unjust Steward and story of Zacchaeus show that it does not exalt poverty for its own sake. If our first gospel pictures Jesus as the fulfilment of God's promises to his people, and Mark, as the man of power at work before our very eyes, astonishing the multitude while winning the few, Luke sets before us the Lord ministering with divine compassion to men subject to like temptations with himself, though, unlike them, he knew no sin.

26. The first three gospels, differing as they do in point of view and aim, present essentially one picture of the ministry of Jesus; for they agree concerning the locality and progress of his Messianic work, and the form and contents of his teaching, showing, in fact, verbal identity in many parts of their narrative. For this reason they are commonly known as the Synoptic Gospels. Yet these gospels exhibit differences as remarkable as their likenesses. They differ perplexingly in the order in which they arrange some of the events in Jesus' life. Which of them should be given preference in constructing a harmonious picture of his ministry? They often agree to the letter in their report of deeds or words of Jesus, yet from beginning to end remarkable verbal differences stand side by side with remarkable verbal identities. Some of the identities of language suggest irresistibly that the evangelists have used, at least in part, the same previously existing written record. One of the clearest evidences of this is found in the introduction, at the same place in the parallel accounts, of the parenthesis " then saith he to the sick of the palsy" which interrupts the words of Jesus in the cure of the paralytic (Mark ii. 10; Matt. ix. 6; Luke v. 24). When the three gospels are carefully compared it appears that Mark contains very little that is not found in Matthew and Luke, and that, with one or two exceptions, Luke presents in Mark's order the matter that he has in common with the second gospel. The same is also true of the relation between the latter part of the Gospel of Matthew (Matt. xiv. 1 to the end) and the parallel portion of Mark; while the comparison of Matthew's arrangement of his earlier half with Mark suggests that the order in the first gospel has been determined by other than chronological considerations. In a sense, therefore, we may say that the Gospel of Mark reveals the chronological framework on which all three of these gospels are constructed.

Comparison discloses further the interesting fact that the matter which Matthew and Luke have in common, after subtracting their parallels to Mark, consists almost entirely of teachings and addresses. Each gospel, however, has some matter peculiar to itself.

27. In considering the problem presented by these facts, it is well to remember that no one of these gospels contains within itself any statement concerning the identity of its author. We are indebted to tradition for the names by which we know them, and no one of them makes any claim to apostolic origin. The earliest reference in Christian literature which may be applied to our gospels comes from Papias, a Christian of Asia Minor in the second century. He reports that an earlier teacher had said, "Mark, having become the interpreter of Peter, wrote down accurately, though not, indeed, in order, whatsoever he remembered of the things said or done by Christ, for he neither heard the Lord nor followed him, but afterward, as I said, he followed Peter, who adapted his teachings to the needs of his hearers, but with no intention of giving a connected account of the Lord's discourses. So that Mark committed no error when he thus wrote some things as he remembered them, for he was careful of one thing, not to omit any of the things which he had heard and not to state any of them falsely. Matthew wrote the oracles of the Lord in the Hebrew language Aramaic, and every one interpreted them as he was able" (Euseb. Ch. Hist. iii. 39). The result of many years' study by scholars of all shades of opinion is the very general conclusion that the writing which Papias attributed to Mark was essentially what we have in our second gospel.

28. It is almost as universally acknowledged that the work ascribed by the second century elder to the apostle Matthew cannot be our first gospel; for its language has not the characteristics which other translations from Hebrew or Aramaic lead us to expect, while the completeness of its narrative exceeds what is suggested by the words of Papias. If, however, the matter which Matthew and Luke have in such rich measure in addition to Mark's narrative be considered, the likeness between this and the writing attributed by Papias to the apostle Matthew is noteworthy. The conclusion is now very general, that that apostolic writing is in large measure preserved in the discourses in our first and third gospels. The relation of our gospels to the two books mentioned by Papias may be conceived, then, somewhat as follows: The earliest gospel writing of which we know anything was a collection of the teachings of Jesus made by the apostle Matthew, in which he collected with simple narrative introductions, those sayings of the Lord which from the beginning had passed from mouth to mouth in the circle of the disciples. At a later time Mark wrote down the account of the ministry of Jesus which Peter had been accustomed to relate in his apostolic preaching. The work of the apostle Matthew, while much richer in the sayings of Jesus, lacked the completeness that characterizes a narrative; hence it occurred to some early disciple to blend together these two primitive gospel records, adding such other items of knowledge as came to his hand from oral tradition or written memoranda. As his aim was practical rather than historical, he added such editorial comments as would make of the new gospel an argument for the Messiahship of Jesus, as we have seen. Since the most precious element in this new gospel was the apostolic record of the teachings of the Lord, the name of Matthew and not of his literary successor, was given to the book.

29. The third gospel is ascribed, by a probably trustworthy tradition, to Luke, the companion of Paul. The author himself says that he made use of such earlier records as were accessible, among which the chief seem to have been the writings of

Mark and the apostle Matthew. To Luke's industry, however, we owe our knowledge of many incidents and teachings from the life of Jesus which were not contained in these two records, and with which we could ill afford to part. Some of these he doubtless found in written form, and some he gathered from oral testimony. His close agreement with Mark in the arrangement of his narrative suggests that he found no clear evidence of a ministry of wider extent in time and place. He therefore used Mark as his narrative framework, and of the rich materials which he had gathered made a gospel, the completest of any written up to his time.

30. Such in the main is the conclusion of modem study of our first three gospels; it explains the general identity of their picture of Jesus and of their report of his teaching; it leaves room for those individual characteristics which give them so much of their charm; and it traces the materials of the gospels far back of the writings as we have them, bringing us nearer to the events which they describe. The dates of these documents can be only approximately known. It is probable that the "logia" collected by the apostle Matthew were written not later than 60 to 65 A. D., while the Gospel of Mark dates from before the fall of Jerusalem in 70. Our first gospel must have been made between 70 and 100, and the Gospel of Luke may be dated about the year 80, â all within sixty or seventy years after the death of Jesus.

31. The fourth gospel gives us a picture of Jesus in striking contrast to that of the other three. These present chiefly the works of the Master and his teachings concerning the kingdom of God and human conduct, leaving the truth concerning the teacher himself to be inferred. John opens the heart of Jesus and makes him disclose his thought about himself in a remarkable series of teachings of which he is the prime topic. This gospel is avowedly an argument (xx. 30, 31); its selection of material is confessedly partial; its aim is to confirm the faith of Christians in the heavenly nature and saving power of their Lord; and its method is that of appeal to testimony, to signs, and to his own self-disclosures. The opening verses of the gospel have a somewhat abstract theological character; the body of the book, however, consists of a succession of incidents and teachings which follow each other in unstudied fashion like a collection of annals. This impression is not compromised by the recognition, at some points, of accidental displacements, like that which has placed xiv. 30, 31 before xv. and xvi., or that which has left a long gap between vii. 23 and the incident of v. 1-9, to which it refers. The theme of tlie gospel is the self-disclosure of Jesus. This seems to have determined the evangelist's choice of material, and, as the gospel is an argument, he does not hesitate to mingle his own comments with his report of Jesus' words, for example (iii. 16-21, 30-36; xii. 37 43). The book is characterized by a vividness of detail which indicates a clear memory of personal experience. While it is evident that the author has the most exalted conception of the nature of his Lord, this seems to have been the result of loving meditation on a friend who had early won the mastery over his heart and life, and who through long years of contemplation had forced upon his disciple's mind the conviction of his transcendent nature. The book discloses a profoundly objective attitude; the Christ whom John portrays is not the creature of his speculations, but the Master who has entered into his experience as a living influence and has compelled recognition of his significance. The Son of God is

for John the human Jesus who, though named at the outset the Word â the Logos, â is the Word who was made flesh, that men through him might become the sons of God.

32. The contrast which the Gospel of John presents to the other three concerns not only the teaching of Jesus, but the scene of his ministry and its historic development as well. Whatever may be the final judgment concerning the fourth gospel, it is manifestly constructed as a simple collection of incidents following each other in what was meant to appear a chronological sequence. It has been seen that the biographical framework of the first three gospels is principally Mark's report of Peter's narrative. Now it is a fact that in portions of Matthew and Luke, derived elsewhere than from Mark, there are various allusions most easily understood if it be assumed that Jesus visited Jerusalem before his appearance there at the end of his ministry. Such, for instance, are the parable of the Good Samaritan (Luke x. 25-37), the story of the visit to Mary and Martha (Luke x. 38-42), and the lamentation of Jesus over Jerusalem (Luke xiii. 34, 35; Matt, xxiii. 37-39). All three gospels, moreover, agree in attributing to emissaries from Jerusalem much of the hostility manifested against Jesus in his Galilean ministry (Luke v. 17; Mark iii. 22; Matt. xv. 1; Mark vii. 1), and presuppose such an acquaintance of Jesus with households in and near Jerusalem as is not easy to explain if he never visited Judea before his passion (Mark xi. 2, 3; xiv. 14; xv. 43 and parallels; compare especially Matt, xxvii. 57; John xix. 38). These all suggest that the narrative of Mark does not tell the whole story, a conclusion quite in accordance with the account of his work given by Papias. It has been assumed that Peter was a Galilean, a man of family living in Capernaum. It is not impossible that on some of the earlier visits of Jesus to Jerusalem he did not accompany his Master, and in reporting the things which he knew he naturally confined himself to his own experiences. If this can explain the predominance of Galilean incidents in the ministry as depicted in Mark, it will explain the predominance of Galilee in the first three gospels, and the contradiction between John and the three is reduced to a divergence between two accounts of Jesus' ministry written from two different points of view.

33. The question of the trustworthiness of the fourth gospel is greatly simplified by the consideration of the one-sidedness of Mark's representation. It is further relieved by the fact that a ministry by Jesus in Jerusalem must have been one of constant self-assertion, for Jerusalem represented at its highest those aspects of thought and practice which were fundamentally opposed to all that Jesus did and taught. Whenever in Galilee, in the ministry pictured by the first three gospels, Jesus came in contact with the spirit and feeling characteristic of Jerusalem, we find him meeting it by unqualified assertion of his own independence and exalted claim to authority, altogether similar to that emphasis of his own signifi- cance and importance which is the chief characteristic of his teachings in the fourth gospel. If it be remembered that that gospel was avowedly an argument written to commend to others the reverent conclusion concerning the Lord reached by a disciple whose thought had dwelt for long years on the marvel of that life, and if we recognize that for such an argument the author would select the instances and teachings most telling for his own purpose, and would do this as naturally as the magnet draws to itself iron filings which are mingled with a pile of sand, the exclusively personal character of the teachings of Jesus in this gospel need cause little perplexity. Nor need it seem

surprising that the words of Jesus as reported in John share the peculiarities of style which mark the work of the evangelist in the prologue to the gospel and in his epistles. His purpose was not primarily biographical but argumentative, and he has set forth the picture of his Lord as it rose before his own heart, his memory of events being interwoven with contemplation on the significance of that life with which his had been so blessedly associated. In a gospel written avowedly to produce in others a conviction like lib own, the evangelist would not have been sensible of any obligation to draw sharp lines between his recollection of his Lord's words and his own contemplations upon them and upon their significance for his life. If these considerations be kept in mind we may accept the uniform tradition of antiquity, confirmed by the plain intimation of the gospel itself, that it is essentially the work of John, the son of Zebedee, written near the close of his life in Ephe-sus, in the last decade of the first century.

34. We have in our gospel records, therefore, two authorities for the general course of the ministry of Jesus, â Mark and John. Even if the fourth gospel should be proved not to be the work of John, its picture of the ministry of Jesus must be recognized as coming from some apostolic source. A forger would hardly have invited the rejection of his work by inventing a narrative which seems to contradict at so many points the tradition of the other gospels. The first and third gospels furnish us from various sources rich additions to Mark's narrative, and it is to these two with the fourth that we turn chiefly for the teachings of Jesus. Each gospel should be read, therefore, remembering its incompleteness, remembering also the particular purpose and individual enthusiasm for Jesus which produced it.

35. A word may be due to two other claimants to recognition as original records from the life of Jesus. One class is represented by that word of the Lord which Paul quoted to the Ephesian elders at Miletus (Acts xx. 35). Scattered here and there in writings of the apostolic and succeeding ages are other sayings attributed to Jesus which cannot be found in our gospels. A few of these so-called Agrapha seem worthy

AGRAPHA AND APOCRYPHA 37 of him, and are recognized as probably genuine. The most important of them is the story of the woman taken in adultery (John vii. 53 to viii. 11), which, though not a part of the gospel of John, doubtless gives a true incident from Jesus' life. They represent the "many other " things which John and the other gospels have omitted, but their small number proves that our gospels have preserved for us practically all that was known of Jesus after the first witnesses fell asleep. It is certainly surprising that so little exists to supplement the story of the gospels, for they are manifestly fragmentary, and leave much of Jesus' public life without any record. The other class of claimants is of a quite different character, â the so-called Apocryphal Gospels. These consist chiefly of legends connected with the birth and early years of Jesus, and with his death and resurrection. They are for the most part crude tales that have entirely mistaken the real character of him whom they seek to exalt, and need only to be read to be rejected.

36. THE church early appreciated the value and the difficulty of having four different pictures of the life and teachings of the Lord. Irenaeus at the close of the second century felt it to be as essential that there should be four gospels as that there should be " four zones of the world, four principal winds, and four faces of the cherubim" (Against Heresies III. ii. 8).

37. Before Irenseus, however, another had sought to obviate the difficulty of having four records which seem at some points to disagree, by making a combination of the gospels, to which he gave the title " Diatessaron." Tatian, the author of this work, was converted from paganism about 152 A. D., and prepared his unified gospel, probably for the use of the Syrian churches, sometime after 172. His work is one of the treasures of the early Christian literature recovered for us within the last quarter-century. It seems to have won great popularity in the Syrian churches, having practically displaced the canonical gospels for nearly three centuries, when, owing to its supposed heretical tendency, it was suppressed by the determined effort of the church authorities. It is a continuous record of Jesus ministry, beginning with the first six verses of the Gospel of John, passing then to the early chapters of Luke. It closes with an account of the resurrection interwoven from all four gospels, concluding with John xxi. 25. The arrangement follows generally the order of Matthew, additional matter from the other gospels being inserted at places which approved themselves to Tatian's judgment. Some portions â in particular the genealogies of Jesus â were omitted altogether, in accordance with views held by the compiler.

38. From Tatian's time to the present there have been repeated attempts to construct a harmonious representation of events and teachings in the ministry of Jesus, generally by setting the parallel accounts side by side, following such a succession of events as seemed most probable. Our evangelists cared little, if they thought at all, about the requirements of strict biography, and they have left us records not easy to arrange on any one chronological scheme. Concerning the chief events, however, the gospels agree. All four report, for instance, the beginning of the work in Galilee (Matt. iv. 12, 17; Mark i. 14, 15; Luke iv. 14, 15; John iv. 43-45); the feeding of the five thousand when Jesus' popularity in Galilee passed its climax (Matt. xiv. 13-23; Mark vi. 30-46; Luke ix. 10-17; John vi. 1-15); the departure from Galilee for the final visit to Jerusalem (Matt. xix. 1, 2; Mark x. 1; Luke ix. 51; John vii. 1-10); and the week of suffering and victory at the end (Matt. xxi. 1 to xxviii. 20; Mark xi. 1 to xvi. 8 20; Luke xix. 29 to xxiv. 53; John xii. 1 to xxi. 25).

39. These facts are enough to give us a clear and unified impression of the course of Jesus' ministry. When, however, we seek to fill in the details given in the different gospels, difficulties at once arise. Thus, first, what shall be done with the long section which John introduces (i. 19 to iv. 42) before Jesus' withdrawal into Galilee? The other gospels make that withdrawal the beginning of his public work. A second difficulty arises from the unnamed feast of John v. 1. By one or another scholar this feast has been identified with almost every Jewish festival known to us. Another problem is furnished by the long section in Luke which is so nearly peculiar to his gospel (ix. 51 to xviii. 14). If the section had no parallels in the other gospels we might easily conclude that it all belongs to a time subsequent to the final departure for Jerusalem; but it contains at least one incident from the earlier ministry in Galilee (Luke xi. 14-36; compare Mark iii. 19-30), and many teachings of Jesus given by Matthew in an earlier connection appear here in Luke. Furthermore, the section has to be adjusted to that portion of the Gospel of John which deals with the same period and yet reports none of the same details.

40. If Mark has furnished the narrative framework adopted in the main by the first and third gospels, the problem of the order of events in Jesus' life becomes a question of the chronological value of Mark, and of the estimate to be placed on the narrative of John. If the fourth gospel is held to be of apostolic origin and trustworthy, the task of the harmonist is chiefly that of combining these two records of Mark and John. The testimony of the Baptist, with which the fourth gospel opens, must have been given some time after he had baptized Jesus, and the ministry which preceded Jesus' return to Galilee (i. 19 to iv. 42) be- longs to a period ignored by the other gospels. The first three gospels contain indications that Jesus must have visited Judea before the close of his life. They give no hint, however, of the time or circumstances of such earlier Judean labor. In giving the emphasis they do to the work in Galilee, they present a onesided picture. When, therefore, we find in John a narrative of work in Judea, confirmed by hints in the other gospels, we may justly assume that the arrangement which fills out the ministry of Jesus by inserting at the proper places in Mark's record the events found in John is essentially true.

41. The consideration of the one-sidedness of Mark's narrative simplifies the problem of harmony, but it does not solve all of the perplexities. Matthew and Luke have much matter, some of it narrative, which Mark has not, and for which he suggests no place. Where shall we put, for instance, the cure of the centurion's servant (Matt. viii. 5-13; Luke vii. 1-10), or John the Baptist's last message (Matt. xi. 2-19; Luke vii. 18-35)? It would simplify matters if we could take Luke's statement that he had " traced the course of all things accurately from the first" (Luke i. 3), as indicating that he had arrived at exact certainty concerning the order of events of Jesus' life. It is probable, however, that his statement was simply a claim that he had carefully gathered material for a record of the whole life of Jesus, from the annunciation of his birth to his ascension. While we may believe that some trustworthy tradition led him to give the place he has to many of the incidents which he adds to Mark's story, it seems impossible to follow him in all respects; for instance, in severing the account of the blasphemy of the Pharisees (xi. 14-36) from the place which it holds in Mark (iii. 19-30).

42. Still more uncertainty exists concerning the historic connection of teachings of Jesus to which Matthew and Luke give different settings; for example, the Lord's Prayer (Matt. vi. 9-15; Luke xi. 1-4), and the exhortations against anxiety (Matt. vi. 25-34; Luke xii. 22-31). We have seen that much of the teaching common to these gospels is probably derived from the collection of the " oracles " of the Lord made by the apostle Matthew. Everything that we can infer concerning such a collection of oracles indicates that, while some of the teachings may have been connected with particular historic situations (compare Luke xi. 1), many would altogether lack such introductory words. A later example of what such a collection may have been has come to light recently in the so-called " Sayings of Jesus," discovered in Egypt and published in 1897. In these the occasion for the teaching has been quite lost; the sole interest centres in the fact that Jesus is supposed to have said the things recorded. If Matthew's book contained such " logia " or " oracles," it is probable that the original connection in which most of them were spoken was a matter of no concern to the apostle, and consequently hr. s been lost. This in no way compromises the genuineness of these

sayings of Jesus. The treatment of Luke ix. 51 to xviii. 14 is much simplified by this consideration. To Luke's industry (i. 1-4) we owe the preservation of some events and very many teachings which no other evangelist has recorded. Some of this new material (for instance, vii. 11-17, 36â 50) he has assigned a place in the midst of Mark's narrative.

Most of it, however, he has gathered together in what seems to be a sort of appendix, which he has inserted between the close of the ministry in Galilee and the final arrival in Judea. For many of the teachings it is now impossible to assign a time or place. That this is so will cause no surprise or difficulty if we remember that in the earliest days the report of what Jesus said and did circulated in the form of oral tradition only. It was the knowledge that first-hand witnesses were passing away that led to the writing of the gospels. During the period of oral tradition many teachings of the Lord were doubtless kept clearly and accurately in memory after the historic situations which led to their first utterance were quite forgotten.

43. This fact helps to explain another perplexity in our gospel narratives. A comparison of the two accounts of the cure of the centurion's servant reveals differences of detail most perplexing, if we ask for minute agreement in records of the same events. When we see that of two accounts evidently reporting the same incident, one can say that the centurion himself sought Jesus and asked the cure of his servant (Matt. viii. 5, 8), while the other makes him declare himself unworthy to come in person to the Lord (Luke vii. 7), the question arises whether other accounts, similar in the main but differing in detail, should not be identified as independent records of one event. Were there two cleansings of the temple (John ii. 13-22; Mark xi. 15-19), two miraculous draughts of fishes (Luke v. 4-11; John xxi. 5-8), two rejections at Nazareth (Mark vi. 1-6; Luke iv. 16-30), two parables of the Leaven, of the Mustard Seed (Matt. xiii. 31-33; Luke xiii. 18-21), and of the Lost Sheep (Matt, xviii. 12-14; Luke xv. 4-7)? Such similar records are often called doublets, and the question of identity or distinctness can be answered only after a special study of each case. It is important to notice that a given teaching, particularly if it took the form of an illustration, would naturally be used by Jesus on many different occasions. When, on the other hand, we find two accounts of specific doings of Jesus similar in detail it is needful to recognize that definite historic situations do not so often repeat themselves as do occasions for similar or identical teachings.

44. All these considerations show that while the general order of events in the life of Jesus may be determined with a good degree of probability, we must be content to remain uncertain concerning the place to be given to many incidents and to more teachings. Such uncertainty is of small concern, since our un-harmonized gospels have not failed during all these centuries to produce one fair picture, to the total impression of which each teaching and deed make definite contribution quite independently of our ability to give to each its particular place in relation to the whole. The degree of certainty attainable justifies, however, a continued interest in the old study of harmony, because of the more comprehensive idea it gives of the ministry depicted in the partial narratives of our several gospels.

45. THE length of the public ministry of Jesus was one of the earliest questions which arose in the study of the four gospels. In the second and third centuries it was

not uncommon to find the answer in the passage from Isaiah (Ixi. 1, 2), which Jesus declared was fulfilled in himself. " The acceptable year of the Lord " was taken to indicate that the ministry covered little more than a year. The fact that the first three gospels mention but one Passover (that at the end), and but one journey to Jerusalem, seems at first to be favorable to this conclusion, and to make peculiarly significant the care taken by Luke to give the exact date for the opening of Jesus' ministry (iii. 1, 2). In fact, the second century Gnostics, relying apparently on Luke, assigned both the ministry and death of Jesus to the fifteenth year of Tiberius Caesar, â an interpretation which may have given rise to the widely spread, early tradition, found, for example, in Tertullian (Ante-nicene Fathers, iii. 160), which placed the death of Jesus in A. D. 29, during the consulship of L. Ru-bellius Geminus and C. Fufius Geminus.

46. The theory that the ministry of Jesus extended over but little more than one year is beset, however, by difficulties that seem insuperable. The first is presented by the three Passovers distinctly mentioned in the Gospel of John (ii. 13; vi. 4; xii. 1). The last of these is plainly identical with the one named in the other gospels. The second gives the time of year for the feeding of the five thousand, and agrees with the mention of " the green grass " in the account of Mark and Matthew (Mark vi. 39; Matt. xiv. 19). John's first Passover falls in a section which demands a place before Mark i. 14 (compare John iii. 24). Hence it must be shown that this first Passover is chronologically out of order in the Gospel of John, or the one year ministry advocated by the second century Gnostics, by Clement of Alexandria, by Origen, and of late years by Keim and others, is seen to be impossible. The fact that at this Passover Jesus cleansed the temple, and that the other gospels assign such a cleansing to the close of the ministry, suggests the possibility that John has set it at the opening of his narrative for reasons connected with his argument. This interpretation falls, however, before the perfect simplicity of structure of John's narrative. The transitions from incident to incident in this gospel are those of simple succession, and indicate, on the writer's part, no suspicion that he was contradicting notions concerning the ministry of Jesus familiar to his contemporaries. Whatever the conclusion reached concerning the authorship of the gospel, the fact that it gained currency very early as apostolic would seem to prove that its conception of the length of Jesus' ministry was not opposed to the recognized apostolic testimony. It is safe to conclude, therefore, that time must be allowed in Jesus' ministry for at least three Passover seasons.

47. With this conclusion most modern discussions of the question rest, and it is possible that it may finally win common consent. The order of Mark's narrative, however, challenges it. This gospel records near the beginning (ii. 23) a controversy with the Pharisees occasioned by the fact that Jesus' disciples plucked and ate the ripening grain as they passed on a Sabbath day through the fields. As Mark places much later (vi. 30-34) the feeding of the five thousand, which occurred at a Passover, that is the beginning of the harvest (Lev. xxiii. 5-11), his order suggests the necessity of including two harvest seasons in the ministry in Galilee, and consequently four Passovers in the public life of Jesus. Two considerations are urged against this conclusion. (1) Papias in his reference to the Gospel of Mark criticises the order of the gospel; (2) Mark ii. 1 to iii. 6 contains a group of five conflicts with the critics of Jesus, which represents a massing of opposition that seems unlikely at the outset

of his Galilean work. The remark of Papias must remain obscure until his standard of comparison is known. Some suggest that he knew John's order and preferred it, others that he agreed with that adopted by Tatian in his Diatessa-ron. Mark is in accord with neither of these. No one, however, knows what order Papias preferred. The early conflict group does appear like a collection drawn from different parts of the ministry. Yet the nucleus of the group â the cure of the paralytic (ii. 1-12) and the call of Levi (ii. 13-17) â is clearly in its right place in Mark (see Holtzmann, Hand-commentar, I. 10). The question about fasting (ii. 18-22) may have been asked much later, and its present place may be due to association in tradition with the criticism of Jesus' fellowship with publicans (ii. 16).

In like manner the cure of the withered hand (iii. 1-6) may have become artificially grouped with the incident of the cornfields. It is possible, also, that both Sabbath controversies owe their early place in the gospel to traditional association with the early conflicts (ii. 1-17). If so, the plucking of the grain actually occurred some weeks after the feeding of the five thousand, and probably after the controversy about tradition (vii. 1-23), with which, according to Mark, Jesus' activity in Galilee practically closed. It is not clear, however, what principle of association drew forward to the early group the Sabbath conflict, and left in its place the controversy about tradition. It is thus possible that the incident of the cornfields belongs also to the early nucleus of the group; and in this case the longer ministry, including four Passovers, must be accepted. The decision of the question is not of vital importance, but it affects the determination of the sequence of events in Jesus' life. Whatever the explanation of the remark of Papias, the more the gospels are studied the more does Mark's order of events commend itself in general as representing the probable fact. Many students have inferred the three year ministry from the Gospel of John alone, identifying the unnamed feast in John v. 1 with a Passover. But John's allusion to that feast is so indefinite that the length of Jesus' ministry must be determined quite independently of it.

48. So long a ministry as three years presents some difficulties, for all that is told us in the four gospels would cover but a small fraction of this time. John's statement (xx. 30) that he omitted many things from Jesus' life in making his book is evidently true of all the evangelists, and long gaps, such as are evident in the fourth gospel, must be assumed in the other three. Recalling the character of the gospels as pictures of Jesus rather than narratives of his life, we may easily acknowledge the incompleteness of our record of the three years of ministry, and wonder the more at the vividness of impression produced with such economy of material. This meagreness of material is not decisive for the shorter rather than the longer ministry, for it is evident that to effect such a change in conviction and feeling as Jesus wrought in the minds of the ardent Galileans who were his disciples, required time. Three years are better suited to effect this change than two.

49. Closely related to the question of the length of Jesus' ministry is another: Can definite dates be given for the chief events in his life? For the year of the opening of his public activity the gospels furnish two independent testimonies: the remark of the Jews on the occasion of Jesus' first visit to Jerusalem, "Forty and six years was this temple in building " (John ii. 20), and Luke's careful dating of the appearance

of John the Baptist, "in the fifteenth year of Tiberius Caesar" (iii. 1, 2). John ii. 20 leads to the conclusion that the first Passover fell in the spring of A. D. 26 or 27, since we learn from Josephus (Ant. xv. 11. 1) that Herod began to rebuild the temple in the eighteenth year of his reign, which closed in the spring of B. c. 19. Luke iii. 1 gives a date contradictory to the one just found, if the fifteenth year of Tiberius is to be counted from the death of his predecessor, for Augustus died August 19, A. D. 14. Reckoned from this time the opening of John's work falls in the year

A. D. 28, and the first Passover of Jesus' ministry could not be earlier than the spring of 29. This is at least two years later than is indicated by the statement in John. The remark in John is, however, so incidental and so lacking in significance for his argument that its definiteness can be explained only as due to a clear historic reminiscence; but it does not follow that Luke has erred in the date given by him. Although Augustus did not die until A. D. 14, there is evidence that Tiberius was associated with him in authority over the army and the provinces not later than January, A. D. 12. One who lived and wrote in the reign of Titus may possibly have applied to the reign of Tiberius a mode of reckoning customary in the case of Titus, as Professor Ramsay has shown (Was Christ born at Bethlehem, 202). If this is the fact, Luke reckoned from the co-regency of Tiberius; hence the fifteenth year would be A. D. 25 or 26, according as the co-regency began before or after the first of January, A. D. 12. This would place the first Passover of Jesus' ministry in the spring of 26 or 27, in agreement with the hint found in John.

50. If the public ministry of Jesus began with the spring of 26 or 27, the close of three years of activity would come at the Passover of 29 or 30. The former of these dates agrees with the early Christian tradition already mentioned. But before accepting that traditional date another matter must be considered. Jesus was crucified on the Friday at the opening of the feast of the Passover. Whether it was the day of the sacri-iice of the Passover (14 Nisan) or the day following (15 Nisan), is not essential for the present question. As the Jewish month began with the first appearance of the new moon, it is evident that, in the year of Jesus' death, the month of Nisan must have begun on a day that would make the 14th or the 15th fall on Friday. Now it can be shown that in the year 30 the 14th of Nisan was Thursday (April 6) or Friday (April 7), for at best only approximate certainty is attainable. The tradition which assigns the passion to 29, generally names March 25 as the day of the month. This date is impossible, because it does not coincide with the full moon of that month. The choice of March 25 by a late tradition may be explained by the fact that it was commonly regarded as the date of the spring equinox, the turning of the year towards its renewing. Mr. Turner has shown (HastbD. I. 415) that another date found in an early document cannot be so explained. Epiphanius was familiar with copies of the Acts of Pilate, which gave March 18 as the date of the crucifixion; and it is remarkable that this date coincides with the full moon, and also falls on Friday. Such a combination gives unusual weight to the tradition, particularly as there is no ready way to account for its rise, as in the case of March 25. From this supplementary tradition the year 29 gains in probability as the year of the passion. Without attempting to arrive at a final conclusion, â a task which must be left for chronological specialists, â it is safe to assume that Jesus died at the Passover of A. D. 29 or 30.

51. Concluding that Jesus' active ministry fell within the years A. D. 26 to 30, is it possible to determine the date of his birth? Four hints are furnished by the gospels: he was born before the death of Herod (Matt. ii. 1; Luke i. 5); he was about thirty years of age at his baptism (Luke iii. 23); he was born during a census conducted in Judea in accordance with the decree of Augustus at a time when Quirinius was in authority in Syria (Luke ii. 1, 2); after his birth wise men from the East were led to visit him by observing "his star" (Matt. ii. 1, 2). From these facts it follows that the birth of Jesus cannot be placed later than B. c. 4, since Herod died about the first of April in that year (Jos. Ant. xvii. 6. 4; 8. 1, 4). The awkwardness of having to find a date Before Christ for the birth of Jesus is due to the miscalculation of the monk, Dionysius the Little, who in the sixth century introduced our modern reckoning from "the year of our Lord."

52. But is it impossible to determine the time of Jesus' birth more exactly? Luke (ii. 1, 2) offers what seems to be more definite information, but his reference to the decree of Augustus and the enrolment under Quirinius are among the most seriously challenged statements in the gospels. It has been said (1) that history knows of no edict of Augustus ordering a general enrolment of "the world; " (2) that a Roman census could not have been taken in Palestine before the death of Herod; (3) that if such an enrolment had been taken it would have been unnecessary for Joseph and Mary to journey from Nazareth to Bethlehem; (4) that the census taken when Quirinius was governor of Syria is definitely assigned by Josephus to the year after the deposition of Archelaus, A. D. 6 (Ant. xviii. 1. 1; see also Acts v. 37); (5) that if Luke's reference to this census as the "first" be appealed to, it must be replied that Quirinius was not governor of Syria at any time during the lifetime of Herod. This array of difficulties is impressive, and has persuaded many conservative students to concede that in his reference to the census Luke has fallen into error. Some recent discoveries in Egypt, however, have furnished new information concerning the imperial administration of that province. Inferring that a policy adopted in Egypt may have prevailed also in Syria, Professor Ramsay has recently put forth a strong argument for Luke's accuracy in respect of this census (Was Christ born at Bethlehem, 95-248). That argument may be condensed as follows: We have evidence of a system of Roman enrolments in Egypt taken every fourteen years, and already traced back to the time of Augustus, the earliest document so far recovered belonging, apparently, to the census of A. D. 20. It is at least possible that this system of Egyptian enrolments may have been part of an imperial policy, of which all other trace is lost excepting the statement of Luke. It is significant that the date of the census referred to by Josephus (A. D. 6) fits exactly the fourteen-year cycle which obtained in Egypt. If the census of A. D. 6 was preceded by an earlier one its date would be B. c. 8; that is, it would be actually taken in B. c. 7, in order to secure the full acts for B. c. 8. ?

53. The statement of Tertullian (Against Marcion, iv. 19) that a census had been taken in Judea under Augustus by Sentius Saturninus, who was governor of Syria about 9 to 7 B. c., certainly comes from some source independent of the gospels, and tends to confirm Luke's account of a census before the death of Herod. That a Roman census might have been taken in Palestine during Herod's life is seen from the fact that in A. D. 36 Vitellius, the governor of Syria, had to send Roman forces into

Cilicia Trachsea to assist Archelaus, the king of that country, to quell a revolt caused by native resistance to a census taken after the Roman fashion (Tacitus, Ann. vi. 41). Herod would almost certainly resent as a mark of subjection the order to enrol his people; and the fact that he was in disfavor with Augustus during the governorship of Saturninus (Josephus, Ant. xvi. 9. 1-3), suggests to Professor Ramsay that he may have sought to avoid obedience to the imperial will in the matter of the census. If after some delay Herod was forced to obey, the enrolment may have been taken in the year 7-6. Since it is probable that the Romans would allow Herod to give the census as distinctly Jewish a character as possible, it is easy to credit the order that all Jews should be registered, so far as possible, in their ancestral homes. Hence the journey of Joseph to Bethlehem; and if Mary wished to have her child also registered as from David's line, her removal with Joseph to Bethlehem is explained. Such a delay in the taking of the census would have postponed it until after the recall of Saturninus. The statement of Tertullian may therefore indicate simply that he knew that a census was taken in Syria by Saturninus.

54. The successor of Saturninus was Varus, who held the governorship until after the death of Herod. How then does Luke refer to the enrolment as taken when Quirinius was in authority? It has for a long time been known that this man was in Syria before he was there as legate of the emperor in A. D. 6. There seems to be evidence that Quirinius was in the East about the year B. c. 6, putting down a rebellion on the borders of Cilicia, a district joined with Syria into one province under the early empire. Varus was at this time governor, but Quirinius might easily have been looked upon as representing for the time the power of the Roman arms. If Herod was forced to yield to the imperial wish by the presence in Syria of this renowned captain, the statement of Luke is confirmed, and the census at which Jesus was born was taken, according to a Jewish fashion, during the life of Herod, but under compulsion of Rome exacted by Quirinius, while he was in command of the Roman forces in the province of Syria-Cilicia. This gives as a probable date for the birth of Jesus B. c. 6, which accords well with the hints previously considered, inasmuch as it is earlier than the death of Herod, and, if born in B. c. 6, Jesus would have been thirty-two at his baptism in A. D. 26.

55. The account given in Matthew of "the star" which drew the wise men to Judea gives no sure help in determining the date of the birth of Jesus, but it is at least suggestive that in the spring and autumn of B. c. 7 there occurred a remarkable conjunction of the planets Jupiter and Saturn. This was first noticed by Kepler in consequence of a similar conjunction observed by him in A. D. 1603. Men much influenced by astrology must have been impressed by such a celestial phenomenon, but that it furnishes an explanation of the star of the wise men is not clear. If it does, it confirms the date otherwise probable for the nativity, that is, not far from B. c. 6.

56. Can we go further and determine the time of year or the month and day of the nativity? It should be borne in mind that our Christmas festival was not observed earlier than the fourth century, and that the evidence is well-nigh conclusive that December 25th was finally selected for the Nativity in order to hallow a much earlier and widely spread pagan festival coincident with the winter solstice. If anything exists to suggest the time of year it is Luke's mention of "shepherds in the field keeping

watch by night over their flock" (ii. 8). This seems to indicate that it must have been the summer season. In winter the flocks would be folded, not pastured, by night.

57. It therefore seems probable that Jesus was born in the summer of B. c. 6; that he was baptized in A. D. 26; that the first Passover of his ministry was in the spring of 26 or 27; and that he was crucified in the spring of 29 or 30.

THE EAKLY YEAES OF JESUS MATT. i. 1 TO ii. 23; LUKE i. 5 TO ii. 52; iii. 23-38 58. IT is surprising that within a century of the life of the apostles, Christian imagination could have so completely mistaken the real greatness of Jesus as to let its thirst for wonder fill his early years with scenes in which his conduct is as unlovely as it is shocking. That he who in manhood was " holy, harmless, unde-filed, separate from sinners " (Heb. vii. 26), could in youth, in a fit of ill-temper, strike a companion with death and then meet remonstrance by cursing his accusers with blindness (Gospel of Thomas, 4, 5); that he could mock his teachers and spitefully resent their control (Pseudo-Matthew, 30, 31); that it could be thought worthy of him to exhibit his superiority to common human conditions by carrying water in his mantle when his pitcher had been broken (same, 33), or by making clay birds in play on the Sabbath and causing them to fly when he was rebuked for naughtiness (same, 27); â these and many like legends exhibit incredible blindness to the real glory of the Lord. Yet such things abound in the early attempts of the pious imagination to write the story of the youth of Jesus, and the account of the nativity and its antecedents fares as ill, being pitifully trivial where it is not revolting.

59. How completely foreign all this is to the apostolic thought and feeling is clear when we notice that excepting the first two chapters of Matthew and Luke the New Testament tells us nothing whatever of the years which preceded John the Baptist's ministry in the wilderness. The gospels are books of testimony to what men had seen and heard (John i. 14); and the epistles are practical interpretations of the same in its bearing on religious life and hope. The apostles found no difficulty in recognizing the divinity and sinlessness of their Lord without inquiring how he came into the world or how he spent his early years; it was what he showed himself to be, not how he came to be, that formed their conception of him. Yet the early chapters of Matthew and Luke should not be classed with the later legends. Notwithstanding the attempts of Keim to associate the narratives of the infancy in the canonical and apocryphal gospels, a great gulf separates them: on the one side there is a reverent and beautiful reserve, on the other indelicate, unlovely, and trivial audacity.

60. The gospel narratives have, however, perplexities of their own, for the two accounts agree only in the main features, â the miraculous birth in Bethlehem in the days of Herod, Mary being the mother and Joseph the foster-father, and Nazareth the subsequent residence. In further details they are quite different, and at first sight seem contradictory. Moreover, while Matthew sheds a halo of glory over the birth of Jesus, Luke draws a picture of humble circumstances and obscurity. These differences, taken with the silence of the rest of the New Testament concerning a miraculous birth, constitute a real difficulty. To many it seems strange that the disciples and the brethren of Jesus did not refer to these things if they knew them to be true. But it must not be overlooked that any familiar reference to the circumstances of the birth of Jesus which are narrated in the gospels would have invited from the Jews simply a challenge of

the honor of his home. Moreover, as the knowledge of these wonders did not keep Mary from misunderstanding her son (Luke ii. 19, 51; compare Mark iii. 21, 31-35), the publication of them could hardly have helped greatly the belief of others. The fact that Mary was so perplexed by the course of Jesus in his ministry makes it probable that even until quite late in her life she " kept these things and pondered them in her heart."

61. No parts of the New Testament are challenged so widely and so confidently as these narratives of the infancy. But if they are not to be credited with essential truth it is necessary to show what ideas cherished in the apostolic church could have led to their invention. That John and Paul maintain the divinity of their Lord, yet give no hint that this involved a miraculous birth, shows that these stories are no necessary outgrowth of that doctrine. The early Christians whether Jewish or Gentile would not naturally choose to give pictorial form to their belief in their Lord's divinity by the story of an incarnation. The heathen myths concerning sons of the gods were in all their associations revolting to Christian feeling, and, while the Jewish mind was ready to see divine influence at work in the birth of great men in Israel (as Isaac, and Samson, and Samuel), the whole tendency of later Judaism was hostile to any such idea as actual incarnation. Some would explain the story of the miraculous birth as a conclusion drawn by the Christian consciousness from the doctrine of the sinlessness of Jesus. Yet neither Paul nor John, who are both clear concerning the doctrine, give any idea that a miraculous birth was essential for a sinless being. Some appeal to the eagerness of the early Christians to exalt the virginity of Mary. This is certainly the animus of many apocryphal legends. But the feeling is as foreign to Jewish sentiment and New Testament teaching as it is contradictory to the evidence in the gospels that Mary had other children born after Jesus.

62. Moreover, the songs of Mary (Luke i. 46-55) and Zachariah (Luke i. 68-79) bear in themselves the evidence of origin before the doctrine of the cross had transformed the Christian idea of the Messiah. That transformed idea abounds in the Epistles and the Acts, and it is difficult to conceive how these songs (if they were later inventions) could have been left free of any trace of specifically Christian ideas. A Jewish Christian would almost certainly have made them more Christian than they are; a Gentile Christian could not have made them so strongly and naturally Jewish as they are; while a non-Christian Jew would never have invented them. Taken with the evidence in Ignatius (Ad Eph. xviii., xix.) of the very early currency of the belief in a miraculous birth, they confirm the impression that it is easier to accept the evidence offered for the miracle than to account for the origin of the stories as legends. The idea of a miraculous birth is very foreign to modern thought; it becomes credible only as the transcendent nature of Jesus is recognized on other grounds. It may not be said that the incarnation required a miraculous conception, yet it may be acknowledged that a miraculous conception is a most suitable method for a divine incarnation.

63. These gospel stories are chiefly significant for us in that they show that he in whom his disciples came to recognize a divine nature began his earthly life in the utter helplessness and dependence of infancy, and grew through boyhood and youth to manhood with such naturalness that his neighbors, dull concerning the things of the spirit, could not credit his exalted claims. He is shown as one in all points like unto

his brethren (Heb. ii. 17). Two statements in Luke (ii. 40, 52) describe the growth of the divine child as simply as that of his forerunner (Luke i. 80), or that of the prophet of old (I. Sam. ii. 26). The clear impression of these statements is that Jesus had a normal growth from infancy to manhood, while the whole course of the later life as set before us in the gospels confirms the scripture doctrine that his normal growth was free from sin (Heb. iv. 15).

64. The knowledge of the probable conditions of his childhood is as satisfying as the apocryphal stories are revolting. The lofty Jewish conception of home and its relations is worthy of Jesus. The circumstances of the home in Nazareth were humble (Matt, xiii. 55; Luke ii. 24; compare Lev. xii. 8). Probably the house was not unlike those seen to-day, of but one room, or at most two or three, â the tools of trade mingling with the meagre furnishings for home-life. We should not think it a home of penury; doubtless the circumstances of Joseph were like those of his neighbors. In one respect this home was rich. The wife and mother had an exalted place in the Jewish life, notwithstanding 1 the trivial opinions of some supercilious rabbis; and what the gospel tells of the chivalry of Joseph renders it certain that love reigned in his home, making it fit for the growth of the holy child.

65. Religion held sway in all the phases of Jewish life. With some it was a religion of ceremony, â of prayers and fastings, tithes and boastful alms, fringes and phylacteries. But Joseph and Mary belonged to the simpler folk, who, while they reverenced the scribes as teachers, knew not enough of their subtlety to have substituted barren rites for sincere love for the God of their fathers and childlike trust in his mercy. Jesus knew not only home life at its fairest, but religion at its best. A father's most sacred duty was the teaching of his child in the religion of his people (Deut. vi. 4â 9), and then, as ever since, the son learned at his mother's side to know and love her God, to pray to him, and to know the scriptures. No story more thrilling and full of interest, no prospect more rich and full of glowing hope, could be found to satisfy the child's spirit of wonder than the story of Israel's past and God's promises for the future. Religious culture was not confined to the home, however. The temple at Jerusalem was the ideal centre of religious life for this Nazareth household (Luke ii. 41) as for all the people, yet practically worship and instruction were cultivated chiefly by the synagogue (Luke iv. 16); there God was present in his Holy Word. Week after week the boy Jesus heard the scripture in its original Hebrew form, followed by translation into Aramaic, and received instruction from it for daily conduct. The synagogue probably influenced the boy's intellectual life even more directly. In the time of Jesus schools had been established in all the important towns, and were apparently under the control of the synagogue. To such a school he may have been sent from about six years of age to be taught the scriptures (compare II. Tim. iii. 15), together with the reading (Luke iv. 16-19), and perhaps the writing, of the Hebrew language. Of his school experience we know nothing beyond the fact that he grew in " wisdom and in stature and in favor with God and man " (Luke ii. 52), â a sufficient contradiction of the repulsive legends of the apocryphal gospels.

66. The physical growth incident to Jesus' develop, ment from boyhood to manhood is a familiar thought. The intellectual unfolding which belongs to this development is readily recognized. Not so commonly acknowledged, but none the less clearly

essential to the gospel picture, is the gradual unfolding of the child's moral life under circumstances and stimulus similar to those with which other children meet (Heb. iv. 15). The man Jesus was known as the carpenter (Matt. xiii. 55). The learning of such a trade would contribute much to the boy's mastery of his own powers. Far more discipline would come from his fellowship with brothers and sisters who did not understand his ways nor appreciate the deepest realities of his life. Without robbing boyhood days of their naturalness and reality, we may be sure that long before Jesus knew how and why he differed from his fellows he felt more or less clearly that they were not like him. The resulting sense of isolation was a school for self-mastery, lest isolation foster any such pride or unloveliness as that with which later legend dared to stain the picture of the Lord's youth. Four brothers of

Jesus are named by Mark (vi. 3), â James, and Joses, and Judas, and Simon,â the gospel adds also that he had sisters living at a later time in Nazareth. They were all subject with him to the same home influences, and apparently were not unresponsive to them. The similarity of thought and feeling between the sermon on the mount and the Epistle of James is not readily explained by the influence of master over disciple, since the days of James's discipleship began after the resurrection of Jesus. In any case there is no reason to think that the companions of Jesus' home were uncommonly irritating or in any way irreligious, only Jesus was not altogether like them (John vii. 5), and the fact of difference was a moral discipline, which among other things led to that moral growth by which innocence passed into positive goodness. If the home was such a school of discipline, its neighbors, less earnest and less favored with spiritual training, furnished more abundant occasion for self-mastery and growth. The very fact that in his later years Jesus was no desert preacher, like John, but social, and socially sought for, indicates that he did not win his manhood's perfection in solitude, but in fellowship with common life and in victory over the trials and temptations incident to it (Heb. ii. IT, 18).

67. Yet he must have been familiar with the life which is in secret (Matt. vi. 1-18). He who in his later years was a man of much prayer, who began (Luke iii. 21) and closed (Luke xxiii. 46) his public life with prayer, as a boy was certainly familiar not only with the prayers of home and synagogue, but also with quiet, personal resort to the presence of God. It would be unjust to think of any abnormal religious precocity. Jesus was the best example the world has seen of perfect spiritual health, but we must believe that he came early to know God and to live much with him.

68. It is instructive in connection with this inwardness of Jesus' life to recall the rich familiarity with the whole world of nature which appears in his parables and other teachings. The prospect which met his eye if he sought escape from the distractions of home and village life, has been described by Renan: " The view from the town is limited; but if we ascend a little to the plateau swept by a perpetual breeze, which stands above the highest houses, the landscape is magnificent. On the west stretch the fine outlines of Carmel, terminating in an abrupt spur which seems to run down sheer to the sea. Next, one sees the double summit which towers above Megiddo; the mountains of the country of Shechem, with their holy places of the patriarchal period; the hills of Gilboa, the small picturesque group to which is attached the graceful or terrible recollections of Shunem and of Endor; and Tabor, with its beautiful rounded

form, which antiquity compared to a bosom. Through a gap between the mountains of Shunem and Tabor are visible the valley of the Jordan and the high plains of Perea, which form a continuous line from the eastern side. On the north, the mountains of Safed, stretching towards the sea, conceal St. Jean d'Acre, but leave the Gulf of Khaifa in sight. Such was the horizon of Jesus. This enchanted circle, cradle of the kingdom of God, was for years his world. Indeed, during his whole life he went but little beyond the familiar bounds of his childhood. For yonder, northwards, one can almost see, on the flank of Hermon, Csesarea-Philippi, his farthest point of advance into the Gentile world; and to the south the less smiling aspect of these Samaritan hills foreshadows the dreariness of Judea beyond, parched as by a burning wind of desolation and death." In the midst of such scenes we are to understand that, with the physical growth, and opening of mind, and moral discipline which filled the early years of Jesus, there came also the gradual spiritual unfolding in which the boy rose step by step to the fuller knowledge of God and himself.

69. That unfolding is pictured in an early stage in the story given us from the youth of Jesus. It was customary for a Jewish boy not long after passing his twelfth year to come under full adult obligation to the law. The visit to Jerusalem was probably in preparation for such assumption of obligation by Jesus. All his earlier training had filled his mind with the sacredness of the Holy City and the glory of the temple. It is easy to feel with what joy he would first look upon Zion from the shoulder of the Mount of Olives, as he came over it on his journey from Galilee; to conceive how the temple and the ritual would fill him with awe in his readiness not to criticise, but to idealize everything he saw, and to think only of the significance given by it all to the scripture; to imagine how eagerly he would talk in the temple court with the learned men of his people about the law and the promises with which in home and school his youth had been made familiar. Nor is it difficult to appreciate his surprise, when Joseph and Mary, only after long searching for him, at last found him in the temple, for he felt that it was the most natural place in which he could be found. In his wondering question to Mary, "Did not you know that I must be in my Father's house? " (Luke ii. 49), there is a premonition of his later consciousness of peculiarly intimate relation to God. The question was, however, a sincere inquiry. It was no precocious rebuke of Mary's anxiety. The knowledge of himself as Son of God was only dawning within him, and was not yet full and clear. This is shown by his immediate obedience and his subjection to his parents in Nazareth through many years. It is safe, in the interpretation of the acts and words of Jesus, to banish utterly as inconceivable anything that savors of the theatrical. We must believe that he was always true to himself, and that the subjection which he rendered to Joseph and Mary sprang from a real sense of childhood's dependence, and was not a show of obedience for any edifying end however high.

70. That question " Did not you know?" is the only hint we possess of Jesus' inner life before John's call to repentance rang through the land. Meanwhile the carpenter's son became himself the carpenter. Joseph seems to have died before the opening of Jesus' ministry. For Jesus as the eldest son, this death made those years far other than a time of spiritual retreat; responsibility for the home and the pressing duties of trade must have filled most of the hours of his days. This is a welcome thought

to our healthiest sentiment, and true also to the earliest Christian feeling (Heb. iv. 15). John the Baptist had his training in the wilderness, but Jesus came from familiar intercourse with men, was welcomed in their homes (John ii. 2), knew their life in its homely ongoing, and was the friend of all sorts and conditions of men. After that visit to Jerusalem, a few more years may have been spent in school, for, whether from school instruction, or synagogue preaching, or simple daily experience, the young man came to know the traditions of the elders and also to know that observance of them is a mockery of the righteousness which God requires. Yet he seems to have felt so fully in harmony with God as to be conscious of nothing new in the fresh and vital conceptions of righteousness which he found in the law and prophets. We may be certain that much of his thought was given to Israel's hope of redemption, and that with the prophets of old and the singer much nearer his own day (Ps. of Sol. xvii. 23), he longed that God, according to his promise, would raise up unto his people, their King, the Son of David.

71. He must also have read often from that other book open before him as he walked upon the hills of Nazareth. The beauty of the grass and of the lilies was surely not a new discovery to him after he began to preach the coming kingdom, nor is it likely that he waited until after his baptism to form his habit of spending the night in prayer upon the mountain. We may be equally sure that he did not first learn to love men and women and long for their good after he received the call, "Thou art my beloved son " (Mark i. 11). He who in later life read hearts clearly (John ii. 25) doubtless gained that skill, as well as the knowledge of human sin and need, early in his intercourse with his friends and neighbors in Nazareth; while a clear conviction that God's kingdom consists in his sover- eignty over loyal hearts must have filled much of his thought about the promised good which God would bring to Israel in due time. Thus we may think that in quietness and homely industry, in secret life with God and open love for men, in study of history and prophecy, in longing for the actual sway of God in human life, Jesus lived his life, did his work, and grew in " wisdom and in stature and in favor with God and man " (Luke ii. 52).

MATT. iii. 1-17; iv. 12; xiv. 1-12; MARK i. 1-14; vi. 14-29; LUKE i. 5-25, 57-80; iii. 1-22; ix. 7-9; JOHN i. 19-37; iii. 22-30.

72. THE first reappearance of Jesus in the gospel story, after the temple scene in his twelfth year, is on the banks of the Jordan seeking baptism from the new prophet. One of the silent evidences of the greatness of Jesus is the fact that so great a character as John the Baptist stands in our thought simply as accessory to his life. For that the prophet of the wilderness was great has been the opinion of all who have been willing to seek him in his retirement. One reason for the common neglect of John is doubtless the meagreness of information about him. But though details are few, the picture of him is drawn in clearest lines: a rugged son of the wilderness scorning the gentler things of life, threatening his people with coming wrath and calling to repentance while yet there was time; a preacher of practical righteousness heeded by publicans and harlots but scorned by the elders of his people; a bold and fearless spirit, yet subdued in the presence of another who did not strive, nor cry, nor cause his voice to be heard in the streets. When the people thought to find in John the promised Messiah, with unparalleled self-effacement he pointed them to his rival and rejoiced

in that rival's growing success. Side by side they worked for a time; then the picture fails, but for a hint of a royal audience, with a fearless rebuke of royal disgrace and sin; a prison life, with its pathetic shaking of confidence in the early certainties; a long and forced inaction, and the question put by a wavering faith, with its patient and affectionate reply; then a lewd orgy, a king's oath, a girl's demands, a martyr's release, the disciples' lamentation and their report to that other who, though seeming a rival, was known to appreciate best the greatness of this prophet. Such is the picture in the gospels.

73. John, unlike his greater successor, has a highly appreciative notice from Josephus: " Now some of the Jews thought that the destruction of Herod's army came from God, and that very justly, as a punishment for what he did against John, who was called the Baptist. For Herod had had him put to death though he was a good man, and commanded the Jews to exercise virtue, both as to justice towards one another, and piety towards God, and so to come to baptism; for baptism would be acceptable to God, if they made use of it not in order to expiate some sin, but for the purification of the body, provided that the soul was thoroughly purified beforehand by righteousness. Now, as many flocked to him, for they were greatly moved by hearing his words, Herod, fearing that the great influence John had over the people might lead to some rebellion (for the people seemed likely to do anything he should advise), thought it far best, by putting him to death, to prevent any mischief he might cause, and not bring himself into difficulties by sparing a man who might make him repent of his leniency when it should be too late. Accordingly he was sent a prisoner, in consequence of Herod's suspicious temper, to Machaerus, the fortress before mentioned, and was there put to death. So the Jews had the opinion that the destruction of this army by Aretas was sent as a punishment upon Herod and was the mark of God's displeasure at him" (Ant xviii. 5. 2). This section is commonly accepted as trustworthy. Superficially different from the gospel record and assigning quite another cause for John's imprisonment and death, it correctly describes his character and his influence with the people, and leaves abundant room for a more intimately personal motive on the part of Antipas for the imprisonment of John. If the jealousy of Herodias was the actual reason for John's arrest, it is highly probable that another cause would be named to the world, and a likelier one than that given by Josephus could not be found.

74. The first problem that offers itself in the study of this man is the man himself. Whence did he come? Everything about him is surprising. He appears as a dweller in the desert, an ascetic, holding aloof from common life and content with the scanty fare the wilderness could offer; yet he was keenly appreciative of his people's needs, and he knew their sins, â the particular ones that beset Pharisees, publicans, soldiers. If a recluse in habit, he was far from such in thought; he was therefore no seeker for his own soul's peace in his desert life. His dress was strikingly suggestive of the old prophet of judgment on national infidelity (I. Kings xvii. 1; II. Kings i. 8), the Elijah whom John would not claim to be. His message was commanding, with its double word " Repent" and " The kingdom is near." His idea of the kingdom was definite, though not at all developed; it signified to him God's dominion, inaugurated by a divine judgment which should mean good for the penitent and utter destruction for the ungodly; hence the prophet's call to repentance. His ministry was one of grace,

but the time was drawing near when the Greater One would appear to complete by a swift judgment the work which his forerunner was beginning. That Greater One would hew down the fruitless tree, winnow the wheat from the chaff on the threshing floor, baptize the penitent with divine power, and the wicked with the fire of judgment, since his was to be a ministry of judgment, not of grace.

75. Whence, then, came this strange prophet? Near the desert region where he spent his youth and where he first proclaimed his message of repentance and judgment was the chief settlement of that strange company of Jews known as Essenes. It has long been customary to think that during his early years John was associated with these fellow-dwellers in the desert, if he did not actually join the order. He certainly may have learned from them many things. Their sympathy with his ascetic life and with his thorough moral earnestness would make them attractive to him, but he was far too original a man to get from them more than some suggestions to be worked out in his own fashion. The simplicity of his teaching of repentance and the disregard of ceremonial in his preaching separate him from these monks. John may have known his desert companions, may have appreciated some things in their discipline, but he remained independent of their guidance.

76. The leaders of religious life and thought in his day were unquestionably the Pharisees. The controlling idea with them, and consequently with the people, was the sanctity of God's law. They were conscious of the sinfulness of the people, and their demand for repentance was constant. It is a rabbinic commonplace that the delay of the Messiah's coming is due to lack of repentance in Israel. But near as this conception is to John's, we need but to recall his words to the Pharisees (Matt. iii. 7) to realize how clearly he saw through the hollowness of their religious pretence. With the quibbles of the scribes concerning small and great commandments, Sabbaths and hand-washings, John shows no affinity. He may have learned some things from these " sitters in Moses seat," but he was not of them.

77. John's message announced the near approach of the kingdom of God. It is probable that many of those who sought his baptism were ardent nationalists,â eager to take a hand in realizing that consummation. Josephus indicates that it was Herod's fear lest John should lead these Zealots to revolt that furnished the ostensible cause of his death. But similar as were the interests of John and these nationalists, the distance between them was great. The prophet's replies to the publicans and to the soldiers, which contain not a word of rebuke for the hated callings (Luke iii. 13, 14), show how fundamentally he differed from the Zealots.

78. But there was another branch of the Pharisees than that which quibbled over Sabbath laws, tradi- tions, and tithes, or that which itched to grasp the sword; they were men who saw visions and dreamed dreams like those of Daniel and the Revelation, and in their visions saw God bringing deliverance to his people by swift and sudden judgment. There are some marked likenesses between this type of thought and that of John, â the impending judgment, the word of warning, the coming blessing, were all in John; but one need only compare John's words with such an apocalypse as the Assumption of Moses, probably written in Palestine during John's life in the desert, to discover that the two messages do not move in the same circle of thought at all; there is something practical, something severely heart-searching, something at home in every-

day life, about John's announcement of the coming kingdom that is quite absent from the visions of his contemporaries. John had not, like some of these seers, a coddling sympathy for people steeped in sin. He traced their troubles to their own doors, and would not let ceremonies pass in place of " fruits meet for repentance." He came from the desert with rebuke and warning on his lips; with no word against the hated Romans, but many against hypocritical claimants to the privileges of Abraham; no apology for his message nor artificial device of dream or ancient name to secure a hearing, but the old-fashioned prophetic method of declaration of truth " whether men will hear or whether they will forbear." " All was sharp and cutting, imperious earnestness about final questions, unsparing overthrow of all fictitious shams in individual as in national life. There are no theories of the law, no new good works, no belief in the old, but simply and solely a prophetic cluteh at men's consciences, a mighty accusation, a crushing summons to contrite repentance and speedy sanctification " (KeimjN. II. 228). We look in vain for a parallel in any of John's contemporaries, except in that one before whom he bowed, saying, "I have need to be baptized of thee."

79. John had, however, predecessors whose work he revived. In Isaiah's words, "Wash you, make you clean" (Isa. i. 16), one recognizes the type which reappeared in John. The great prophetic conception of the Day of the Lord â the day of wrath and salvation (Joel ii. 1-14) â is revived in John, free from all the fantastic accompaniments which his contemporaries loved. The invitations to repentance and new fidelity which abound in Isaiah, Ezekiel, Hosea, and Joel; the summons to simple righteousness, which rang from the lips of Micah (vi. 8), and of the great prophet of the exile (Isa. Iviii.), these tell us where John went to school and how well he learned his lesson. It is hard for us to realize how great a novelty such simplicity was in John's day, or how much originality it required to attain to this disciple-ship of the prophets. From the time when the curtain rises on the later history of Israel in the days of the Maccabean struggle to the coming of that " voice crying in the wilderness," Israel had listened in vain for a prophet who could speak God's will with author-it '. The last thing that people expected when John came was such a simple message. He was not the creature of his time, but a revival of the older type; yet, as in the days of Elijah God had kept him seven thousand in Israel that had not bowed the knee to Baal, so, in the later time, not all were bereft of liv- ing faith. These devout souls furnished the soil which could produce a life like John's, gifted and chosen by God to restore and advance the older and more genuine religion.

80. If John was thus a revival of the older prophetic order, a second question arises: Whence came his baptism, and what did it signify? The gospels describe it as a " baptism of repentance for the remission of sins " (Mark i. 4). John's declaration that his greater successor should baptize with the Holy Spirit and fire (Matt. iii. 11) shows that he viewed his baptism as a symbol, rather than as a means, of remission of sin. But it was more than a sign of repentance, it was a confession of loyalty to the kingdom which John's successor was to establish. It had thus a twofold significance: (a) confession of and turning from the old life of sin, and (b) consecration to the coming kingdom. Whence, then, came this ordinance? Not from the Essenes, for, unlike John's baptism, the bath required by these Jewish ascetics was an oft-repeated act. Further, John's rite had a far deeper religious significance than the Essene washings.

These performed their ablutions to secure ritual cleanness as exemplary disciples of the Mosaic ideal. The searching of heart which preceded John's baptism, and the radical change of life it demanded, seem foreign to Essenism. The baptism of John, considered as a ceremony of consecration for the coming kingdom, was parallel rather to the initiatory oaths of the Essene brotherhood than to their ablutions. Their custom may have served to suggest to John a different application of the familiar sacred use of the bath; indeed John could hardly have been uninfluenced by the usage of his contemporaries; yet in this, as in his thought, he was not a product of their school.

81. John's baptism was equally independent of the pharisaic influence. The scribes made much of "divers washings," but not with any such significance as would furnish to John his baptism of repentance and of radical change of life. That he was not following a pharisaic leading appears in the question put to him by the Pharisees, "Why, then, baptizest thou? " (John i.   25). They saw something unique in the ceremony as he conducted it.

82. Many have held that he derived his baptism from the method of admitting proselytes into the Jewish fellowship. It is clear, at least, that the later ritual prescribed a ceremonial bath as well as circumcision and sacrifice for all who came into Judaism from the Gentiles, and it is difficult to conceive of a time when a ceremonial bath would not seem indispensable, since Jews regarded all Gentile life as defiling. While such an origin for John's baptism would give peculiar force to his rebuke of Jewish confidence in the merits of Abraham (Matt. iii. 9), it is more likely, as Keim has shown (JN. II. 243 and note), that in this as in his other thought John learned of his predecessors rather than his contemporaries. Before the giving of the older covenant from Sinai, it is said that Moses was required " to sanctify the people and bid them wash their garments" (Ex. xix. 10). John was proclaiming the establishment of a new covenant, as the prophets had promised. That the people should prepare for this by a similar bath of sanctification seems most natural. John appeared with a revival of the older and simpler religious ideas of Israel's past, deriving his rite as well as his thought from the springs of his people's religious life.

83. This revival of the prophetic past had nothing scholastic or antiquarian about it. John was a disciple, not an imitator, of the great men of Israel; his message was not learned from Isaiah or any other, though he was educated by studying them. What he declared, he declared as truth immediately seen by his own soul, the essence of his power being a revival, not in letter but in spirit, of the old, direct cry, "Thus saith the Lord." Inasmuch as John's day was otherwise hopelessly in bondage to tradition and the study of the letter, by so much is his greatness enhanced in bringing again God's direct message to the human conscience. John's greatness was that of a pioneer. The Friend of publicans and sinners also spoke a simple speech to human hearts; he built on and advanced from the old prophets, but it was John who was appointed to prepare the people for the new life, 44 to make ready the way of the Lord" (Mark i. 3). The clearness of his perception of truth is not the least of his claims to greatness. His knowledge of the simplicity of God's requirements in contrast with the hopeless maze of pharisaic traditions, and his insight into the characters with whom he had to deal, whether the sinless Jesus or the hypocritical Pharisees, show a man marvellously gifted by God who made good use of his gift. This greatness appears in superlative

degree in the self-effacement of him who possessed these powers. Greatness always knows itself more or less fully. It was not self-ignorance that led John to claim to be but a voice, nor was it mock humility. The confession of his unworthiness in com- parison with the mightier one who should follow is unmistakably sincere, as is the completed joy of this friend of the bridegroom rejoicing greatly because of the bridegroom's voice, even when the bridegroom's presence meant the recedence of the friend into ever deepening obscurity (John iii. 30).

84. But John had marked limitations. He knew well the righteousness of God; he knew, and, in effect, proclaimed God's readiness to forgive them that would turn from their wicked ways; he knew the simplicity as well as the exceeding breadth of the divine commandment; but beyond one flash of insight (John i. 29-36), which did not avail to remould his thought, he did not know the yearning love of God which seeks to save. It is not strange that he did not. Some of the prophets had more knowledge of it than he, his own favorite Isaiah knew more of it than he, but it was not the thought of John's day. The wonder is that the Baptist so far freed himself from current thought; yet he did not belong to the new order. He thundered as from Sinai. The simplest child that has learned from the heart its "Our Father" has reached a higher knowledge and entered a higher privilege (Matt. xi. 11). John's self-effacement, wonderful as it was, fell short of discipleship to his greater successor; in fact, at a much later time there was still a circle of disciples of the Baptist who kept themselves separate from the church (Acts xix. 1-7). He was doubtless too strenuous a man readily to become a follower. He could yield his place with unapproachable grace, but he remained the prophet of the wilderness still. He seemed to belong consciously to the old order, and, by the very circumstances ordained of

God who sent Mm, he could not be of those who, sitting at Jesus' feet, learned to surrender to him their preconceptions and hopes, and in heart, if not in word, to say, "To whom shall we go, thou hast the words of eternal life? " (John vi. 68).

THE MESSIANIC CALL

MATT. iii. 13 TO iv. 11; MARK!. 9-13; LUKE iii. 21, 22; iv. 1-13; JOHN i. 30-34

85. IN the circle about John all classes of the people were represented: Pharisees and Sadducees, jealous of innovation and apprehensive of popular excitement; publicans and soldiers, interested in the new preacher or touched in conscience; outcasts who came in penitence, and devout souls in consecration. The wonder of the new message was carried throughout the land and brought great multitudes to the Jordan. Jesus in Nazareth heard it, and recognized in John a revival of the long-silent prophetic voice. The summons appealed to his loyalty to God's truth, and after the multitudes had been baptized (Luke iii. 21) he too sought the prophet of the wilderness.

86. The connection which Luke mentions (i. 36) between the families of Jesus and John had not led to any intimacy between the two young men. John certainly did not know of his kinsman's mission (John i. 31), nor was his conception of the Messiah such that he would look for its fulfilment in one like Jesus (Matt. iii. 10-12). One thing, however, was clear as soon as they met, â John recognized in Jesus one holier than himself (Matt. iii. 14). With a prophet's

spiritual insight he read the character of Jesus at a glance, and although that character did not prove him to be the Messiah, it prepared John for the revelation which was soon to follow.

87. The reply of Jesus to the unwillingness of John to give him baptism (Matt. iii. 15) was an expression of firm purpose to do God's will; the absence of any confession of sin is therefore all the more noticeable. In all generations the holiest men have been those most conscious of imperfection, and in John's message and baptism confession and repentance were primary demands; yet Jesus felt no need for repentance, and asked for baptism with no word of confession. But for the fact that the total impression of his life begat in his disciples the conviction that "he did no sin" (I. Pet. ii. 22; compare John viii. 46; II. Cor. v. 21), this silence of Jesus would offend the religious sense. Jesus, however, had no air of self-sufficiency, he came to make surrender and "to fulfil all-righteousness" (Matt. iii. 15). It was the positive aspect of John's baptism that drew him to the Jordan. John was preaching the coming of God's kingdom. The place held by the doctrine of that kingdom in the later teaching of Jesus makes it all but certain that his thought had been filled with it for many years. In his reading of the prophets Jesus undoubtedly emphasized the spiritual phases of their promises, but it is not likely that he had done much criticising of the ideas held by his contemporaries before he came to John. As already remarked he seems to have been quicker to discover his affinity with the older truth than to be conscious of the novelty of his own ways of apprehending it (Matt. v. 17). When, then, Jesus heard John's call for consecration to the approaching kingdom he recognized the voice of duty, and he sought the baptism that he might do all that he could to "make ready the way of the Lord."

88. This act of consecration on Jesus' part was one of personal obedience. There were no crowds present (Luke iii. 21), and his thoughts were full of prayer. It was an experience which concerned his innermost life with God, and it called him to communion with heaven like that in which he sought for wisdom before choosing his apostles (Luke vi. 12), and for strength in view of his approaching death (Luke ix. 28, 29). His outward declaration of loyalty to the coming kingdom was thus not an act of righteousness " to be seen of men," but one of personal devotion to him who is and who sees in secret (Matt. vi. 1, 6). As the transfiguration followed the prayer on Hermon, so this initial consecration was answered from heaven. A part of the answer was evident to John, for he saw a visible token of the gift of the divine Spirit which was granted to Jesus for the conduct of the work he had to do, and he recognized in Jesus the greater successor for whom he was simply making preparation (Mark i. 10; John i. 32-34). To Jesus there came also with the gift of the Spirit a definite word from heaven, "Thou art my beloved Son, in thee I am well pleased" (Mark i. 11). The language in Mark and Luke, and the silence of the Baptist concerning the voice from heaven (John i. 32-34), indicate that the word came to Jesus alone, and was his summons to undertake the work of setting up that kingdom to which he had just pledged his loyalty. The expression " My beloved Son " had clear Messianic signifi- cance for Jesus' contemporaries (comp. Mark xiv. 62), and the message can have signified for him nothing less than a Messianic call. It implied more than that

child-relation to God which was the fundamental fact in his religious life from the beginning: it had an official meaning.

89. For Jesus the sense of being God's child was normally human, and in his ministry he invited all men to a similar consciousness of sonship. Yet his early years must have brought to him a realization that he was different from his fellows. That in him which made a confession at the baptism unnatural and which led to John's word, "I have need to be baptized by thee," was ready to echo assent when God said, "Thou art my Son." He accepted the call and the new office and mission which it implied, and he must have recognized that it was for this moment that all the past of his life had been making preparation.

90. The gift of the Spirit to Jesus, which furnished to John the proof that the Greater One had appeared, was not an arbitrary sign. The old prophetic thought (Isa. xi. 2; xlii. 1; Ixi. 1) as well as a later popular expectation (Ps. of Sol. xvii. 42) provided for such an anointing of the Messiah; and in the actual conduct of his life Jesus was constantly under the leading of this Spirit (see Matt. xii. 28 and John iii. 34). The temptation which followed the baptism, and in which he faced the difficulties in his new task, was the first result of the Spirit's control. Its later influence is not so clearly marked in the gospels, but they imply that as the older servants of God were guided and strengthened by him, so his Son also was aided, â with this difference, however, that he possessed com- pletely the heavenly gift (John iii. 34). Jesus uniform confession of dependence on God confirms this teaching of the gift of the divine Spirit; and his uniform consciousness of complete power and authority confirms the testimony that he had the Spirit " without measure."

91. The temptation to which the Spirit "drove" Jesus after his baptism gives proof that the call to assume the Messianic office came to him unexpectedly; for the three temptations with which his long struggle ended were echoes of the voice which he had heard at the Jordan, and subtle insinuations of doubt of its meaning. Some withdrawal to contemplate the significance of his appointment to a Messianic work was a mental and spiritual necessity. As has often been said, if the gospels had not recorded the temptation, we should have had to assume one. Jesus being the man he was, could not have thought that his call was a summons to an entire change in his ideals and his thoughts about God and duty. Yet he must have been conscious of the wide differences between his conceptions of God's kingdom and the popular expectation. Those differences, by the measure of the defi-niteness of the popular thought and the ardor of the popular hope, were the proof of the difficulty of his task. The call meant that the Messiah could be such as he was; it meant that the kingdom could be and must be a dominion of God primarily in the hearts of men and consequently in their world; it meant that his work must be religious rather than political, and gracious rather than judicial. These essentials of the work which he could do contradicted at nearly every point the expectations of his people. How could he succeed in the face of such opposition? His long meditation during forty days doubtless showed him the difficulty of his task in all its baldness, yet it did not shake his certainty that the call had come to him from God, nor his faith that what God had called him to do he could accomplish.

92. The gospels show no hesitation in calling the experience of these days a temptation, nor had the Christian feeling of the first century any difficulty in thinking of its Lord as actually suffering temptation (Heb. ii. 18; iv. 15). A temptation to be real cannot be hypothetical; evil must actually present itself as attractive to the tempted soul. A suggestion of evil that takes no hold concretely of the heart is no temptation, nor is the resistance of it any victory. The sin-lessness of him who sought baptism with no confession on his lips nor sense of penitence in his heart offers no barrier to his experience of genuine temptation, unless we think him incapable of sin, and therefore not " like unto his brethren." Not only do the gospels repeatedly refer to his temptations (Luke iv. 13; Mark viii. 31-33; Luke xxii. 28; compare Heb. v. 7-9), but they also depict clearly the reality of these initial testings. The account as given in Matthew and Luke represents the experience with which the forty days' struggle culminated. The absorption of Jesus' mind had been so complete that he had neglected the needs of his body, and when he turned to think of earthly things he was pressed by hunger. A popular notion at a later time, and probably also in Jesus' day, was that the Messiah would be able to feed his people as Moses had given them manna in the wilderness (John vi. 30-32; see EderslJM. I. 176). He had just been endowed with the divine Spirit for the work before him; it was therefore no fantastic idea when the suggestion came that he should use his power to supply his own needs in the desert. Nor was the temptation without attractiveness; his own physical nature urged its need, and Jesus was no ascetic who found discomfort a way of holiness. The evil in the suggestion was that it asked him to use his newly given powers for the supply of his own needs, as if doubting that God would care for him as for any other of his children. There was more than distrust of God suggested; the temptation came with a hint of another doubt, â "If thou art God's Son." A miracle would prove to himself his appointment and his power. The suggested doubt of his call he passed unnoticed; distrust of God he repudiated instantly, falling back on his faith in the God he had served these many years (Deut. viii. 3). His victory is remarkable because his spirit conquered unhesitatingly after a long ecstasy which would naturally have induced a reaction and a surrender for the moment to the demand of lower needs. 93. This firmness of trust opened the way for another evil suggestion. In the work before him as God's Anointed many difficulties were on either side and across his path. He knew his people, their prejudices, and their hardness of heart; and he knew how far he was from their ideal of a Messiah. He knew also the watchful jealousy of Rome. Others before him, like Judas of Galilee, had tried the Messianic rôle and had failed. He, however, was confident of his divine call: should he not, therefore, press forward with his work, heedless of all danger and regardless of the dicfe tes of prudence, â as heedless as if, trust- ing God's promised care, he should cast himself down from a pinnacle of the temple to the rocks in Kidron below? A fanatic would have yielded to such a temptation. Many another than Jesus did so, â Theudas (Acts v. 36), the Egyptian (Acts xxi. 38); and Bar Cochba (Dio Cassius, Ixix. 12-14; Euseb. Ch. Hist. iv. 6). Jesus, however, showed his perfect mental health, repudiating the temptation by declaring that while man may trust God's care, he must not presumptuously put it to the test (Matt. iv. 7). The after life of Jesus was a clear commentary on this reply. He constantly sought to avoid situations which would compromise his mission or cut

short his work (see John vi. 15), and when at the end he suffered the death prepared for him by his people's hatred, it was because his hour had come and he could say, "I lay down my life of myself " (John x. 18). His marvellous control of enthusiasm and his self-mastery in all circumstances separate Jesus from all ecstatics and fanatics. Yet presumption must have seemed the easier course, and could readily wear the mask of trust. He was tempted, yet without sin.

94. As the refusal to doubt led to the temptation to presume, so the determination to be prudent opened the way for a third assault upon his perfect loyalty to God. The world he was to seek to save was swayed by passions; his own people were longing for a Messiah, but they must have their kind of a Messiah. If he would acknowledge this actual supremacy of evil and self-will in the world, the opposition of passion and prejudice might be avoided. If he would own the evil inevitable for the time, and accommodate his work to it, he might then be free to lead men to higher and more spiritual views of God's kingdom. His knowledge of his people's grossness of heart and materialism of hope made a real temptation of the suggestion that he should not openly oppose but should accommodate himself to them. Jesus did not underestimate the opposition of "the kingdoms of the world," but he truly estimated God's intolerance of any rivalry (Matt. iv. 10), and he was true to God and to his own soul. Again, in this as in the preceding temptations, Jesus conquered the evil suggestions by appropriating to himself truth spoken by God's servants to Israel. Tempted in all points like his brethren, he resisted as any one of them could have resisted, and won a victory possible, ideally considered, to any other of the children of men.

95. It is not idle curiosity which inquires whence the evangelists got this story of the temptation of Jesus. Even if the whole transaction took place on the plane of outer sensuous life, and Jesus was bodily carried to Jerusalem and to the mountain-top, there is no probability that any witnesses were at hand who could tell the tale. But the fact that in any case the vision of the kingdoms of the world in a moment of time (Luke iv. 5) could have been spiritual only, since no mountain, however high (Matt. iv. 8), could give, physically, that wide sweep of view, suggests that the whole account tells in pictorial language an intensely real, inner experience of Jesus. This in no respect reduces the truthfulness of the narratives. Temptation never becomes temptation till it passes to that inner scene of action and debate. Since Jesus shows in all his teaching a natural use of parabolic language to set forth spiritual truth, the inference is almost inevitable that the gospels have in like manner adopted the language of vivid picture as alone adequate to depict the essential reality of his inner struggle. In any case the narrative could have come from no other source than himself. How he came to tell it we do not know. On one of the days of private converse with his disciples after the confession at Cæsarea Philippi he may have given them this account of his own experience, in order to help his loyal Galileans to understand more fully his work and the way of it, and to prepare them for that disappointment of their expectations which they were so slow to acknowledge as possible.

96. From this struggle in the wilderness Jesus came forth with the clear conviction that he was God's Anointed, and in all his after life no hesitation appeared. The kingdom which he undertook to establish was that dominion of simple righteousness

which he had learned to know and love in the years of quiet life in Nazareth. He set out to do his work fearlessly, but prudently, seeking to win men in his Father's way to acknowledge that Father's sovereignty. There is no evidence that, beyond such firm conviction and purpose, he had any fixed plan for the work he was to do, nor that he saw clearly as yet how his earthly career would end. The third temptation, however, shows that he was not unprepared for seeming defeat. The struggle had been long and serious, â for the three temptations of the end are doubtless typical of the whole of the forty days, â and the victory was great and final. With the light of victory as well as the marks of warfare on his face, he took his way back towards Galilee.

THE FIRST DISCIPLES JOHN i. 19 TO ii. 12 97. AFTER the withdrawal of Jesus into the wilderness, John the Baptist continued his ministry of preaching and baptizing, moving northward up the Jordan valley to Bethany, on the eastern side of the river, near one of the fords below the Sea of Galilee (John i. 28). Here Galilee, doubtless, contributed more to his audience than Judea. It is certain that some from the borders of the lake were at this time among his constant attendants: Andrew and Simon of Bethsaida, John the son of Zebedee, and perhaps his brother James, probably also Philip of Bethsaida and Nathan-ael of Cana (John i. 40, 41, 43-45; compare xxi. 2).

98. The leaders in Jerusalem, becoming apprehensive whither this work would lead, sent an embassy to question John. They chose for this mission priests and Levites of pharisaic leaning as most influential among the people. The impression John and his message were making on the popular mind is seen in the questions put to him, "Art thou the Messiah? " "Elijah?" "The prophet?" (see Deut. xviii. 15), and in the challenge, "Why, then, baptizest thou?" when John disclaimed the right to any of these names. John's reply is the echo of his earlier proclamation of the one mightier than he who should baptize with the Spirit (Mark i. 7, 8), only now he added that this one was present among them (John i. 26, 27).

99. This interview occurred several weeks after Jesus' baptism, for upon the next day John saw Jesus (John i. 29), now returned from the temptation, and pointed him out to a group of disciples. Something in Jesus' face or in his bearing, as he came from his temptation, must have impressed John even more than at their first meeting; for he was led to think of a prophetic word for the most part ignored by the Messianic thought of his day, "He was brought as a lamb to the slaughter " (Isa. liii. 7). As he looked on Jesus the mysterious oracle was illuminated for him, and he cried, "Behold the lamb of God which taketh away the sin of the world." Once again on the next day the same thought rushed to his lips when, with two disciples, he saw Jesus passing by (John i. 35, 36). Then as Jesus left John's neighborhood and took up again the round of ordinary life, John seems to have reverted to his more ordinary Messianic thought, his momentary insight into highest truth standing as a thing apart in his life. Such a moment's insight, caused by extraordinary circumstances, no more requires that John should retain the high thought constantly than does Peter's confession of Christ at Csesarea Philippi exclude his later rebuke of his Lord (Mark viii. 32, 33), or his denials (Mark xiv. 66-72).

100. The disciples who heard these testimonies from John understood them to be Messianic (John i. 30-34), though their later consternation, when the cross seemed

to shatter their hopes (John xx. 9,10, 24, 25), shows that they did not comprehend their deeper meaning. Two of these disciples at once attached themselves to Jesus, and one of them, Andrew of Bethsaida, was so impressed by the new master that, having sought out his brother Simon, he declared that they had found the Messiah. The other of these earliest followers was John the son of Zebedee, and it is possible that he also found his brother and introduced James from the very first into the circle of the disciples. Jesus was about to take his departure for Galilee, and on the next day, as he was leaving, added Philip of Bethsaida to the little company of followers. Philip, impressed as Andrew had been, brought Nathan-ael of Cana to Jesus. The undefined something about Jesus which drew noble hearts irresistibly to himself, and his marvellous knowledge of this new comer, produced the same effect in Nathanael, as was seen earlier in Andrew and Philip, and he acknowledged the new master as " Son of God, King of Israel " (John i. 49).

101. These early confessions in the fourth gospel present a difficulty in view of Jesus' warm approval of Peter's acknowledgment of him at Csesarea Philippi (Matt. xvi. 13-20). Jesus saw in that confession a distinct advance in the disciples' thought and faith. Yet the religious feeling which early questioned whether the Baptist even were not the Messiah (Luke iii. 15) would almost certainly have concluded that John's greater successor must be God's anointed. The veiy fact that men's thoughts about the Messiah were varied and complex made them ready for some modifications of their preconceptions. One with such subtle personal power as Jesus had exercised was almost sure to be hailed by some with enthusiasm as the looked- for representative of God. In fact, it is probable that at any time in the early days of his ministry Jesus could have been proclaimed Messiah, provided he had accepted the people's terms. Such a confession would have been merely the outcome of enthusiasm. The people, even the disciples, did not know Jesus. They all had high hopes and somewhat fixed ideas about the Messiah, nearly every one of which was destined to rude shock. How little they knew him Jesus realized (John i. 51), and his self-mastery is manifest in his attitude to this early enthusiasm. He was no visionary; he had a great work to do and a long lesson to teach, and he was patient enough to teach it little by little. He did not rebuke the ill-informed faith of a Nathanael, but sought gradually to supplant the old thought of the Messiah and of the kingdom by new truth, and to bind men's affections to himself for his own sake and the truth's sake, not simply for the idea which he impersonated to them.

102. The visit to Cana seems to have found a place in the fourth gospel, because there the new disciples discovered in their master miraculous powers which were to them a sign that he was in truth God's anointed. It is probable that at the time of this miracle the disciples thought only of the power and the marvel, yet the sharp contrast between John's ascetic habit and Jesus' use of his divine resources to relieve embarrassment at a wedding feast must have impressed every man among them. Their minds, however, were as yet too full of Messianic hopes to leave much room for reflection. They were content to have a sign, for in the view of Jesus' contemporaries signs were essential marks of the Messiah (John vi. 30; vii. 31;

Mark viii. 11). They did their reflecting later (John ii. 22).

103. Miracles are as great a stumbling-block to modern thought as they were a help to the contemporaries of Jesus. The study of Jesus' life cannot ignore this fact, nor make little of it. It is fair to insist, however, that the question is one of evidence, not of metaphysical possibility. Men are wisely slow to-day to claim that they can tell what are the limits of the possible. If the question is one of evidence, it is in an important sense true that the evidence for miracle in the life of Jesus is appreciable only when that life is viewed in its completeness. The miracles attributed to Jesus may be studied, however, for the disclosure which they give of his character, and of his relation to common human need. So it is with this first sign at Cana. Jesus had just heard the call to be Messiah, and in his lonely struggle in the wilderness had given a loyal answer to that call, and had set out to do his Father's business in his Father's way. He who by the Jordan still carried the marks of struggle, so that the Baptist saw in him the suffering Saviour of Isaiah liii., now returned to the ordinary daily life in Galilee, and as a guest at a wedding feast he commenced that ministry of simple human friendliness (Matt. xi. 19; compare Mark ii. 15-17; Luke xv. 1, 2), which set him in sharp contrast alike with John's asceticism and with the ritualism and pedantry of the Pharisees.

104. His human friendliness is all the more worthy of note, inasmuch as on his return to Cana Jesus did not take up again the old relations of life as they existed before his baptism. This is clear from his reply to his mother when she reported the scarcity of wine (John ii. 3-5). While it is true that the title by which Jesus addressed Mary was neither disrespectful nor unkind (John xix. 26), the reply itself was a warning that now he was no longer hers in the old sense. A new mission had been given him, which henceforth would determine all his conduct, and in that mission she could not now share. Here is one of the many indications (compare Mark iii. 21, 31-35; Luke ii. 48) that Mary did not understand her son nor his work until much later (John xix. 25; Acts i. 14). That with such a clear sense of his new and serious mission Jesus' first official act was one of kindly relief for social embarrassment is most significant. He chose to show his divine authority to his new disciples in a way that brought joy to a festal company. Little as the disciples were likely to appreciate it at the time, it was beautifully indicative of the simplicity and everyday lovableness of Jesus' idea of the earnest service of God.

105. With the disciples thus strengthened in faith, and the mother not separated from him though unable to know his deepest thoughts, and the brethren who could not yet nor later understand their kinsman and his work, Jesus went down to Capernaum (John ii. 12), which proved thenceforth to be the centre of his greatest work and teaching. There for a time, how long cannot be known, he continued in quiet fellowship with his new friends, until the approach of the Passover drew him to Jerusalem to make formal opening of his Messianic work in that centre of his people's religious life.

106. THE attempt to arrange an orderly account of the way in which Jesus set about the work to which he was called at his baptism is met at the outset by a problem. The vivid and familiar words of Mark (i. 14), seconded by the representation in both Matthew (iv. 12) and Luke (iv. 14), indicate the imprisonment of John as the occasion, and Galilee as the scene of the inauguration of Jesus' public ministry. The fourth gospel, on the other hand, tells of a work of Jesus and his disciples in Judea prior to the

imprisonment of John (iii. 24), and makes this work follow at some interval after the inauguration of the Messianic ministry in Jerusalem. The minuteness of detail of time and place in the early chapters of John (i. 19 to iv. 43), together with the vividness of their narrative, give them strong claim to credence. They thus record a ministry earlier than that narrated in the other gospels, proving that the actual inauguration of Jesus' work occurred in Jerusalem at a Passover season previous to the imprisonment of John. This is known as the Early Judean Ministry.

107. The fact that Peter was wont to tell the story of Jesus' life in such a way as to lead Mark to set the opening of the ministry after the close of John's activ- ity, indicates that that beginning of work in Galilee seemed to the disciples to be in a way the actual inauguration of Jesus' constructive and successful work. Peter cannot have been ignorant of the labors in Judea, though he may not himself have accompanied Jesus to the Passover. A new stage in the life of Jesus began, therefore, with his withdrawal to Galilee.

108. The story of the Galilean ministry is given chiefly by the first three gospels, John contributing but two incidents to the period covered by that ministry,â a second miracle at Cana (iv. 46-54), and a visit to Judea (v. 1-47), â and relating more fully the story of the feeding of the multitudes (vi. 1-71). The journey from Judea through Samaria (John iv. 1-45) should be identified with the removal to Galilee which stands at the beginning of Mark's record (i. 14; Matt. iv. 12; Luke iv. 14). Mark's account of the Galilean activity of Jesus (i. 14 to ix. 50) is one of such simple and steady progress that the whole period must be considered as a unit.

109. In the use which Matthew (iv. 12 to xviii. 35) and Luke (iv. 14 to ix. 50) make of Mark's record this unity is emphasized. Their treatment of the matter which they add, however, makes it best to study the period topically rather than attempt to follow closely a chronological sequence. As it is probable that the early writing ascribed by Papias to the apostle Matthew failed to preserve in many cases any record of the time and place of the teachings of Jesus, so is it certain that the first and third evangelists have distributed quite differently the material which they seem to have derived from that apostolic document. Mention need only be made of the exhor- tation against anxiety which Matthew places in the sermon on the mount (vi. 19-34), and which Luke has given after the close of the Galilean activity (xii. 22-34). It is possible to form some judgment of the general relations of such discourses from the character of their contents, but in the absence of positive statement by the evangelists it is hopeless to seek to give them a more definite historical setting. A topical study can consider them as contributions to the period to which they belong, while a chronological study would be lost in uncertain conjectures. A topical study may, however, disclose the fact that sequence of time was identical with development of method. This is, in general, the case with the Galilean ministry. The new lesson which Jesus began to teach after the confession at Csesarea Philippi marked the supreme turning point in his whole public activity. Before that crisis the work of Jesus was a constructive preparation for the question which called forth Peter's confession. Subsequently his work was that of making ready for the end, which from that time on he foretold. As has been stated, the Galilean ministry is the story of the first three gospels, except for two incidents and a discourse added by John. The visit to the feast of Tabernacles (John vii. 1 to viii.

59) stands on the border between the work in Galilee and that which followed. It was one of Jesus' many attempts to win Jerusalem, and is evidence that the author of the fourth gospel â either because of special interest in the capital, or because of superior knowledge of the work of his Master in Judeaâ gave emphasis to a side of the life of Jesus which the other gospels have neglected.

110. With the close of the constructive ministry in Galilee, the account of Mark (x. 1; compare Matt xix. 1; Luke ix. 51) turns towards Jerusalem and the cross. The journey was not direct, but traversed Perea, the domain of Antipas beyond Jordan, and was accompanied by continued ministry of teaching and healing (Mark x. 1-52; Matt. xix. 1 to xx. 34). It is at this point that Luke has inserted the long section peculiar to his gospel (ix. 51 to xviii. 14), becoming again parallel with Mark as Jesus drew near to Jerusalem (xviii. 15 to xix. 28; compare Mark x. 13-52). Much of that which Luke adds gives evidence that in all probability it should be placed before the change in method at Csesarea Philippi, while much of it undoubtedly belongs to the last months of Jesus' life. Since the last journey to Jerusalem is reported with considerable fulness, it is natural in a study of Jesus' life to treat that journey by itself. At this point John contributes important additions to the record (ix. 1 to xi. 57) showing that the journey was not continuous, but was interrupted by several more or less hurried visits to the capital, renewed efforts of Jesus to win the city.

111. With the final arrival in Jerusalem the four gospels come together in a record of the last days and the crucifixion (Mark xi. 1 to xv. 47; Matt. xxi. 1 to xxvii. 66; Luke xix. 29 to xxiii. 56; John xi. 55 to xix. 42). The evangelists, in their accounts of the last week, seem to have had access to completer and more varied information than for any other part of the ministry. This causes some difficulties in constructing an ordered conception of the events, yet it greatly adds to the fulness of our knowledge. It is easier, therefore, to consider the period in three parts, â the final controversies in Jerusalem, the Last Supper, and the betrayal, trial, and crucifixion.

112. In a sense the resurrection and ascension form the conclusion of the final visit to Jerusalem, and should be treated with the last week. In a larger sense, however, they form the culmination of the whole ministry, and therefore constitute a final stage in the study of Jesus' life. At this point the record of the gospels is supplemented by the first chapter of the Acts and by Paul's concise report of the appearances of the risen Christ (I. Cor. xv. 3-8). The various accounts exhibit perplexing independence of each other. In total impression, however, they agree, and show that the tragedy, by which the enemies of Jesus thought to end his career, was turned into signal triumph.

The first Passover of the public ministry: Cleansing of the temple â John ii. 13-22.

Early results in Jerusalem: Discourse with Nicodemus â John ii. 23 to iii. 15.

Withdrawal into rural parts of Judea to preach and baptize â John iii. 22-30; iv. 1, 2.

Imprisonment of John the Baptist â Matt. iv. 12; Mark i. 14.

Withdrawal from Judea through Samaria â John iv. 1-42.

Unlooked-for welcome in Galilee â John iv. 43-45.

? Second sign at Cana: Cure of the Nobleman's son â John iv. 46-54 (see sect. A 41).

Retirement at Nazareth, the disciples resuming their accustomed calling. Inferred from Matt. iv. 13; Luke iv. 31; Matt, iv. 18-22 and s.

Events marked? should possibly be given a different place; s stands for "parallel accounts;" for sections marked JLâ as A 41 â see Appendix.

THE EAELY MINISTRY IN JUDEA 113. WE owe to the fourth gospel our knowledge of the fact that Jesus began his general ministry in Jerusalem. The silence of the other records concerning this beginning cannot discredit the testimony of John. For these other records themselves indicate in various ways that Jesus had repeatedly sought to win Jerusalem before his final visit at the end of his life (compare Luke xiii. 34; Matt, xxiii. 37). Moreover, the fourth gospel is confirmed by the probability, rising almost to necessity, that such a mission as Jesus conceived his to be must seek first to win the leaders of his people. The temple at Jerusalem was the centre of worship, drawing all Jews sooner or later to itself â even as Jesus in early youth was accustomed to go thither at the time of feasts (Luke ii. 41). Worshippers of God throughout the world prayed with their faces towards Jerusalem (Dan. vi. 10). Moreover, at Jerusalem the chief of the scribes, as well as the chief of the priests, were to be found. Compared with Jerusalem all other places were provincial and of small influence. A Messiah, who had not from the outset given up hope of winning the capital, cannot have long delayed his effort to find a following there.

114. Arriving at Jerusalem at the Passover season, in the early spring, Jesus remained in Judea until the following December (John iv. 35). Evidently the record which John gives of these months is most fragmentary, and from his own statement (xx. 30, 31) it seems highly probable that it is one sided, emphasizing those events and teachings in which Jesus disclosed more or less clearly his claim to be the Messiah. Doubtless the full record would show a much closer similarity between this early work in Judea and that later conducted in Galilee than a comparison of John with the other gospels would suggest; yet it is evident that Jesus opened his ministry in Jerusalem with an unrestrained frankness that is not found later in Galilee.

115. It is a mistake to think of the cleansing of the temple as a distinct Messianic manifesto. The market in the temple was a licensed affront to spiritual religion. It found its excuse for being in the require- ment that worshippers offer to the priests for sacrifice animals levitically clean and acceptable, and that gifts for the temple treasury be made in no coin other than the sacred " shekel of the sanctuary." The chief priests appreciated the convenience which worshippers coming from a distance would find if they could obtain all the means of worship within the temple enclosure itself. The hierarchy or its representatives seem also to have appreciated the opportunity to charge good prices for the accommodation so afforded. The result was the intrusion of the spirit of the market-place, with all its disputes and haggling, into the place set apart for worship. In fact, the only part of the temple open to Gentiles who might wish to worship Israel's God was filled with distraction, unseemly strife, and extortion (compare Mark xi. 17). Such despite done the sanctity of God's house must have outraged the pious sense of many a devout Israelite. There is no doubt of what an Isaiah or a Micah would have said and done in such a situation. This is exactly what Jesus did. His act was the assumption of a full prophetic authority. In itself considered it was nothing more. In his expulsion of the traders he had the conscience of the people

for his ally. There is no need to think of any use of miraculous power. His moral earnestness, coupled with the underlying consciousness on the part of the traders themselves that they had no business in God's house, readily explains the confusion and departure of the intruders. Even those who challenged Jesus' conduct did not venture to defend the presence of the market in the temple. They only demanded that Jesus show his warrant for disturbing a condition of things authorized by the priests.

116. The temple cleansing is recorded in the other gospels at the end of Jesus' ministry, just before the hostility of the Jews culminated in his condemnation and death. Inasmuch as these gospels give no account of a ministry by Jesus in Jerusalem before the last week of his life, it is easy to see how this event came to be associated by them with the only Jerusalem sojourn which they record. The definite place given to the event in John, together with the seeming necessity that Jesus should condemn such authorized affront to the very idea of worship, mark this cleansing as the inaugural act of Jesus' ministry of spiritual religion, rather than as a final stern rebuke closing his effort to win his people. Against the conclusion commonly held that Jesus cleansed the temple both at the opening and at the close of his course is the extreme improbability that the traders would have been caught twice in the same way. The event fits in closely with the story of the last week, because it actually led to the beginning of opposition in Jerusalem to the prophet from Galilee. At the first the opposition was doubtless of a scornful sort. Later it grew in bitterness when it saw how Jesus was able to arouse a popular enthusiasm that seemed to threaten the stability of existing conditions.

117. The reply of Jesus to the challenge of his authority for his high-handed act shows that he offered it to the people as an invitation; he would lead them to a higher idea and practice of worship (compare John iv. 21-24). When they demanded the warrant for his act, he saw that they were not ready to follow him, and could not appreciate the only warrant he needed for his course. He cleansed the temple because they were destroying it as a place where men could worship God in spirit. In reply to the challenge, he who later taught the Samaritan woman that 'the worship of God is not dependent on any place however sacred, answered that they might finish their work and destroy the temple as a house of God, yet he would speedily re-establish a true means of approach to the Most High for the souls of men. He clothed his reply in a figurative dress, as he was often wont to do in his teaching, â " Destroy this temple, and in three days I will raise it up." To his unsympathetic hearers it must have been completely enigmatic. Even the disciples did not catch its meaning until after the resurrection had taught them that in their Master a new chapter in God's dealing with men had begun.

118. The unreadiness of the Jewish leaders to receive the only kind of message he had to offer produced in Jesus a decided reserve. He did not lack a certain kind of success in Jerusalem. His cures of the sick won him many followers who seemed ready to believe almost anything of him. But the attitude taken by the leaders made it evident that Jesus must make disciples who should understand in some measure at least his idea of God's kingdom, and, understanding, must be ready to be loyal to it through good report and evil. For the position taken by the leaders of the people had an ominous significance. It could mean but one thing for Jesus, â unrelenting

conflict. If they could not be won, they who would so legalize the desecration of God's house would not hesitate at any extreme in opposing his messenger. This possibility confronted Jesus at the very outset; therefore he held the popular enthusiasm in check, knowing that as yet it had little of that kind of faith which could endure seeming defeat.

119. One of those who were drawn to him, however, gave Jesus opportunity to lay aside his reserve and speak clearly of the truth he came to publish. He was a member of the Jewish sanhedrin, a rabbi apparently held in high regard in Jerusalem. While his associates were dismissing the claims of Jesus with a wave of the hand, Nicodemus sought out the new teacher by night, and showed his desire to learn what Jesus held to be truth concerning God's kingdom. Jesus first reminded the teacher of Israel of the old doctrine of the prophets, that Israel must find a new heart before God's kingdom can come (Jer. xxxi. 31-34; Ezek. xxxvi. 25-27), and then declared that the heavenly truth which God now would reveal to men is that all can have the needed new life as freely as the plague-stricken Israelites found relief when Moses lifted up the brazen serpent. This conversation serves to introduce the evangelist's interpretation of Jesus as the only begotten Son of God sent in love to redeem the world (John iii. 16-21).

120. John's record suggests that Jesus left Jerusalem shortly after the conversation with Nicodemus. His work there was not without success, for Nicodemus seems to have been henceforth his loyal advocate (compare John vii. 50-52; xix. 39); and it may be that at the time of this sojourn he won the hearts of his friends in Bethany, for the first picture the gospels give of this household seems to presuppose a somewhat intimate relation of Jesus to the family (Luke x. 38-42). It would be idle to speculate whether it was at this time or later that he became acquainted with Joseph of Arimathea, or the friends who during the last week of his life showed him hospitality (Mark xi. 2-6; xiv. 12-16).

121. For a time after his withdrawal from Jerusalem he lingered in Judea, carrying on a simple ministry of preparation like that of John the Baptist. In this way the summer and early autumn seem to have passed, Jesus growing more popular as a prophet than John himself had been. The fact that Jesus' disciples administered b. iptism in connection with his work roused the jealousy of some of John's followers, and attracted again the attention of Jerusalem to the new activity of th.3 bold disturber of the temple market. John's disciples complained to him of Jesus' rivalry, and received his self-effacing confession, "He must increase, I must decrease." The Pharisees, on the other hand, made Jesus feel that further work in Judea was for the time unwise, and he withdrew into Galilee for retirement, since u a prophet has no honor in his own country " (John iv. 1-3, 44). Baffled in his first effort to win his people, this journey back from the region of the holy city must have been one of no little sadness for Jesus. Some urgency for haste led him by the direct road through despised Samaria. A seemingly chance conversation with a woman at Jacob's well, where he was resting at noonday, gave him an opportunity for ministry which was more ingenuously received than any which he had been able to render in Judea; and to this woman he declared himself even more plainly than to Nicodemus, and preached to her that spiritual idea of worship which he had sought to enforce by cleansing Jerusalem's temple. Samaria was so isolated from all Jewish interest that Jesus felt no need for reserve in this "

strange " land. The few days spent there must have been peculiarly welcome to his heart, fresh from rejection in Judea.

122. One reason why he wished to hasten from Judea seems to have been his knowledge of the hostile movement which was making against John the Baptist. Either before or soon after Jesus started for Galilee Herod had arrested John, ostensibly as a measure of public safety owing to John's undue popularity (Jos. Ant. xviii. 5. 2). Herod may have been encouraged to take this step by the hostility of the Pharisees to the plain-spoken prophet of the desert (see John iv. 1-3). The fourth gospel leaves its readers to infer that the imprisonment took place somewhere about this time (compare iii. 24 and v. 35), while the other gospels unite in giving this arrest as the occasion for Jesus' withdrawal into Galilee.

123. Arrived in Galilee, Jesus seems to have returned to his home at Nazareth, while his disciples went back to their customary occupations, until he summoned them again to join him in a new ministry (see sect. 125). John assigns to this time the cure of a nobleman's son. The father sought out Jesus at Cana, having left his son sick at Capernaum. At first Jesus apparently repelled his approach, even as he had dealt with seekers after marvels at Jerusalem; but on hearing the father's cry of need and trust, he at once spoke the word of healing. This event is in so many ways a duplicate of the cure of a centurion's servant recorded in Matthew and Luke, that to many it seems but another version of the same incident. Considering the variations in the story reported by Matthew and Luke, it is clearly not possible to prove that John tells of a different case. Yet the simple fact of similarity of some details in two events should not exclude the possibility of their still being quite distinct. The reception which Jesus gave the two requests for help is very different, and the case reported in John is in keeping with the attitude of Jesus before he began his new ministry in Galilee. On his arrival in Galilee he wished to avoid a mere wonder faith begotten of the enthusiasm he excited in Jerusalem, yet this wish yielded at once when a genuine need sought relief at his hands.

124. The apparent result of this first activity in Judea was disappointment and failure. He had won no considerable following in the capital. He had definitely excited the jealousy- and opposition of the leading men of his nation. Even such popular enthusiasm as had followed his mighty works was of a sort that Jesus could not encourage. The situation in Judea had at length become so nearly untenable that he decided to withdraw into seclusion in Galilee, where, as a prophet, he could be " without honor." He had gone to Jerusalem eager to begin there, where God should have had readiest service, the ministry of the kingdom of God. Challenge, cold criticism, and superficial faith were the results. A new beginning must be made on other lines in other places. Meanwhile Jesus retired to his home and his followers to theirs.

The imprisonment of John and the withdrawal of Jesus into Galilee â Matt. iv. 12-17; Mark i. 14,15; Luke iv. 14,15. Removal from Nazareth to Capernaum â Matt. iv. 13-16; Luke iv. 31'. The call of Simon and Andrew, James and John â Matt. iv. 18-22; Mark i. 16-20; Luke v. 1-11. First work in Capernaum â Matt. viii. 14-17; Mark i. 21-34; Luke iv. 31-41. First circuit of Galilee â Matt. iv. 23; viii. 2-4; Mark i. 35-45;

Luke iv. 42-44; v. 12-16. Cure of a paralytic in Capernaum â Matt. ix. 2-8; Mark ii.

1-12; Luke v. 17-26. The call of Matthew â Matt. ix. 9-13; Mark ii. 13-17; Luke v. 27-32.? The question about fasting â Matt. ix. 14-17; Mark ii. 18-22;

Luke v. 33-39 (see sects. 47; A 54).? Sabbath cure at Jerusalem at the unnamed feast â John v 1-47 (see sect. A 53).? The Sabbath controversy in the Galilean grain fields â Matt.

xii. 1-8; Mark ii. 23-28; Luke vi. 1-5 (see sects. 47; A 54).? Another Sabbath controversy: cure of a withered hand â

Matt. xii. 9-14; Mark Hi. 1-6; Luke vi. 6-11 (see sects. 47;

A 54). Jesus followed by multitudes from all parts â Matt. iv. 23-25; xii. 15-21; Mark iii. 7-12; Luke vi. 17-19. The choosing of the twelve â Matt. x. 2-4; Mark iii. 13-19;

Luke vi. 12-19. The sermon on the mount â Matt. v. 1 to viii. 1; Luke vi. 20 to vii. 1 (see sect. A 55). The cure of a centurion's servant â Matt. viii. 5-13; Luke vii-1-10; Johniv. 46-54.

The restoration of the widow's son at Nain â Luke vii. 11-17. The message from John in prison â Matt. xi. 2-19 j Luke vii.

18-35.

The anointing of Jesus by a sinful woman â Luke vii. 36-50. The companions of Jesus on his second circuit of Galileeâ Luke viii. 1-3. Cure of a demoniac in Capernaum and blasphemy by the

Pharisees â Matt. xii. 22-45; Mark iii. 19 b-30; Luke xi.

14-36. The true kindred of Jesus â Matt. xii. 46-50; Mark iii. 31-35;

Luke viii. 19-21. The parables by the seaâ Matt. xiii. 1-53; Mark iv. 1-31;

Luke viii. 4-18 (see sect. A 56). The tempest stilled â Matt. viii. 18, 23-27; Mark iv. 35-11;

Luke viii. 22-25. Cure of the Gadarene demoniac â Matt. viii. 28-34; Mark v.

1-20; Luke viii. 26-39. The restoration of the daughter of Jairus and cure of an invalid womanâ Matt. ix. 1, 18-26; Mark v. 21-43; Luke viii.

40-56.

Cure of blind and dumb â Matt. ix. 27-34. Rejection at Nazareth â Matt. xiii. 54-58; Mark vi. 1-6'; Luke iv. 16-30 (see sect. A 52).

Third circuit of Galilee â Matt. ix. 35; Mark vi. 6 b. The mission of the twelve â Matt. ix. 36 to xi. 1; Mark vi.

7-13; Luke ix. 1-6 (see sect. A 57). The death of John the Baptist â Matt. xiv. 1-12; Mark vi.

14-29; Luke ix. 7-9.

Withdrawal of Jesus across the sea and feeding of the five thousandâ Matt, xiv. 13-23; Mark vi. 30-46; Luke ix. 10-17:

John vi. 1-15. Return to Capernaum, Jesus walking on the water â Matt. xiv.

24-36; Mark vi. 47-56; John vi. 16-21. Teaching about the Bread of Life in the synagogue at Capernaum â John vi. 22-71 (see sect. A 59). Controversy concerning tradition: handwashing, etc. â Matt.

xv. 1-20; Mark vii. 1-23. Withdrawal to regions of Tyre and Sidon: the Syrophoenician woman's daughter â Matt. xv. 21-28; Mark vii. 24-30-

Return through Decapolis â Matt. xv. 29-31; Mark vii. 31-37.? The feeding of the four thousand â Matt. xv. 32-38; Mark viii. 1-9 (see sect. A 58). Pharisaic challenge in Galilee, and warning against the leaven of the Pharisees â Matt. xv. 39 to xvi. 12; Mark viii. 10-21. Cure of blind man near Bethsaida â Mark viii. 22-26. Peter's confession of Jesus as Christ near Caesarea Philippi â

Matt. xvi. 13-20; Mark viii. 27-30; Luke ix. 18-21. The new lesson, that the Christ must die â Matt. xvi. 21-28;

Mark viii. 31 to ix. 1; Luke ix. 22-27. The transfigurationâ Matt. xvii. 1-13; Mark ix. 2-13; Luke ix. 28-36. Cure of the epileptic boy â Matt. xvii. 14-20; Mark ix. 14-29;

Luke ix. 37-43". Second prediction of approaching death and resurrection â Matt. xvii. 22, 23; Mark ix. 30-32; Luke ix. 43 b-45. Return to Capernaum: the temple tax â Matt. xvii. 24-27;

Mark ix. 33". Teachings concerning humility and forgiveness â Matt, xviii.

1-35; Mark ix. 33-50; Luke ix. 46-50. Visit of Jesus to Jerusalem at the feast of Tabernacles â John vii. 1-52; viii. 12-59 (see sect. A 60).? The woman taken in adultery â John vii. 53 to viii. 11 (see sect. 163).

The following probably belong to the Galilean ministry before the confession at Caesarea Philippi (see sect. 168): â

The disciples taught to pray â Matt. vi. 9-15; vii. 7-11; Luke xi. 1-13.

The cure of an infirm woman on the Sabbath â Luke xiii. 10-17. Two parables: mustard-seed and leaven â Matt xiii. 31- 3;

Luke xiii. 18-21 (see sect. A 56). The parable of the rich fool â Luke xii. 13-?: Cure on a Sabbath and teaching at a Pharisee's ruble Luke xiv.

1-24.

Five parables â Luke xv. 1 to xvi. 31. Certain disconnected teachings â Luke xvii. 1-4.

125. THE work of Jesus in Galilee, which is the principal theme of the first three gospels, began with a removal from Nazareth to Capernaum, and the calling of four fishermen to be his constant followers. The ready obedience which Simon and Andrew and James and John gave to this call is an interesting evidence that they did not first come to know Jesus at the time of this summons. The narrative presupposes some such earlier association as is reported in John, followed by a temporary return to their old homes and occupations, while Jesus sought seclusion after his work in Judea. The first evangelist has most vividly indicated the development of the Galilean ministry, directing attention to two points of beginning, â the beginning of Jesus' preaching of the kingdom (Matt. iv. 17) and the beginning of his predictions of his own sufferings and death (xvi. 21). Between these two beginnings lies the ministry of Jesus to the enthusiastic multitudes, the second of them marking his choice of a more restricted audience and a less popular message. Within the first of these periods two events mark epochs, â the mission of the twelve (Matt. ix. 36; x. 1) to preach the coming kingdom of God and to multiply Jesus' ministry of healing, and the feeding of the five thousand when the popular enthusiasm reached its climax (John vi. 14, 15). These events fall

not far apart, and mark two different phases of the same stage of development in his work. The first is emphasized by Matthew, the second by John; both help to a clearer understanding of the narrative which Mark has furnished to the other gospels for their story of the Galilean ministry. The table at the head of this chapter indicates in outline the probable succession of events in the Galilean period. The order adopted is that of Mark, supplemented by the other gospels. Luke's additions are inserted in his order where there is not some reason for believing that he himself disregarded the exact sequence of events. Thus the rejection at Nazareth is placed late, as in Mark. Much of the material in the long section peculiar to Luke is assigned in general to this Galilean period, since all knowledge of its precise location in time and place has been lost for us, as it not unlikely was for Luke. Although Matthew is the gospel giving the clearest general view of the Galilean work, it shows the greatest disarrangement of details, and aids but little in determining the sequence of events. The material from that gospel is assigned place in accordance with such hints as are discoverable in parallel or associated parts of Mark or Luke. Of John's contributions one â the feeding of the multitudes â is clearly located by its identity with a narrative found in all the other gospels. The visit to Jerusalem at the unnamed feast can be only tentatively placed.

126. Viewing this gospel story as a whole, the parallel development of popular enthusiasm and official hostility at once attracts attention. Jesus' first cures in the synagogue at Capernaum roused the interest and wonder of the multitudes to such an extent that he felt constrained to withdraw to other towns. On his return to Capernaum he was so beset with crowds that the friends of the paralytic could get at him only by breaking up the roof. It was when Jesus found himself followed by multitudes from all parts of the land that he selected twelve of his disciples "that they might be with him and that he might send them forth to preach," and addressed to them in the hearing of the multitudes the exacting, although unspeakably winsome teaching of the sermon on the mount. This condition of things continued even after Herod had killed John the Baptist, for when Jesus, having heard of John's fate, sought retirement with his disciples across the sea of Galilee, he was robbed of his seclusion by throngs who flocked to him to be healed and to hear of the kingdom of God.

127. The popular enthusiasm was not indifferent to the question who this new teacher might be. At first Jesus impressed the people by his authoritative teaching and cures. After the raising of the widow's son at Nain the popular feeling found a more definite declaration, â "a great prophet has risen up among us." The cure of a demoniac in Capernaum raised the further incredulous query, "Can this be the Son of David?" The notion that he might be the Messiah seems to have gained acceptance more and more as Jesus' popularity grew, for at the time of the feeding of the multitudes the enthusiasm burst into a flame of determination to force him to undertake the work for which he was so eminently fitted, but from which for some inexplicable reason he seemed to shrink (John vi. 15).

128. Parallel with the growth of popular enthusiasm, and in part because of it, the religious leaders early assumed and consistently maintained an attitude of opposition. The gospels connect the critics of Jesus now and again with the Pharisees of the capital â the Galilean Pharisees being represented as more or less friendly. At the first appearance of Jesus in Capernaum even the Sabbath cure in the synagogue passed

unchallenged; but on the return from his first excursion to other towns, Jesus found critics in his audience (Luke connects them directly with Jerusalem). From time to time such censors as these objected to the forgiveness by Jesus of the sins of the paralytic (Mark ii. 6, 7), criticised his social relations with outcasts like the publicans (Mark ii. 16), took offence at his carelessness of the Sabbath tradition in his instruction of his disciples (Mark ii. 24), and sought to turn the tide of rising popular enthusiasm by ascribing his power to cure to a league with the devil (Mark iii. 22). Baffled in one charge, they would turn to another, until, after the feeding of the multitudes, Jesus showed his complete disregard of all they held most dear, replying to a criticism of his disciples for carelessness of the ritual of hand-washing by an authoritative setting aside of the whole body of their traditions, as well as of the Levitical ceremonial of clean and unclean meats (Mark vii. 1-23).

129. The wonder is, not that popular enthusiasm for Jesus was great, but that it was so hesitating in its judgment about him. The province which provided a following to Judas of Galilee a generation earlier than the public ministry of Jesus, and which under John of Gischala furnished the chief support to the revolt against Rome a generation later, could have been excited to uncontrollable passion by the simple idea that a leader was present who could be made to head a movement for Jewish liberty. But there was something about Jesus which made it impossible to think of him as such a Messiah. He was much more moved by sin lurking within than by wrong inflicted from without. He looked for God's kingdom, as did the Zealots, but he looked for it within the heart more than in outward circumstances. Even the dreamers among the people, who were as unready as Jesus for any uprising against Rome, and who waited for God to show his own hand in judgment, found in Jesus â come to seek and to save that which was lost â something so contradictory of their idea of the celestial judge that they could not easily think of him as a Messiah. Jesus was a puzzle to the people. They were sure that he was a prophet; but if at any time some were tempted to query, "Can this be the Son of David?" the incredulous folk expected ever a negative reply.

130. This was as Jesus wished it to be. An unreasoning enthusiasm could only hinder his work. When his early cures in Capernaum stirred the ardent feelings of the multitudes, he took occasion to withdraw t" other towns and allow popular feeling to cool. When later he found himself pressed upon by crowds from all quarters of the land, by the sermon on the mount he set them thinking on strange and highly spiritual things, far removed from the thoughts of Zealots and apocalyptic dreamers.

131. The manifest contradiction of popular Messianic ideas which Jesus presented in his own person usually served to check undue ardor as long as he was present. But when some demoniac proclaimed the high station of Jesus, and thus seemed to the people to give supernatural testimony; or when some one in need sought him apart from the multitudes, Jesus frequently enjoined silence. These injunctions of silence are enigmas until they are viewed as a part of Jesus' effort to keep control of popular feeling. In his absence the people might dwell on his power and easily come to imagine him to be what he was not and could not be. Jesus was able by these means to restrain unthinking enthusiasm until the multitudes whom he fed on the east side of the sea determined to force him to do their will as a Messiah. Then he refused to follow where they called, and that happened which would doubtless have happened

at an earlier time but for Jesus' caution, â the popular enthusiasm subsided, and his active work with the common people was at an end. But he had held off this crisis until there were a few who did not follow the popular defection, but rather clung to him from whom they had heard the words of eternal life (John vi. 68).

132. Jesus' caution brings to light one aspect of his aim in the Galilean ministry, â he sought to win acceptance for the truth he proclaimed. His message as reported in the synoptic gospels was the near approach of the kingdom of God. Any such proclamation was sure of eager hearing. At first he seems to have been content to gather and interest the multitudes by this preaching and the works which accompanied it. But he early took occasion to state his ideas in the hearing of the multitudes, and in terms so simple, so concerned with every-day life, so exacting as respects conduct, and so lacking in the customary glowing picture of the future, that the people could not mistake such a teacher for a simple fulfiller of their ideas. In this early sermon in effect, and later with increasing plainness, he set forth his doctrine of a kingdom of heaven coming not with observation, present actually among a people who knew it not, like a seed growing secretly in the earth, or leaven quietly leavening a lump of meal. By word and deed, in sermon and by parable, he insisted on this simple and every-day conception of God's rule among men. With Pharisee, Zealot, and dreamer, he held that "the best is yet to be," yet all three classes found their most cherished ideals set at nought by the new champion of the soul's inner life in fellowship with the living God. In all his teaching there was a claim of authority and a manifest independence which indicate certainty on his part concerning his own mission. Yet so completely is the personal question retired for the time, that in his rebuke of the blasphemy of the Pharisees he took pains to declare that it was not because they had spoken against the Son of Man, that they were in danger, but because they had spoken against the Spirit of God, whose presence was manifest in his works. He wished, primarily, to win disciples to the kingdom of God.

133. Yet Jesus was not indifferent in Galilee to what the people thought about himself. The question at Cæsarea Philippi shows more fully the aim of his ministry. During all the period of the preaching of the kingdom he never hesitated to assert himself whenever need for such self-assertion arose. This was evident in his dealing with his pharisaic critics. He rarely argued with them, and always assumed a tone of authority which was above challenge, asserting that the Son of Man had authority to forgive sins, was lord of the Sabbath, was greater than the temple or Jonah or Solomon. Moreover, in his positive teaching of the new truth he assumed such an authoritative tone that any who thought upon it could but remark the extraordinary claim involved in his simple "I say unto you." He wished also to win disciples to himself.

134. The key to the ministry in Galilee is furnished in Jesus' answer to the message from John the Baptist. John in prison had heard of the works of his successor. Jesus did so much that promised a fulfilment of the Messianic hope, yet left so much undone, contradicting in so many ways the current idea of a Messiah by his studied avoidance of any demonstration, that the older prophet felt a momentary doubt of the correctness of his earlier conviction. It is in no way strange that he experienced a reaction from that exalted moment of insight when he pointed out Jesus as the Lamb of God, particularly after his restless activity had been caged within the walls of his prison. Jesus showed

that he did not count it strange, by his treatment of John's question and by his words about John after the messengers had gone. Yet in his reply he gently suggested that the question already had its answer if John would but look rightly for it. He simply referred to the things that were being done before the eyes of all, and asked John to form from them a conclusion concerning him who did them. One aid he offered to the imprisoned prophet, â a word from the

Book of Isaiah (xxxv. 5f., Ixi. If.), â and added a blessing for such as " should find nothing to stumble at in him." Here Jesus emphasized his works, and allowed his message to speak for itself; but he frankly indicated that he expected people to pass from wonder at his ministry to an opinion about himself. At Caesarea Philippi he showed to his disciples that this opinion about himself was the significant thing in his eyes. Throughout the ministry in Galilee, therefore, this twofold aim appears. Jesus would first divert attention from himself to his message, in order that he might win disciples to the kingdom of God as he conceived it Having so attached them to his idea of the kingdom, he desired to be recognized as that kingdom's prince, the Messiah promised by God for his people. He retired behind his message in order that men might be drawn to the truth which he held dear, knowing that thus they would find themselves led captive to himself in a willing devotion.

135. This aim explains his retirement when popularity pressed, his exacting teaching about the spirituality of the kingdom of God, and his injunctions of silence. He wished to be known, to be thought about, to be accepted as God's anointed, but he would have this only by a genuine surrender to his leadership. His disciples must own him master and follow him, however much he might disappoint their misconceptions. This aim, too, explains his frank self-assertions and exalted personal claims in opposition to official criticism. He would not be false to his own sense of masterhood, nor allow people to think him bold when his critics were away, and cowardly in their presence. Therefore, when needful, he invited attention to him- self as greater than the temple or as lord of the Sabbath. This kind of self-assertion, however, served his purpose as well as his customary self-retirement, for it forced people to face the contradiction which he offered to the accepted religious ideas of their leaders.

136. The method which Jesus chose has already been repeatedly indicated, â teaching and preaching on the one hand, and works of helpfulness to men on the other. The character of the teaching of this period is shown in three discourses, â the Sermon on the Mount, the Discourse in Parables, and the Instructions to the Twelve. The sermon on the mount is given in different forms in Matthew and Luke, that in Matthew being evidently the more complete, even after deduction has been made of those parts which Luke has assigned with high probability to a later time. This address was spoken to the disciples of Jesus found among the multitudes who flocked to him from all quarters. It opened with words of congratulation for those who, characterized by qualities often despised, were yet heirs of God's kingdom. The thought then passed to the responsibility of such heirs of the kingdom for the help of a needy world. Next, since much in the words and works of Jesus hitherto might have suggested to men that he was indifferent to the older religion of his people, he carefully explained that he came, not to set aside the old, but to realize the spiritual idea for which it stood, by establishing a more exacting standard of righteousness. This more

exacting righteousness Jesus illustrated by a series of restatements of the older law, and then by a group of criticisms of current religious practice. The sermon closed with warnings against complacent censoriousness in judging other men's failures, and a solemn declaration of the vital seriousness of "these sayings of mine." The righteousness required by this new law is not only more exacting but unspeakably worthier than the old, being more simply manifested in common life, and demanding more intimate filial fellowship with the living God.

137. The teachings included in the sermon by the first gospel, but placed later by Luke, supplement the sermon by bidding God's child to lead a trustful life, knowing that the heavenly Father cares for him. That Luke has omitted much which from Matthew's account clearly belonged to the original sermon may be explained by the fact that Gentile readers did not share the interest which Jesus' hearers had, and which the readers of the first gospel had, in the relation of the new gospel to the older law. Hence the restatement of older commands and the criticism of current practice was omitted. Similar to the teachings which the first gospel has included in the sermon, are many which Luke has preserved in the section peculiar to himself. It is not unlikely that they belong also to the Galilean ministry. They urge the same sincere, reverent life in the sight of God, the same trust in the heavenly Father, the same certainty of his love and care; and they do not have that peculiar note of impending judgment which entered into the teachings of Jesus after the confession at Caesarea Philippi.

138. In the story of Mark, which is reproduced in the first and third gospels, the use of parable was first introduced in a way to attract the attention of the disciples, after pharisaic opposition to Jesus had become somewhat bitter and there was need of checking a too speedy culmination of opposition. He chose at that time a form of parable which was enigmatic to his disciples, and could but further puzzle hearers who had no sympathy with him and his message. Mark (iv. 12) states that this perplexity was in accordance with the purpose of Jesus. But it is equally clear that Jesus meant to teach the teachable as well as to perplex the critical by these illustrations, for in explaining the Sower he suggested that the disciples should have understood it without explanation (Mark iv. 13). Many of Jesus' parables, however, had no such enigmatic character, but were intended simply to help his hearers to understand him. He made use of this kind of teaching from first to last. The pictures of the wise and foolish builders with which the sermon on the mount concludes show that it was not the use of illustration which surprised the disciples in the parables associated with the Sower, but his use of such puzzling illustrations. Some of the parables of Luke's peculiar section may belong to the Galilean ministry, and even to the earlier stages of it. These have none of the enigmatic character; the parables of the last days of Jesus' life also seem to have been simple and clear to his hearers. The Oriental mind prefers the concrete to the abstract, and its teachers have ever made large use of illustration. Jesus stands unique, not in that he used parables, but in the simplicity and effective beauty of those which he used. These illustrations, whether Jesus intended them for the moment to enlighten or to confound, served always to set forth concretely some truth concerning the relation of men to God, or concerning his kingdom and their relation to it. The form of teaching was welcome to his hearers, and served as one of the attractions to draw men to him.

139. The first gospel assigns another extended discourse to this Galilean period, â the Instructions to the Twelve. The mission of the twelve formed a new departure as Jesus saw the Galilean crisis approaching. He sought thereby to multiply his own work, and commissioned his disciples to heal and preach as he was doing. The restriction of their field to Israel (Matt. x. 5, 6) simply applied to them the rule he adopted for himself during the Galilean period (Matt. xv. 24). Comparison with the accounts in Mark and Luke, as well as the character of the instructions found in Matthew, show that here the first evangelist has followed his habit of gathering together teachings on the same general theme from different periods in Jesus' life. Much in the tenth chapter of Matthew indicates clearly that the ministry of Jesus had already passed the period of popularity, and that his disciples could now look for little but scorn and persecution. This was the situation at the end of Jesus' public life, and parallel sayings are found in the record of the last week in Jerusalem.

140. When the teaching of the sermon and the parables is compared with Jesus' self-assertion in his replies to pharisaic criticism and blasphemy, the difference is striking. Ordinarily he avoided calling attention to himself, wishing men to form their opinion of him after they had learned to know him as he was. Yet when one looks beneath the surface of his teaching, the tone of authority which astonished the multitudes is identical with the calm self-confidence which replied to pharisaic censure: "The
Son of Man hath authority on the earth to forgive sins."

141. Jesus drew the multitudes after him not only by his teachings, but also by his mighty works. He certainly was for his contemporaries a wonder-worker and healer of disease, and, in order to appreciate the impression which he made, the miracles recorded in the gospels must be allowed to reveal what they can of his character. The mighty works which enchained attention in Galilee were chiefly cures of disease, with occasional exhibitions of power over physical nature, â such as the stilling of the tempest and the feeding of the five thousand. The significant thing about them is their uniform beneficence of purpose and simplicity of method. Nothing of the spectacular attached itself to them. Jesus repeatedly refused to the critical Pharisees a sign from heaven. This was not because he disregarded the importance of signs for his generation, â witness his appeal to his works in the reply to John (Matt. xi. 4-6); but he felt that in his customary ministry to the needy multitudes he had furnished signs in abundance, for his deeds both gave evidence of heavenly power and revealed the character of the Father who had sent him.

142. One of the commonest of the ailments cured by Jesus is described in the gospels as demoniac possession, the popular idea being that evil spirits were accustomed to take up their abode in men, speaking with their tongues and acting through their bodies, at the same time afflicting them with various physical diseases. Six specific cures of such possession are recorded in the story of the Galilean ministry, besides general references to the cure of many that were pos- sessed. Of these specific cases the Gadarene demoniac shows symptoms of violent insanity; the boy cured near Caesarea Philippi, those of epilepsy; in other cases the disease was more local, showing itself in deafness, or blindness, or both. In the cures recorded Jesus addressed the possessed with a command to the invading demon to depart. He was ordinarily

greeted, either before or after such a command, with a loud outcry, often accompanied with a recognition of him as God's Holy One.

143. The record of such maladies and their cure is not confined to the New Testament. The evil spirit which came upon King Saul is a similar case, and Josephus tells of Jewish exorcists who cured possessed persons by the use of incantations handed down from King Solomon. The early Christian fathers frequently argued the truth of Christianity from the way in which demons departed at the command of Christian exorcists, while in the middle ages and down to modern times belief in demoniac possession has been common, particularly among some of the more superstitious of the peasantry in Europe. Moreover, from missionaries in China and other eastern lands it is learned that diseases closely resembling the cases of possession recorded in the New Testament are frequently met with, and are often cured by native Christian ministers.

144. The similarity of the symptoms of so-called possession to recognized mental and physical derangements such as insanity, epilepsy, and hysteria, suggests the conclusion that possession should be classed with other ailments due to ill adjustment of the relations of the mental and physical life. If this conclu- sion is valid, the idea of actual possession by evil spirits becomes only an ancient effort to interpret the mysterious symptoms in accordance with wide-spread primitive beliefs. This explanation would doubtless be generally adopted were it not that it seems to compromise either the integrity or the knowledge of Jesus. The gospels plainly represent him as treating the supposed demoniac influence as real, addressing in his cures not the invalid, but the invading demon. If he did this knowing that the whole view was a superstition, was he true to his mission to release mankind from its bondage to evil and sin? If he shared the superstition of his time, had he the complete knowledge necessary to make him the deliverer he claimed to be? These questions are serious and difficult, but they form a part of the general problem of the extent of Jesus' knowledge, and can be more intelligently discussed in connection with that whole problem (sects. 249-251). It is reasonable to demand, however, that any conclusion reached concerning the nature of possession in the time of Jesus must be considered valid for similar manifestations of disease in our own day.

145. What astonished people in Jesus' cures was not so much that he healed the sick as that he did it with such evidence of personal authority. His cures and his teachings alike served to attract attention to himself and to invite question as to who he could be. Yet a far more powerful means to the end he had in view was the subtle, unobtrusive, personal influence which without their knowledge knit the hearts of a few to himself. In reality both his teaching and his cures were only means of self-disclosure. His permanent work during this Galilean period was the winning of personal friends. His chief agency in accomplishing his work was what Renan somewhat too romantically has called his " charm." It was that in him which drew to his side and kept with him the fishermen of Galilee and the publican of Capernaum, during months of constant disappointment of their preconceived religious ideas and Messianic hopes; it was that which won the confidence of the woman who was a sinner, and the constant devotion of Mary Magdalene and Susanna and the others who followed him " and ministered to him of their substance." The outstanding wonder of early Christianity is

the complete transformation not only of life but of established religious ideas by the personal impress of Jesus on a Peter, a John, and a Paul. The secret of the new element of the Christian religion â salvation through personal attachment to Jesus Christ â is simply this personal power of the man of Nazareth. The multitudes followed because they saw wonderful works or heard wonderful words; many because they hoped at length to find in the new prophet the champion of their hopes in deliverance from Roman bondage. But these sooner or later fell away, disappointed in their desire to use the new leader for their own ends. It was only because from out the multitudes there were a few who could answer, "To whom shall we go? thou hast the words of eternal life," when Jesus asked, "Will ye also go away?" that the work in Galilee did not end in complete failure. These few had felt his personal power, and they became the nucleus of a new religion of love to a personal Saviour.

146. The test of the personal attachment of the few came shortly after the execution of John the Baptist by Antipas. Word of this tragedy was brought to Jesus by John's disciples about the time that he and the twelve returned to Capernaum from their tour of preaching. At the suggestion of Jesus they withdrew to the eastern side of the lake in search of rest. It is not unlikely that the little company also wished to avoid for the time the territory of the tyrant who had just put John to death, for Jesus was not yet ready for the crisis of his own life. Such a desire for seclusion would be intensified by the continued impetuous enthusiasm of the multitudes who flocked about him again in Capernaum. In fact, so insistent was their interest in Jesus that they would not allow him the quiet he sought, but followed around the lake in great numbers when they learned that he had taken ship for the other side. He who came not to be ministered unto but to minister could not repel the crowds who came to him, and he at once "welcomed them, and spake to them of the kingdom of God, and them that had need of healing he healed" (Luke ix. 11). The day having passed in this ministry, he multiplied the small store of bread and fish brought by his disciples in order to feed the weary people. This work of power seemed to some among the multitudes to be the last thing needed to prove that Jesus was to be their promised deliverer, and they " were about to come and take him by force and make him king " (John vi. 15), when he withdrew from them and spent the night in prayer.

147. This sudden determination on the part of the multitudes to force the hand of Jesus was probably due to the prevalence of an idea, found also in the later rabbinic writers, that the Messiah should feed his people as Moses had provided them manna in the desert. The rebuff which Jesus quietly gave them did not cool their ardor, until on the following day, in the synagogue in Capernaum, he plainly taught them that they had quite missed the significance of his miracle. They thought of loaves and material sustenance. He would have had them find in these a sign that he could also supply their spirits' need, and he insisted that this, and this alone, was his actual mission. From the first the popular enthusiasm had had to ignore many contradictions of its cherished notions. But his power and the indescribable force of his personality had served hitherto to hold them to a hope that he would soon discard the perplexing role which he had chosen for the time to assume, and take up avowedly the proper work of the Messiah. This last refusal to accept what seemed to them to be his evident duty caused a revulsion in the popular feeling, and " many of his disciples turned

back and walked no more with him" (John vi. 66). The time of sifting had come. Jesus had known that such a rash determination to make him king was possible to the Galilean multitudes, and that whenever it should come it must be followed by a disillusionment. Now the open ministry had run its course. As the multitudes were turning back and walking no more with him, he turned to the twelve with the question, "Will ye also go away?" and found that with them his method had borne fruit. They clung to him in spite of disillusionment, for in him they had found what was better than their preconceptions.

148. It is the fourth gospel that shows clearly the critical significance of this event. The others tell nothing of the sudden determination of the multitude, nor of the revulsion of feeling that followed Jesus' refusal to yield to their will. Yet these other gospels indicate in their narratives that from this time on Jesus avoided the scenes of his former labors, and show that when from time to time he returned to the neighborhood of Capernaum he was met by such a spirit of hostility that he withdrew again immediately to regions where he and his disciples could have time for quiet intercourse.

149. The months of toil in Galilee show results hardly more significant than the grain of mustard seed or the little leaven. Popular enthusiasm had risen, increased, reached its climax, and waned. Official opposition had early been aroused, and had continued with a steadily deepened intensity. The wonderful teaching with authority, and the signs wrought on them that were sick, had been as seed sown by the wayside or in thorny or in stony ground, except for the little handful of hearers who had felt the personal power of Jesus and had surrendered to it, ready henceforth to follow where he should lead, whether or not it should be in a path of their choice. These, however, were the proof that those months had been a time of rewarded toil.

150. WITH the crisis in Capernaum the ministry in Galilee may be said in one sense to have come to an end. Yet Jesus did not immediately go up to Jerusalem. Once and again he was found in or near Capernaum, while the time between these visits was spent in regions to the north and northwest. In fact, the disciples were far from ready for the trial their loyalty was to meet before they had seen the end of the opposition to their Lord. The time intervening between the collapse of popularity and Jesus' final departure from Galilee may well be thought of, then, as a time of further discipline of the faith of his followers and of added instruction concerning the truth for which their Master stood. The length of this supplementary period in Galilee is not definitely known. It extended from the Passover to about the feast of Tabernacles (April to October, see John vi. 4 and vii. 2). The record of what Jesus did and said in this time is meagre, only enough being reported to show that it was a time of repeated withdrawals from Galilee and of private instruction for the disciples.

151. The disciples were trained in faith by further exhibitions of the complete break between their Master and the leaders of the people. This break appeared most clearly, soon after the feeding of the multitudes, in his reply to a criticism of the disciples for disregard of pharisaic traditions concerning hand-washing (Mark vii. 1-23). The critics insisted on the sacredness of their traditions. Jesus in reply scored them for disregard for the plain demands of God's law, and with a word freed men

from bondage to the whole ritual of ceremonial cleanness and uncleanness (Mark vii. 19), thus attacking Judaism in its citadel.

152. It was immediately after this that he withdrew with his disciples to the regions of Tyre. On his return a little later to the west side of the sea of Galilee he was met by hostile Pharisees with a demand for a sign (Mark viii. 11-13), and after refusing to satisfy the unbelieving challenge, â signs in plenty having been before their eyes since the opening of his work among them, â he and his disciples withdrew again from Galilee towarls Caesarea Philippi. As they went on their way, Jesus distinctly warned them against the influence of their leaders, religious and political (Mark viii. 14 f.). So far as our records tell us Jesus was but once again in Capernaum. Then he was met with the demand that he pay the temple tax (Matt. xvii. 24-27). This tax was usually collected just before the Passover. As this last visit to Capernaum was probably not far from the feast of Tabernacles, Jesus seems to have been in arrears. This may have been due to his absence from Capernaum at the time of the collection. The prompt answer of Peter may indicate that he knew that in other years Jesus had paid this tax, as it is altogether probable that he did. The question, however, implies official suspicion that Jesus was seeking to evade pay- ment, and exhibits further the straining of the relations between him and the Jewish leaders. The conversation of Jesus with Peter served to show his clear consciousness of superiority, and was a further summons to the disciples to choose between him and his opponents.

153. Within the limits of the Holy Land the faith of the disciples had been constantly tested by the increasing opposition between their master and their old leaders. When the little company withdrew to Gentile regions, however, Jesus had regard for their Jewish feeling. The time would come when he would send them forth to make disciples of all the nations. For the present he made it his business to nurture their faith in him, and when appealed to for help by one of these foreigners, he refused to " take the children's bread and cast it to the dogs " (Mark vii. 27). Jesus had assumed a different attitude to the Samaritans before the opening of his work in Galilee, and in general had shown ready sympathy for all in distress. In fact it seems as if he welcomed the Syro-phoenician woman's great faith with a feeling of relief from a restriction that he had felt it wise to adopt for his work in Phoenicia. It appears from his later attitude in the Gentile regions of the Decapolis (Mark yii. 31-37; Matt. xv. 21-31) that, having once shown his regard for the limitations of his disciples' faith in the case of the Syrophcenician, he felt no longer obliged to check his natural readiness to help the needy who sought him out. Although in one instance, for reasons no longer known to us, Jesus charged a man whom he had cured to keep it secret (Mark vii. 32-37), in general his work in these heathen regions seems, after the visit to Phoenicia, to have been quite unrestrained, and to have produced the same enthusiasm that had earlier brought the multitudes to him in Galilee (Mark viii. If.).- 154. This continued activity of healing must have served greatly to strengthen the determination of the disciples to cling to Jesus, let the leaders say what they would. We can only conjecture what various teachings filled the days, and what personal fellowship the disciples had with him who spake as never man spake. There was need for advance in the faith of these loyal friends. Their enthusiastic declaration when the multitudes turned away could easily have been followed by reaction. Each new exhibition of the irrevocableness

of the break between Jesus and the leaders was a severe test of their loyalty. These weeks of withdrawal were doubtless filled, therefore, with new proofs that Jesus had the words of eternal life.

155. Before he put to his disciples the crucial question, he who knew what was in man (John ii. 25) was confident that they were ready for it. It was after the rebuff in Galilee, when the unbelieving Pharisees had again demanded a sign of his authority, and after he had definitely warned the disciples against the influence of their leaders, that Jesus led his little company far to the north towards the slopes of Hermon. There, near the recently built Cresarea Philippi, Jesus plainly asked his disciples what the people thought of him (Mark viii. 27-30). We have seen how gradually sentiment in Galilee concerning the new teacher crystallized until, from thinking him a prophet, the people, first timidly, then boldly, con- eluded that such a teacher and worker of signs must be the promised king. We have seen also how the popular estimate changed when Jesus refused to be guided by the popular will. Now, after the lapse of a few weeks, in answer to his inquiry concerning the common opinion of him, he is told that the people look on him as a prophet, in whom the spirit of the men of old had been revived; but not a whisper remains of the former readiness to hail him as the Messiah. It was in the face of such a definite revulsion in the popular feeling, in the face, too, of the increasing hostility of all the great in the nation, that Peter answered for the twelve that they believed Jesus to be the Messiah, God's appointed Deliverer of his people (Matt. xvi. 16 if.). In form this confession was no more than Nathanael had rendered on his first meeting with Jesus (John i. 49), and was practically the same as the report made by Andrew to Simon his brother, and by Philip to Nathanael (John i. 41, 45). In both idea and expression the reply to Jesus' question, "Will ye also go away?" (John vi. 68, 69), was virtually equivalent to this later confession of Peter. Yet Jesus found in Peter's answer at Caesarea Philippi something so significant and remarkable that he declared that the faith that could answer thus could spring only from a heavenly source (Matt. xvi. 17). The early confessions were in fact no more than expressions of more or less intelligent expectation that Jesus would fulfil the confessor's hopes. The confession at Capernaum followed one of Jesus' mightiest exhibitions of power, and was given before the disciples had had time to consider the extent of the defection from their Master. Here at Csesarea Philippi, however, the word was spoken immediately after an acknowledgment that the people had no more thought of finding in Jesus their Messiah. It was spoken after the disciples had had repeated evidence of the determined hostility of the leaders to Jesus. All the disappointment he had given to their cherished ideas was emphasized by the isolation in which the little company now found itself. One after another their ideas of how a Messiah should act and what he should be had received contradiction in what Jesus was and did. Yet after the weeks of withdrawal from Galilee, Peter could only in effect assert anew what he had declared at Capernaum, â that Jesus had the words of eternal life. It was a faith chastened by perplexity, and taught at length to follow the Lord let him lead where he would. It was an actual surrender to his mastery over thought and life. Here at length Jesus had won what he had been seeking during all his work in Galilee, â a corner-stone on which to build up the new community of the kingdom of

God. Peter was the first to confess openly to this simple surrender to the full mastery of Jesus. He was the first stone in the foundation of the new " building of God."

156. In his commendation of Peter Jesus revealed the secret of his method in the work which, because of this confession, he could now proceed to do more rapidly. He cuts loose utterly from the method of the scribes. He, the new teacher, commits to them no body of teaching which they are to give to others as the key to eternal life. The salvation they are to preach is a salvation by personal attachment; that is, by faith. The rock on which he will build his church is personal attachment, faith that is ready to leave all and follow him. Peter, not the substance of his confession, was its corner-stone, but Peter, as the first clear confessor of a faith that is ready to leave all, a faith whose very nature it is to be contagious, and associate with itself others of "like precious faith." His faith was as yet meagre, as he showed at once; but it was genuine, the surrender of his heart to his Lord's guidance and control. This was the distinctive mark of the new religious life inaugurated by Jesus of Nazareth.

157. If anything were needed to prove that the idea that he was the Messiah was no new thought to Jesus, it could be found in the new lesson which he at once began to teach his disciples. The confession of Peter indicated to him simply that the first stage in his work had been accomplished. He immediately began to prepare the disciples for the end which for some time past he had seen to be inevitable. He taught them more than that his death was inevitable; he declared that it was divinely necessary that he should be put to death as a result of the hostility of the Jews to him ("the Son of Man must suffer"). All the contradictions which he had offered to the Messianic ideas of his disciples paled into insignificance beside this one. When they saw how he failed to meet the hopes that were commonly held, they needed only to urge themselves to patience, expecting that in time he would cast off the strange mask and take to himself his power and reign. But it was too much for the late confessed and very genuine faith of Peter to hear that the Messiah must die. So unthinkable was the idea, that he assumed that Jesus had become unduly discouraged by the relentlossness of the opposition which had driven him first out of Judea and later out of Galilee. Accordingly Peter sought to turn his Master's mind to a brighter prospect, asserting that his forebodings could not be true. It is hard for us to conceive the chill of heart which must have followed the glow of his confession when he heard the stern rebuke of Jesus, who found in Peter's later words the voice of the Evil One, as before in his confession he had recognized the Spirit of God.

158. The sternness of Jesus' rebuke escapes extravagance only in view of the fact that the words of Peter had greatly affected Jesus himself. At the outset of his public life he had faced the difficulty of doing the Messiah's work in his Father's way, and had withstood the temptation to accommodate himself to the ideas of his world, declaring allegiance to God alone (Matt. iv. 10). Yet once and again in the course of his ministry he showed that this allegiance cost him much. Luke reports a saying in which Jesus confessed that, in view of this prospect of death which Peter was opposing so eagerly, he was greatly " straitened " (xii. 50), and at the near approach of the end " his soul was exceeding sorrowful" (Mark xiv. 34). It should never be forgotten that Jesus was a Jew, and heir to all the Messianic ideas of his people. In these, glory, not rejection and death, was to be the Messiah's portion. That he was always superior to current

expectations is no sign that he did not feel their force. They quite mistake who find the bitterness of Jesus' " cup " simply in his physical shrinking from suffering. The temptation was ever with him to find some other way to the goal of his work than that which led through death. What Peter said had a force greater than any word of the disciple's. It voiced the crucial temptation of Jesus' life. The answer addressed to Peter showed that his words had drawn the thought of Jesus away from the disciple to that earlier temptation which was never absent from him more than " for a season " (Luke iv. 13).

159. Jesus was not content with a mere rebuke of his impulsive disciple. In his first announcement of his death as necessary he had also declared that it would not be a tragedy, but would be followed by a resurrection. This the disciples could not appreciate, as they found the idea of the Messiah's death unthinkable. Jesus, however, saw in it the general law, that life must ever win its goal by disregard of itself, and called his disciples also to walk in the path of self-sacrifice. In order that the new lesson might not quite overwhelm the yet feeble faith of these followers, Jesus assured them that after his death and resurrection he would come as Messianic Judge and fulfil the hopes which his prediction of death seemed to blot out utterly (Mark viii. 34 to ix. 1).

160. That this new lesson was a difficult one for master as well as disciple seems to be shown by the experience which came a few days later to Jesus and his three closest friends. He had withdrawn with them to a "high mountain" for prayer (Luke ix. 28f.). While he prayed the light of heaven came into his face, and his disciples were granted a vision of him in celestial glory, conversing with Moses and Elijah, representatives of Old Testament law and prophecy. The theme of the discourse was that death which had so troubled the disciples, and which then and later weighed heavily on Jesus' own spirit (Luke ix. 31).

At the conclusion of the vision came a divine injunction to hear him who now was superseding law and prophets. The effect of the transfiguration can only be inferred. It doubtless brought strengthening to Jesus for his difficult task (compare Heb. v. 7), and at least a silencing of remonstrance when he spoke again to his disciples of his approaching death. This he did while the little company was making its way back towards Capernaum (Mark ix. 30-32), and repeatedly later before the end came (Mark x. 32-34; Matt. xxvi. If.).- 161. On Jesus' return from the mountain, he was met by the despairing plea of a father and healed his epileptic son, out of whom the disciples were unable to cast the demon (Mark ix. 14-29; compare vi. 7, 13). It may have been the shock which the new lesson had given the disciples that accounted for the reproof of their lack of faith. The new evidence of Jesus' power, coupled with this reproof, seems to have restored their confidence in him. Perhaps, too, there was something contagious about the spirit of hope with which the three came from their vision of the Master's glory. For, although they were not free to tell what they had seen (Mark ix. 9), they could not have concealed the fact that their faith had received great encouragement. Whatever the cause, hope revived for the disciples, for on the way back to Capernaum a dispute arose among them concerning personal precedence in the kingdom which their Master should soon set up. In this rapid reaction from unbelief to faith the disciples seem to have forgotten the lesson of self-denial recently given them (Mark viii. 34, 35). In Peter's confession the corner-stone of the church was laid; but the superstructure was yet far out of sight. Although his own soul, taking its way down into the valley of shadows, might rightly have asked for sympathy and complained of its lack, Jesus simply set a little child in the midst of them, and taught them again the first lessons of faith, â gentle humility and trust. Thereby he rebuked the spirit of rivalry and asked of his disciples a generous, unselfish, and forgiving spirit (Matt, xviii. 1-35).

162. It was possibly at this time, certainly near the end of the Galilean ministry, that Jesus was approached by his own brethren, who urged him to try to win the capital. Their attitude was not one of indifference, though clearly not one of actual faith in his claim (John vii. 2-6). They seem to have felt that Jesus had not made adequate effort to secure a following in Jerusalem, and that he could not hope for success in his work if he continued to confine his attention to Galilee. Jesus knew conditions in Jerusalem far better than they did, and had no idea as yet of resuming a general ministry there. He therefore dismissed the suggestion, and left his brethren to go up to the feast disappointed in their desire that he make a demonstration at that time. Yet Jesus still yearned over Jerusalem. He knew in what organized opposition a general demonstration would result. There were some, however, in the capital who had real faith in him. His repeated efforts to win Jerusalem mean nothing if we do not recognize that he hoped against hope that many of the people might yet turn and let him lead them. With some suck purpose, therefcia, he went up a little later without ostentation, and quietly appeared in the temple teaching. The effect of this unannounced arrival was that the opposition was not ready for him. The multitude was compelled to form an opinion of him for itself, and he had opportunity to make his own impression for a time, inde pendently of official suggestion as to what ought to be thought of him. This course resulted in a division of sentiment among the people, so much so that when the leaders, both secular and religious, sought to compass his arrest, the officers sent to take Jesus were themselves entranced by his teaching. In spite of the wish of the leaders Jesus continued to teach, and many of the people began to think of him with favor. When, however, he tried to lead them on to become "disciples indeed," they took offence, and showed that they were not ready yet to follow him. This effort to " gather the children of Jerusalem" resulted in new proof that they preferred his death to his message (John vii. 2 to viii. 59).

163. Interesting evidence of the fact that " Jesus did many other signs which are not written " in our accepted gospels is found in the story of his dealing with an adulteress whom the Pharisees brought to him for judgment (John vii. 53 to viii. 11). This narrative had no secure place in any of the gospels in the earliest days, yet was so highly regarded that men would not let it go. Hence in the manuscripts which contain it, it is found in various places. Some give it in Luke after chapter xxi., some at the end of the Gospel of John, one placing it after John vii. 36. Many considerations combine to prove that it was no part of the Gospel of John, but as many show that it preserves a true incident in the ministry of Jesus. In scene it belongs to the temple, therefore in time to one of the Jerusalem visits. To which of those visits it should be assigned is not now discoverable. The ancient copyists who assigned it to this feast of Tabernacles, chose as well as later students can. If the incident belongs to this visit, it

illustrates the patience and the keen insight of Jesus in his effort to win self-satisfied Jerusalem.

164. John is silent concerning the doings of Jesus after the feast of Tabernacles. In x. 22 he notes that Jesus was at Jerusalem at the feast of Dedication, which followed two months later. It seems probable that after his hurried and private journey to the feast of Tabernacles (John vii. 10) he returned to Galilee and gathered to himself again the little company of his loyal followers, preparatory to that final journey to Jerusalem which should bring the end foreseen, unless, perchance, Israel should yet repent and turn unto the Lord. As the shadow deepened over his own life, and the persistency of the unbelief of his people appeared more and more clearly, the teachings of Jesus took on a new note of tragedy which was not characteristic of the earlier preaching in Galilee. Even when his topic was similar and his treatment of it not unlike some earlier discourse, there appeared in it here and there a warning of impending judgment. This is seen as early as the reply to the criticism of the disciples for disregard of traditions (Matt. xv. 13f.). Many discourses in the section peculiar to Luke show by the presence of this note of doom that they belong to this later time rather than to the Galilean period proper. (See the table prefixed to Chapter V.) 165. Two years had nearly passed since Jesus withdrew from Judea to stnrt his ministry anew in a differ- ent region and following a different method. The fruit of that ministry was small, but significant. His proclamation of the coming kingdom and his call to a deeper righteousness, coupled as they were with his works of heavenly power, had won at first an enthusiastic following. Realizing that an uncontrolled enthusiasm would thwart his purpose to introduce a kingdom of the spirit, Jesus had kept his Messianic claim in the background, seeking first to win disciples to the kingdom that he was proclaiming. Yet emphasize his message as he would, he could not conceal his personal significance. In fact he wished by winning disciples to his doctrine of the kingdom to attach followers to himself, the bearer of the words of eternal life. The great development of popular enthusiasm did not deceive him, nor did he hesitate, when the multitude would force him to do its will, to show clearly how far he was from being a fulfiller of their desires. By successive disappointments of the popular ideas he sifted his followers until a few were read ' to follow him whithersoever he might lead. With these he allowed time for the fact of his unpopularity to appear, giving them opportunity to consider the relentless hostility of their national leaders to the teacher from Galilee. Then when the time was ripe he drew from the loyal few thsir declaration that they would follow him in spite of disappointments and unpopularity, their confession that he had come to be to them more than their cherished preconceptions, that he had won the mastery over their thought and life. He began then to prepare them for the end he had long foreseen, and at length, after giving them time for that perplexing mystery to find place in their hearts, he was ready to move on toward the crisis which he knew his public appearance in Jerusalem would precipitate. Before setting out on this journey his desire still to seek to win Jerusalem, if perchance it would repent, led him to visit the capital unannounced at the feast of Tabernacles. This taught him that, however ready some might be superficially to believe in him, he could as yet win in Jerusalem only hatred and plots against his life, and he returned to his faithful friends in Galilee.

The final departure from Galilee â Matt. xix. 1, 2; viii. 19-22;

Mark x. 1; Luke ix. 51-62.

The mission of the seventy â Matt. xi. 20-30; Luke x. 1-24. The visit to the feast of Dedication â John ix. 1 to x. 39. Possibly at this time:

The parable of the Good Samaritan â Luke x. 25-37. The visit to Mary and Martha â Luke x. 38-42. Return to Perea â John x. 40-42.

The visit to Bethany and the raising of Lazarus â John xi. 1-46. The withdrawal to Ephraim â John xi. 47-54. Events connected with the last journey to Jerusalem, which cannot be more definitely located:

The question whether few are saved â Luke xiii. 22-30. Reply to the warning against Herod, probably near the close â

Luke xiii. 31-35.

The cure of ten lepers â Luke xvii. 11-19. The question of the Pharisees concerning divorce â Matt. xix.

3-12; Mark x. 2-12. The blessing of little children â Matt. xix. 13-15; Mark x. 13-16; Lukexviii. 15-17. The question of the rich young ruler â Matt. xix. 16 toxx. 16;

Mark x. 17-31; Luke xviii. 18-30. The third prediction of death and resurrection â Matt. xx.

17-19; Mark x. 32-34; Luke xviii. 31-34. The ambitious request of the sons of Zebedee â Matt. xx.

20-28; Mark x. 35-45. The last stage, Jericho to Jerusalem:

The blind men near Jericho â Matt. xx. 29-34; Mark x. 46-52; Luke xviii. 35-43.

The visit to Zacchreus â Luke xix. 1-10. The parable of the pounds (minae) â Luke xix. 11-28. Events and discourses found in Luke ix. 51 to xviii. 14, which probably belong after the confession of Peter, and very likely to some stage of the journey to Jerusalem: Woes against the Pharisees, uttered at a Pharisee's table â

Luke xi. 37-54.

Warnings against the spirit of pharisaism â Luke xii. 1-59. Comment on the slaughter of Galileans by Pilate â Luke xiii. 1-9. Discourse on counting the cost of discipleship â Luke xiv.

25-35.

Discourse on the coming of the kingdom â Luke xvii. 20-37. Parable of the Unjust Judge â Luke xviii. 1-8. Parable of the Pharisee and the Publican â Luke xviii. 9-14.

THE JOURNEY THROUGH PEREA TO JERUSALEM 166. THE fourth gospel says that after the visit to Jerusalem at the feast of Dedication Jesus withdrew beyond Jordan to the place where John at the first was baptizing (x. 40). Matthew and Mark also say that at the close of the ministry in Galilee Jesus departed and came into the borders of Judea and beyond Jordan, and that in this new region the multitudes again flocked to him, and he resumed his ministry of teaching (Matt. xix. If.; Mark x. 1). What he did and taught at this time is not shown at all by John, and only in scant fashion by the other two. They tell of a discussion with the Pharisees concerning divorce (Mark x. 2-12); of the welcome extended by Jesus to certain little children (Mark x. 13-16); of the disappointment of a rich young ruler, who wished to learn from Jesus the way of life, but loved better his great possessions (Mark x. 17-31); of a further manifestation of the unlovely spirit of rivalry among the disciples in the request of James and John for the best places in the kingdom (Mark x. 35-45), â a request following in the records directly after another prediction by Jesus of his death and resurrection (Mark x. 32-34). Then, after a visit to Jericho (Luke xviii. 35 to xix. 28), these records come into coincidence with John in the account of the Messianic entry into Jerusalem just before the last Passover.

167. The fourth gospel tells in addition of a considerable activity of Jesus in and near Jerusalem during this period. In making the journey beyond Jordan start from Jerusalem (x. 40), John shows that Jesus must have returned to the capital after his withdrawal from the feast of Tabernacles. When and how this took place is not indicated. Later, after his retirement from the feast of Dedication Jesus hastened at the summons of his friends from beyond Jordan to Bethany when Lazarus died (xi. 1-7). From Bethany he went not to the other side of Jordan again, but to Ephraim (xi. 54), a town on the border between Judea and Samaria, and from there he started towards Jerusalem when the Passover drew near. This record of John has, as Dr. Sanday has recently remarked (HastbD II. 630), so many marks of verisimilitude that it must be accepted as a true tradition. It demands thus that in our conception of the last journey from Galilee room be found for several excursions to Jerusalem or its neighborhood. One of these at least â to the feast of Dedication (x. 22) â represents another effort to "gather the children of Jerusalem,"

While not without success, for at least the blind man restored by Jesus gave him the full faith he sought (ix. 35-38), it showed with fuller clearness the determined hostility to Jesus of the influential class (x. 39).

168. It has been customary to find in the long section peculiar to Luke (ix. 51 to xviii. 14) a fuller account of the Perean ministry, as it has been called. For it opens with a final departure from Galilee, and comes at its close into parallelism with the record of Matthew and Mark. Yet some parts of this section in Luke belong in the earlier Galilean ministry. The blasphemy of the Pharisees (xi. 14-36) is clearly identical with the incident recorded in Mark iii. 22-30, and Matt. xii. 22-45; while several incidents and discourses (see outline prefixed to Chapter III.) bear so plainly the marks of the ministry before the revulsion of popular favor, that it is easiest to think of them as actually belonging to the earlier time, but assigned by Luke to this peculiar section because he found no clear place offered for them in the record of Mark. Not a little, however, of what Luke records here manifestly belongs to the time when Jesus referred openty to his rejection by the Jewish people. The note of tragedy characteristic of later discourses appears in the replies of Jesus to certain would-be disciples (ix. 57-62), and in his warning that his followers count the cost of discipleship (xiv. 25-35). The woes spoken at a Pharisee's table (xi. 37-52), the warning to the disciples against pharisaism (xii. 1-12), and the encouragement of the " little flock " (xii. 22-34), with many other paragraphs from this part of the gospel (see outline at the head of this chapter), evidently were spoken at the time of the approaching end. Some narratives reflect the neighborhood of Jerusalem, and naturally corroborate the indications in the fourth gospel that Jesus was repeatedly at the capital during this time. The parable of the good Samaritan, for instance, must have been spoken in Judea, else why choose the road from Jerusalem to Jericho for the illustration? The visit to Mary and Martha

shows Jesus at Bethany, and the parable of the Pharisee and the Publican, naming the temple as the place of prayer, belongs naturally to Judea.

169. The effort to find the definite progress of events in this part of Luke has not been successful. There are three hints of movement towards Jerusalem, â the introductory mention of the departure from Galilee (ix. 51); a statement that Jesus went on his way through cities and villages, journeying on unto Jerusalem (xiii. 22); and again a reference to passing through the midst of Samaria and Galilee on the way to Jerusalem (xvii. 11). The attempt to make the third of these belong actually to the last stages of the final journey seems artificial. Confessedly the expression " through the midst of Samaria and Galilee" is obscure. It is much easier to understand, however, if the journey so described is identified with the visit to Samaria with which the departure from Galilee opened. It seems probable that Luke found these records of events and teachings in Jesus' life, and was unable to learn exactly their connection in time and place, so placed them after the close of the Galilean story and before the account of the passion, much as later some copyist found the story of the adulteress (John vii. 53 to viii. 11), and, certain that it was a true incident, gave it a place in connection with the visit to the feast of Tabernacles (perhaps influenced by John viii. 15). It must always be remembered that the earliest apostolic writing â Matthew's Logia â probably consisted of just such disconnected records (see sects. 28, 42), and that, as Julicher (Einlei-tung i. d. NT. 235) has said, the early church was not interested in when Jesus said or did anything. Its interest was in what he said and did.

170. The time of the departure from Galilee for Jerusalem may be set with much probability not long before the feast of the Dedication in December; for at that feast Jesus was again in Jerusalem, and from it he returned to Perea (John x. 22, 40-42). He started southward through Samaria (Luke ix. 51 ff.), and probably in connection with the early stages of the journey he sent out the seventy " into every city and place whither he himself was about to come " (Luke x. 1). It is not unlikely that, after the sending out of these heralds, he went with a few disciples to make one more effort to turn the heart of Jerusalem to himself (John ix., x.). It is impossible to determine whither the seventy were sent. The " towns and cities" whither Jesus was about to come may have included some from all portions of the land, not excepting Judea. The matter must be left in considerable obscurity. This, however, may be said, that the reasons offered for holding that the story of the sending out of the seventy is only a " doublet" of the mission of the twelve are not conclusive (see sect. A 68). The connection in Luke of the woes against Capernaum, Bethsaida, and Chorazin with the instruction of the seventy is very natural, and marks this misoion as belonging to the close of the Galilean period, while the mission of the twelve belongs to the height of Jesus' popularity. 171. Our knowledge of Jesus' visit to the feast of Dedication is due to John's interest in the cure at about that time of one born blind (John ix., x.). The prejudice of the sanhedrists who excommunicated the man for his loyalty to Jesus led him in indignation to contrast their method of caring for God's " sheep" with his own love and sympathy and genuine ministry to their needs. He saw clearly that his course must end in death, unless a great change should come over his enemies; yet, as the Good Shepherd, he was ready to lay down his life for the sheep, rather than leave them to the heartlessness of leaders who cared only for themselves (x. 11-18).

The critics of Jesus could not, or would not, understand his charge against them, and accused him of madness for his extraordinary claims. There were some, however, who could not credit the notion that Jesus had a devil (John x. 21). It is possible that it was at this time that the lawyer questioned him about the breadth of interpretation to be given to the word " neighbor" in the law of love, and was answered by the parable of the Good Samaritan (Luke x. 25-37). Possibly the parable of the Pharisee and the Publican (Luke xviii. 9-14) belongs also to this time. In general, however, the visit proved anew that Jerusalem was in no mood to accept Jesus (John x. 24-39). His enemies sought to draw from him a declaration of his claim to be the Messiah, and Jesus appealed to his works, asserting that only their incorrigible prejudice prevented their recognizing his claims. He added that his Father, with whom he was ever in perfect accord, had drawn some faithful followers to him, and thereupon, angered by his claim to close kinship with God, they appealed to the rough logic of violence (John x. 31-39; compare viii. 59).

172. After this added attempt to win Jerusalem Jesus withdrew to the region beyond Jordan, where John had carried on his ministry to the eager multitudes. Here he anew attracted great attention, causing people to contrast his ministry with the less remarkable work of John, and to acknowledge that John's testimony to him was true (John x. 40-42). Possibly it was in this place that the seventy found Jesus when they returned to report the success of their mission (Luke x. 17-24), for the thanksgiving which Jesus rendered for the faith of the common people in contrast with the unbelief of the " wise and prudent" might well express his feeling after the fresh evidence he had at the feast of Dedication that Jerusalem would none of his mission. The invitation to all the heavy laden to take his yoke illustrates, though under another figure, his claim to be the Good Shepherd (Matt. xi. 28-30). We have no means of knowing how much more of what the gospels assign to the last journey to Jerusalem should be put in connection with this sojourn across the Jordan. The multitudes that came to him there may have included the Pharisees who questioned him about divorce (Mark x. 2-12), and the young ruler who loved his great possessions (Mark x. 17-31), as well as the parents who eagerly sought the Lord's blessing for their children (Mark x. 13-16). Some parts of Luke's narrative seem to belong still later in this journey, yet s, uch a section as the reply of Jesus to the report of Pilate's slaughter of the Galileans (xiii. 1-9), or the parable of the Great Supper (xiv. 15-24), is suitable to any stage of it.

173. This sojourn on the other side of Jordan was brought to a close by the summons to come to the aid of his friends in Bethany (John xi.). It is not strange that the disciples feared his return to Judea, nor that Jesus did not hesitate when he recognized the call of duty as well as of friendship. In no recorded miracle of Jesus is his power more signally set forth, yet here more clearly than anywhere else he is represented as dependent on his Father in his exercise of that power. The words of Jesus at the grave (John xi. 41, 42) show that he was confident of the resurrection of Lazarus, because he had prayed and was sure he was heard. It may be that his delay after hearing of the sickness of his friend (xi. 6) was a time of waiting for answer, and that this explains his confidence of safety when the time came for him to expose himself again to the hostility of Judea. Jesus indicated not only that on this occasion

he had help from above in doing his miracles, but that it was the rule in his life to seek such help and guidance (xi. 42). In fact, at a later time he ascribed all his works to the Father abiding in him (John xiv. 10; compare x. 25). The effect of the resurrection of Lazarus was such as to intensify the determination of the leaders in Jerusalem â both Pharisees and Sadducees â to get rid of Jesus as dangerous to the quiet of the nation (John xi. 47-54). In this it simply served to fix a determination already present (John vii. 25, 32; viii. 59; x. 31, 39). The miracle does not appear in John as the cause of the apprehension of Jesus, but rather as one influence leading to it. It was indeed the total contradiction between Jesus and all current and cherished ideas that led to his condemnation; the raising of Lazarus only showed that he was becoming dangerously popular, and made the priestly leaders feel the necessity of haste. The silence of the first three gospels concerning this event is truly perplexing, yet it is not any more difficult of explanation, as Beyschlag (LJ I. 495) has shown, than the silence of all four evangelists concerning the appearance of the risen Jesus to James, or to the five hundred brethren (I. Cor. xv. 6, 7). Room must be allowed in our conception of the life of Jesus for many things of which no record remains, all the more, therefore, for incidents to which but one of the gospels is witness. Moreover, after the collapse of popularity in Galilee, the great enthusiasm of the multitudes over Jesus when he entered Jerusalem (Luke xix. 37-40; Mark xi. 8-10) is most easily understood if he had made some such manifestation of power as the restoration of Lazarus.

174. After the visit to Bethany Jesus withdrew to a little town named Ephraim, on the border between Judea and Samaria, and spent some time there in seclusion with his disciples (John xi. 54), doubtless strengthening his personal hold on them preparatory to the shock their faith was about to receive. Of the length of this sojourn nothing is told us, nor of the road by which Jesus left Ephraim for Jerusalem (John xii. 1). The first three gospels show that he began his final approach to the Holy City at Jericho (Mark x. 46). It may be that he descended from Ephraim direct to Jericho some days before the Passover, rejoining there some of the people who had been impressed by his recent ministry in the region " where John at the first was baptizing." It is natural to suppose that it was on this journey to Jericho that he warned his disciples again of the fate which he saw before him in Jerusalem (Mark x. 32-34), and quite probably it was at this time that he rebuked the crude ambition of the sons of Zebedee by reminding them that his disciples must be more ambitious to serve than to rule, since even " the Son of Man came not to be ministered unto but to minister, and to give his life a ransom for many" (Mark x. 35-45). At Jericho he was at once crowded upon by enthusiastic multitudes. The feeling they had for him may perhaps be inferred from the cry of blind Bartimeus, "Thou son of David, have mercy on me" (Mark x. 48). This enthusiasm received a shock when Jesus chose to be guest in Jericho of a chief of the publicans, a shock which Jesus probably intended to give, for much the same reason that led him afterwards on his way up to Jerusalem to teach his followers in the parable of the pounds that they must be ready for long delay in his actual assumption of his kingly right (Luke xix. 11-28). Finally, six days before the Passover, he and his disciples left Jericho and went up to Bethany preparatory to his final appearance in Jerusalem (John xii. 1).

175. The interval between the final departure from Galilee and the public entry into Jerusalem was given to three different tasks: the renewed proclamation of the coming of the kingdom, further efforts to win acceptance in Jerusalem, if perchance she might learn to know the things that belonged to her peace; and continued training of the disciples, specially needed because of the ill-considered enthusiasm with which they were inclined to view the probable issue of this journey to Jerusalem. The first of these tasks was conducted as the earlier work in Galilee had been, both by teaching and healing, in which Jesus used his disciples even more extensively than before. It proved that here as in Galilee the common people were ready to hear him gladly, until he showed too radical a disappointment of their hopes. In this new ministry to the people Jesus spoke very frankly of the seriousness of the opposition which the leaders of the people were manifesting, and of the need that those who would be his disciples should count the cost of their allegiance (Luke xiii. 22-30; xiv. 25-35; xii. 1-59). He did not hesitate to administer the most scathing rebuke to the Pharisees for the superficiality and hypocrisy of their religious life and teaching (Luke xi. 37-54), â a rebuke which is emphasized by the parable in which, on another occasion, he taught God's preference for a contrite sinner over a complacent saint (Luke xviii. 9-14). When reminded of Pilate's outrage upon certain Galilean worshippers, he used the calamity to warn his hearers that personal godliness was the only protection which could secure them against a more serious outbreak of the hostility of the Roman power (Luke xiii. 1-9); and it was probably in reply to such an appeal as accompanied this report of Pilate's cruelty that Jesus spoke the parable of the Unjust Judge (Luke xviii. 1-8), teaching that God's love may be trusted to be no less regardful of his people's cry than a selfish man's love of ease would be.

176. The second of these tasks must not be held to be perfunctory, even though each new effort for Jerusalem proved that genuine acceptance of its saviour was increasingly improbable. As the denunciations of the older prophets ever left open a way of escape if Israel would return and seek the Lord, so the anticipation of rejection and death which filled the heart of Jesus does not banish a like if from his own thought of Jerusalem in his repeated efforts to " gather her children." The combination" of the new popular enthusiasm and the fresh proofs of the hopelessness of winning Jerusalem made more important the third task, â the founding of the faith of the disciples on the rock of personal certainty, from which the rising floods of hatred and seeming ruin for the Master's cause could not sweep it. It was for them that much of his instruction of the multitudes was doubtless primarily intended; they needed above all others to count the cost of discipleship (Luke xiv. 25-35), and the warnings against the spirit of Pharisaism (Luke xii.) were addressed principally to them, even as it was to them that Jesus confessed the " straitening " of his own soul in view of the " fire which he had come to cast upon the earth" (Luke xii. 49-53), â a confession which had another expression when he found it needful to rebuke the personal ambition of the sons of Zebedee (Mark x. 35-45). As for Jesus himself, the popular enthusiasm had not deceived him, nor the obdurate unbelief of Jerusalem daunted him, nor his disciples' misconception of his kingdom disheartened him; he still stedfastly set his face to go to Jerusalem.

Saturday (?). The anointing in Bethany six days before the

Passover â Matt. xxvi. 6-13; Mark xiv. 3-9; Johnxi. 55 to xii. 11. Sunday (?). The Messianic entry â Matt. xxi. 1-11; Mark xi.

1-11; Luke xix. 29-44; John xii. 12-19. Monday (?). Visit to the temple: the cursing of the barren fig-treeâ Matt. xxi. 18-19, 12-17; Mark xi. 12-14, 15-18;

Luke xix. 45Â, 47, 48. Return to Bethany for the night â Matt. xxi. 17; Mark xi. 19;

Luke xxi. 37, 38. Tuesday (?). Visit to the temple: the fig-tree found withered â

Matt. xxi. 20-23; Mark xi. 20-27; Luke xx. 1. Challenge of Jesus' authority â Matt. xxi. 23-27; Mark xi.

27-33; Luke xx. 1-8. Three parables against the religious leaders â Matt. xxi. 28 to xxii. 14; Mark xii. 1-12; Luke xx. 9-19. The question about tribute â Matt. xxii. 15-22; Mark xii.

13-17; Luke xx. 20-26. The question of the Sadducees about the resurrection â Matt.

xxii. 23-33; Mark xii. 18-27; Luke xx. 27-40. The question of the Pharisees about the great commandmentâ â

Matt. xxii. 34-40; Mark xii. 28-34. Jesus' counter-question about David's son and Lord â Matt.

xxii. 41-46; Mark xii. 35-37; Luke xx. 41-44. Jesus' denunciation of the scribes and Pharisees â Matt, xxiii.

1-39; Mark xii. 38-40; Luke xx. 45-47. The widow's two mites â Mark xii. 41-44; Luke xxi. 1-4. The visit of the Greeks â John xii. 20-36'. Final departure from the temple â John xii. 36 b (-50).

Discourse concerning the destruction of Jerusalem and the end of the world â Matt. xxiv. 1 to xxvi. 2; Mark xiii. 1-37; Luke xxi. 5-38. Plot of Judas to betray Jesus â Matt. xxvi. 3-5, 14-16; Mark xiv. 1, 2, 10, 11; Luke xxii. 1-6. Wednesday. Retirement at Bethany. (?) Thursday. The Last Supperâ Matt. xxvi. 17-30; Mark xiv.

12-26; Luke xxii. 7-30; John xiii. 1-30. The farewell words of admonition and comfort â John xiii. 31 to xvi. 33.

The intercessory prayer â John xvii. 1-26. Friday. The agony in Gethsemane â Matt. xxvi. 30, 36-46;

Mark xiv. 26, 32-42; Luke xxii. 39-46; John xviii. 1. The betrayal and arrest â Matt. xxvi. 47-56; Mark xiv. 43-52;

Luke xxii. 47-53; John xviii. 1-12. Trial before the high-priests and sanhedrin â Matt. xxvi. 57 to xxvii. 10; Mark xiv. 53 to xv.!â; Luke xxii. 54-71; John xviii. 12-27. Trial before Pilate â Matt, xxvii. 11-31; Mark xv. 1-20; Luke xxiii. 1-25; John xviii. 28 to xix. 16'. The crucifixion â Matt, xxvii. 32-56; Mark xv. 21-41; Luke xxiii. 26-49; John xix. 16-37. The burial â Matt, xxvii. 57-61; Mark xv. 42-47; Luke xxiil 50-56; John xix. 38-42.

Saturday. The Sabbath rest â Luke xxiii. 56 b. The watch at the tomb â Matt, xxvii. 62-66.

THE FINAL CONTROVERSIES IN JERUSALEM 177. THE early Christians were greatly interested in the teachings of Jesus and in his deeds, but they thought oftenest of the victory which by his resurrection he won out of seeming defeat. This is proved by the fact that of the first two gospels over one third, of Luke over one fifth, and of the fourth gospel nearly one half are devoted to the story of the passion and resurrection. This preponderance is not strange in view of the shock which the death of Jesus caused his disciples, and the new life which the resurrection brought to their hearts. The resurrection was the fundamental theine of apostolic preaching, the supreme evidence that Jesus was the Messiah. Hence the cross early became the object of exultant Christian joy and boasting; and in this the church entered actually into the Lord's own thought, for through the cross he looked for his exaltation and glory (Mark viii. 31; John xii. 23-36). From the time of the confession at Csesarea Philippi, he had had his death avowedly in view, and had repeatedly checked the ambitious and unthinking enthusiasm of his disciples by reminding them of what he must receive at the hands of the leaders of the people. The few months preceding his final appearance in Jerusalem had been devoted to the journey to the cross. This explains the note of tragedy which appears in his teachings at this period. The people had shown that they would none of his ministry. In this they had written their national and religious death warrant, and as he approached Jerusalem for the final crisis he declared, though with almost breaking heart, "Your house is left unto you desolate " (Luke xiii. 31-35). Each new effort of Jesus to turn aside the impending judgment of his people by winning their acceptance of himself and his message resulted in a new certainty of his ultimate rejection, and thus in confirmation of the early recognized necessity, that, if he continued the work God had given him to do, he should suffer many things, and die at the hands of his own people.

178. The last chapter in his public ministry began with his arrival at Bethany six days before the Passover. It is probable that the caravan with which Jesus was travelling reached Bethany not far from the sunset which marked the beginning of the Sabbath preceding the feast. Jesus had friends there who gladly gave him entertainment, and the Sabbath was doubtless spent quietly in this retreat. The holy day closed with the setting sun, and then his hosts were able to show him the special attention which they desired. The general cordiality of welcome expressed itself in a feast given in the house of one Simon, a leper who had probably experienced the power of Jesus to heal. He may have been a relative also of Lazarus, for Martha assisted in the entertainment, and Lazarus was one of the guests of honor (Mark xiv. 3; John xii. 2). During the feast, Mary, the sister of Lazarus, poured forth on the head and feet of Jesus a box of the rarest perfume. This act of costly adoration seemed extravagant to some, particularly to one of Jesus' disciples, who complained that the money could have been better spent. This criticism of one who had not counted cost in her service was rebuked by Jesus, who defended and commended Mary; for in the act he recognized her fear that he might not be long with her (Mark xiv. 8; John xii. 7). It is probable that this rebuke, with the clear reference to his approaching death, led Judas to decide to abandon the apparently waning cause of his Master, and bargain with the leaders in Jerusalem to betray him (Mark xiv. 3-11).

179. The day following the supper at Bethany â that is, the first day of the week â witnessed the welcome of Jesus to Jerusalem by the jubilant multitudes.

His mode of entering the city affords a marked contrast to his treatment of the determination to make him king after he had fed the multitudes in Galilee (John vi. 15). In some respects the circumstances were similar. A multitude of the visitors to the feast, healing that Jesus was at Bethany on his way to Jerusalem, went out to meet him with a welcome that showed their enthusiastic confidence that at last he would assume Messianic power and redeem Israel (John xii. 12,13). Jesus was now ready for a popular demonstration, for the rulers were unwilling longer to tolerate his work and his teaching. He had never hesitated to assert his superiority to official criticism, and at length the hour had come to proclaim the full significance of his independence. In fact it was for this that some months before he had set his face steadfastly to go to Jerusalem. When, therefore, the crowd from Jerusalem appeared, Jesus took the initiative in a genuine Messianic demonstration. He sent two of his disciples to a place near by to borrow an ass's colt, on which he might ride into the city, fulfilling Zechariah's prophecy of the " king that cometh meek, and riding upon an ass " (see Matt. xxi. 4, 5). At this, the enthusiasm of his followers, and of those who had come to meet him, became unbounded, and without rebuke from Jesus they proceeded towards Jerusalem crying, "Hosanna; Blessed is he that cometh in the name of the Lord" (Mark xi. 9, 10). Notwithstanding the remonstrances of certain Pharisees among the multitude (Luke xix. 39), Jesus accepted the hosannas, for they served to emphasize the claim which he now wished, without reserve or ambiguity, to make in Jerusalem. The time for reserve had passed. The mass of the people with their leaders had shown clearly that for his truth, and himself as bearer of it, they had no liking; while the few had become attached to him sufficiently to warrant the supreme test of their faith. He could not continue longer his efforts to win the people, for both Galilee and Judea were closed to him. Even if he had been content, without contradicting popular ideas, to work wonders and proclaim promises of coming good, he could with difficulty have continued this work, for Herod had already been regarding him with suspicion (Luke xiii. 31). He had run his course and must measure strength with the hostile forces in Jerusalem. For the last encounter he assumed the aggressive, and entered the city as its promised deliverer, the Prince of Peace. The very method of his Messianic proclamation was a challenge of current Jewish ideas, for they were riot looking for so meek and peaceful a leader as Zech-ariah had conceived; this entrance emphasized the old contradiction between Jesus and his people's expectations. He accepted the popular welcome with full knowledge of the transitoriness of the present enthusiasm. As he advanced he saw in thought the fate to which the city and people were blindly hurrying, and his day of popular triumph was a day of tears (Luke xix. 41-44). The city was stirred when the prophet of Nazareth thus entered it; but he simply went into the temple, looked about with heavy heart, and, as it was late, returned to Bethany with the twelve for the night.

180. On the following day Jesus furnished to his disciples a parable in action illustrating the fate awaiting the nation; for it is only as a parable that the curse of the barren fig-tree can be understood. The idea that Jesus showed resentment at disappointment of his hunger when he found no figs on the tree out of season is too petty for consideration. He was drawn to it by the early foliage, for it was not yet the season for either fruit or leaves. One is tempted to believe, as Dr. Bruce has suggested, that he had small expectation of finding fruit, and that even before he reached the tree with its early leaves he felt a likeness between it and the nation of hypocrites whose fate was so clear in his mind. The withering of the fig-tree set his disciples thinking;

and Jesus showed that it was an object lesson, promising that the disciples, by the exercise of but a little faith, could do more, even remove mountains, â such mountains of difficulty as the opposition of the whole Jewish nation would offer to the success of their work in their Master's name.

181. The curse upon the barren fig-tree was spoken as Jesus was going from Bethany to Jerusalem on the morning after his Messianic entry, that is, on Monday, and it was Tuesday when the disciples found it withered away (Mark xi. 12-14, 20-25). On Monday Jesus entered into the temple and taught and healed (Luke xix. 47; Matt. xxi. 14-16). It is at this point that Mark inserts the cleansing of the temple which John shows to belong rather to Jesus' first public visit to Jerusalem. The place which this incident holds in the first three gospels has already been explained by the fact that it furnished one cause for the official hostility to Jesus, and that Mark's story included no earlier visit to the holy city (sect. 116; see A 39).

182. Tuesday, the last day of public activity, ex- hibits Jesus in four different lights, according as he had to do with his critics, with the devout widow, with the inquiring Greeks, and with his own disciples. The opposition to him expressed itself, after the general challenge of his authority, in three questions put in succession by Pharisees and Herodians, by Sadducees, and by a scribe, more earnest than most, whom the Pharisees put forward after they had seen how Jesus silenced the Sadducees. Jesus met the opening challenge by a question about John's baptism (Mark xi. 29-33) which completely destroyed the complacency of his critics, putting them on the defensive. This was more than a clever stroke, they could not know what his authority was unless they had a quick sense for spiritual things. His question would have served to bring this to the surface if they had possessed it. Their reply showed them incapable of receiving a real answer to their question. It also gave him opportunity to say in three significant parables (Matt. xxi. 28 to xxii. 14) what their spiritual blindness signified for them and their nation, giving thus a turn to the interview not at all to their minds. As Jesus' rebuke was spoken in the hearing of the people, a determined effort was at once made to discredit him in the popular mind. The question (Mark xii. 13-17) with which the Pharisees and Herodians hoped to ensnare him was most subtle, for the popular feeling was as sensitive to the mark of subserviency which the payment of tribute kept ever before them as the Roman authorities were to the slightest suspicion of revolt against their sway. In none of his words had Jesus so clearly asserted the simple other-worldliness of his doctrine of the kingdom of God as in his answer to the question about tribute. For him loyalty to the actual earthly sovereign was quite compatible with loyalty to God, the lower obligation was in fact a summons to be scrupulous also to render to God his due, â a duty in which this nation was sadly delinquent. The reply gave no ground for an accusation before the governor; but the popular feeling against Rome was so strong that it is not unlikely that it contributed somewhat to the readiness of the multitude a few days later to prefer Barabbas to Jesus.

183. A second assault was made by some Sadducees who put to him a crude question about the relations of a seven-times married woman in the resurrection (Mark xii. 18-27). If this question was asked with the expectation of making Jesus ridiculous in the sight of the people it was a marked failure, for his reply was so simple

and straightforward that he won the admiration even of some of the Pharisees. The most significant feature of it was his argument from God's reference to himself as God of Abraham, Isaac, and Jacob; for in that he taught that the fact of fellowship with God implies that God's servants share with him a life that death cannot vanquish. The skill with which Jesus met these two questions interested some of his hearers and showed to his opponents that they must put forward their ablest champions to cope with him. The next test was more purely academic in character, â as to what class of commands is greatest in the law (Mark xii. 28-34). For the pharisaic scholars this was a favorite problem. For Jesus, however, the question contained no problem, since all the law is summed up in the two commandments of love. His contemporaries were not without power to see the truth of his generalization, and their champion in this last attack was moved with admiration for the fineness and sufficiency of Jesus' answer.

184. All of the assaults served only to show freshly the clearness and profoundness of his thought; his critics were quite discomfited in their effort to entangle him. They had done with him, but he had still a word for them. The business of these scribes was the study of the scriptures. They furnished the people with authoritative statements of truth. One of the common-places of the current thought was that the Messiah should be David's son. Jesus did not deny the truth of this view, yet he showed them how partial their ideas were by quoting a word of scripture in which the Messiah is shown as David's Lord. If they had been open-minded they might have inferred from this that perhaps the man before them was not so impossible a Messiah as they thought. This last question closed the colloquy; there awaited yet, however, Jesus' calm, scathing arraignment of the hypocrisy of these religious leaders. There was no longer any need for prudence and every reason for a clear indication of the difference between himself and the scribes in motive, in teaching, and in character. The final conflict was on, and Jesus freely spoke his mind concerning their whole life of piety without godliness. Never have sharper words of reproach fallen from human lips than these which Jesus directed against the scribes and Pharisees; they are burdened with indignation for the misleading of the people, with rebuke for the misrepresentation of God's truth, and with scorn for their hollow pretence of righteousness. Through it all breathes a note of sorrow for the city whose house was now left to her desolate. The change of scene which introduces the widow offering her gift in the temple treasury heightens the significance of the controversies through which Jesus had just passed. In his comment on the worth of her two mites we hear again the preacher of the sermon on the mount, and are assured that it is indeed from him that the severe rebukes which have fallen on the scribes have come. There is again a reference to the insight of him who sees in secret, and who judges as he sees; while allusion is not lacking to the others whose larger gifts attracted a wider attention. The whole scene is like a commentary on Matt. vi. 2-4.

185. Still a different side of Jesus' life appears when the Greeks seek him in the temple. They were probably proselytes from some of the Greek cities about the Mediterranean where the synagogue offered to the earnest-minded a welcome relief from the foolishness and corruption of what was left of religion in the heathen world. Having visited Jerusalem for the feast, they heard on every hand about the new teacher. They were not so bound to rabbinic traditions as the Jews themselves, they had been

drawn by the finer features of Judaism, â its high morality and its noble idea of God. What they heard of Jesus might well attract them, and they sought out Philip, a disciple with a Greek name, to request an interview with his Master. The evangelist who has preserved the incident (John xii. 20-36) evidently introduced it because of what it showed of Jesus' inner life; hence we have no report of the conversation between him and his visitors. The effect of their seeking him was marked, however, for it offered sharp contrast to the rejection which he already felt in his dealings with the people who but two days before had hailed him as Messiah. This foreign interest in him did not suggest a new avenue for Messianic work, it only brought before his mind the influence which was to be his in the world which these inquirers represented, and immediately with the thought of his glorification came that of the means thereto, â the cross whose shadow was already darkening his path. Excepting Gethse-mane, no more solemn moment in Jesus' life is reported for us. A glimpse is given into the inner currents of his soul, and the storm which tossed them is seen. It is in marked contrast to the calmness of his controversy with the leaders, and to the gentleness of his commendation of the widow. The agitation passed almost at once, but it left Jesus in a mood which he had not shown before on that day; in it his own thoughts had their way, and the doctrine of the grain of wheat dying to appear in larger life, of the Son of Man lifted up to draw all men unto him, had utterance, greatly to the perplexity of his hearers. It seems to have been one of the few times when Jesus spoke for his own soul's relief.

186. In all the earlier events of the day the disciples of Jesus appear but little. He is occupied with others, accepting the challenge of the leaders, and completing his testimony to the truth they refused to hear. The quieter hours of the later part of the day gave time for further words with his friends. The comment on the widow's gift was meant for them, and the uncovering of his own soul when the Greeks sought him was in their presence. After he had left the temple and the city he gave himself to them more ex- clusively. His disciples were perplexed by what they saw and felt, for the temper of the people toward their Master could not be mistaken. Yet they were sure of him. The leaders among them, therefore, asked him privately to tell them when the catastrophe should come, to which during the day he had made repeated reference. The conversation which followed is reported for us in the discourse on the destruction of Jerusalem and the end of the world (Mark xiii. and parallels), in which Jesus taught his disciples to expect trouble in their ministry, as he was meeting trouble in his; and to be ready for complete disappointment of their inherited hopes for the glory of their holy city. He also taught them to expect that his work would shortly be carried to perfection, and to live in expectancy of his coming to complete all that he was now seeming to leave undone. This lesson of patience and expectancy is enforced in a group of parables preserved for us in Matthew (chap, xxv.), closing with the remarkable picture of the end of all things when the Master should return in glory as judge of all to make final announcement of the simplicity of God's requirement of righteousness, as it had been exhibited in the life which by the despite of men was now drawing to its close.

187. The bargain made by Judas to betray his Lord has always been difficult to understand. The man must have had fine possibilities or Jesus would not have chosen

him for an apostle, nor would the little company have made him its treasurer (John xii. 6; xiii. 29). The fact that Jesus early discovered his character (John vi. 64) does not compel us to think that his selection as an apostle was not perfectly sin- cere; the man must have seemed to be still savable and worthy thus to be associated with the eleven others who were Jesus' nearest companions. It has often been noticed that he was probably the only Judean among the twelve, for Kerioth, his home, was a town in southern Judea. The effort has frequently been made to redeem his reputation by attributing his betrayal to some high motive â such as a desire to force his Master to use his Messianic power, and confound his opponents by escaping from their hands and setting up the hoped-for kingdom. But the remorse of Judas, in which De Quincey finds support for this theory of the betrayal, must be more simply and sadly understood. It is more likely that the traitor illustrates Jesus' words: "No man can serve two masters; for either he will hate the one and love the other; or else he will hold to the one and despise the other. Ye cannot serve God and mammon" (Matt. vi. 24). The beginning of his fall may have been his disappointment when Jesus showed clearly that he would not establish a kingdom conformed to the popular ideas. As the enthusiasm which drew him to Jesus cooled, personal greed, with something of resentment at the cause of his disappointment, seem to have taken possession of him, and they led him on until the stinging rebuke which Jesus administered to the criticism of Mary at Bethany prompted the man to seek a bargain with the authorities which should insure him at least some profit in the general wreck of his hopes. His remorse after he saw in its bald hid-eousness what he had done was psychologically inevitable. Although Jesus was aware of Judas' character from the beginning (John vi. 64), he that came to seek and to save that which was lost was no fatalist; and this knowledge was doubtless â like that which he had of the fate hanging over Jerusalem â subject to the possibility that repentance might change what was otherwise a certain destiny. As the event turned he could only say, "Good were it for that man if he had not been born " (Mark xiv. 21).

188. With this the curtain falls on the public ministry of Jesus. The gospels suggest a day of quiet retirement following these controversies and warnings, with their fresh demonstration of the irreconcilable hostility of people of all classes to him and his work. After the seclusion of that day, he returned to give final proof of complete obedience to his Father's will.

189. OK Thursday Jesus and his disciples returned to Jerusalem for the last time. Knowing the temper of the leaders, and the danger of arrest at any time,-Jesus was particularly eager to eat the Passover with his disciples (Luke xxii. 15), and he sent two of them â Luke names them as Peter and John â to prepare for the supper. In a way which would give no information to such a one as Judas, he directed them carefully how to find the house where a friend would provide them the upper room that was needed for an undisturbed meeting of the little band, and the two went on in advance to make ready. When the hour was come Jesus with the others went to the appointed place and sat down for the supper (Mark xiv. 17; Luke xxii. 14; Matt. xxvi. 20).

190. The gospels all report the last evening which the little company spent together. There is a perplexing divergence, however, between John and the others concerning the relation of this supper to the feast of the Passover. In their introduction of the

storj', Mark and his companion gospels indicate that the supper which Jesus ate was the Passover meal itself. John, on the other hand, declares that it was " before the feast of the Passover " (xiii. 1) that Jesus took this meal with his disciples. John's account is consistent throughout, for he states that on the next day the desire of the Jews to "eat the Passover" forbade them to enter the house of the governor lest they should incur defilement (xviii. 28). The other gospels, moreover, hint in several ways that the day of Jesus' death could not have been the day after the Passover; that is, the first day of the feast of unleavened bread. Dr. Sanday has recently enumerated these afresh, remarking that 44 the Synoptists make the Sanhedrin say beforehand that they will not arrest Jesus on the feast day," and then actually arrest him on that day; that not only the guards, but one of the disciples (Mark xiv. 47), carries arms, which on the feast day was not allowed; that the trial was also held on the feast day, which would be unlawful; that the feast day would not be called simply Preparation (see Mark xv. 42, and compare John xix. 31); that the phrase ' coming from the field' (Mark xv. 21 Greek) means properly Â coming from work;' that Joseph of Arimathea is represented as buying a linen cloth (Mark xv. 46) and the women as preparing spices and ointments (Luke xxiii. 56), all of which would be contrary to law and custom" (HastbD ii. 634). In these particulars the first three gospels seem to confirm the representation of the fourth that the day of the last supper was earlier than the regular Jewish Passover. On the other hand, a strong argument, though one that has not commended itself to other specialists in Jewish archaeology, has been put forth by Dr. Edersheim (LJM ii. 567 f.) to prove that John also indicates that the last supper was eaten at the time of the regular Passover. In the present condition of our knowledge certainty is impossible. If John does from the others, his testimony has the greatest weight. While not conclusive, it has some significance that Paul identified Christ with the sacrifice of the pass-over (I. Cor. v. 7), a statement which may indicate that he held that Jesus died about the time of the killing of the paschal lamb. If John be taken to prove that the last supper occurred a day before the regular Passover, Jesus must have felt that the anticipation was necessary in order to avoid the publicity and consequent danger of a celebration at the same time with all the rest of the city.

191. Whatever the conclusion concerning the date of the last supper, and conse-quently of the crucifixion, the last meal of Jesus with his disciples. was for that little company the equivalent of the Passover supper. Luke states that the desire of Jesus had looked specially to eating this feast with his disciples (xxii. 15). The reason must be found in his certainty of the very near end, and in his wish to make the meal a preparation for the bitter experiences which were overhanging him and them.

192. It is customary to connect as occasion and consequence the dispute con-cerning precedence which Luke reports (xxii. 24â 30), and the rebuke which Jesus administered by washing the disciples' feet (John xiii. 1-20). The jealousies of the disciples may have arisen over the allotment of seats at the table, as Dr. Edersheim has most fully shown (LJM ii. 492-503); such a controversy would be the natural sequel of earlier disputes concerning greatness, and particularly of the request of James and John for the best places in the coming kingdom (Mark x. 35-45), and would lead as naturally to the distress of heart with which Jesus declared that one of the disciples should betray him, and that another of them should deny him. The narrative in Mark

favors the withdrawal of Judas before the new rite was appointed. This must seem to be the probability in the case, for the presence of Judas would be most incongruous at such a memorial service. John's mention of his departure before the announcement of Peter's approaching fall confirms this interpretation of Mark (Mark xiv. 18-21; John xiii. 21-30).

193. The paschal memories furnished to Jesus an opportunity to establish for his disciples an institution which should symbolize the new covenant which he was soon to seal with his blood. Jesus regarded this new covenant as that which was promised by the prophets, especially Jeremiah (xxxi. 31-34), and his thought, like that of the prophets, goes back to the story of the covenant established at Sinai (Ex. xxiv. 1-11). In this way he gave to his disciples a conception of his death, which later, if not immediately, would help them to regard it as a necessary part of his work as Messiah. They were now oppressed by the evident certainty that the near future would bring their Master to death; he accordingly gave them a sacred reminder of himself and of his death as an essential part of his self-giving " for them; " for whatever the conclusion concerning the disputed text of Luke (xxii. 19), the institutional character of the act and words of Jesus is clear. As Holtzmann remarks (Ntth i. 304): " The words ' this do in remembrance of me' were perhaps not spoken; all the more certainly do they of themselves express what lay in the situation and made itself felt with incontestable collusiveness."

194. Several hints in the records seem to connect the meal in various details with what is known of ancient custom in the celebration of the Passover. The hymn with which according to Mark and Matthew the supper closed is easily identified with the last part (Psalms cxv. to cxviii.) of the so called Hallel, which was sung at the close of the Passover meal. The mention of two cups in the familiar text of Luke (xxii. 17-20) agrees with the repeated cups of the Passover ritual; so also do the sop and the dipping of it with which Jesus indicated to John who the traitor was (John xiii. 23-26; Mark xiv. 20). If it could be proved that the customs recorded in the Talmud correctly represent the usage in Jesus' time it would be of extreme interest to seek to connect what is told us of the last supper with that Passover ritual as Dr. Edersheim has done (LJM ii. 490-512). The antiquity of the rabbinic record is so uncertain, however, that it is only useful as showing what possibly may have been the case. All that can be asserted is that the rabbinic ritual probably originated long before it was recorded, and that as the last supper was a meal which Jesus and his disciples celebrated as a Passover, it is probable that some such ritual was more or less closely followed.

195. Luke and John give the fullest reports of what was said at the table. All the gospels tell of Peter's declaration of superior loyalty and the prediction of his threefold denial; Luke, however, adds that in connection with it Jesus assured Peter of his restoration, and charged him to strengthen his brethren (Luke xxii. 31-34). John alone gives the long and full discourse of admonition and comfort, followed by Jesus' prayer for his disciples (xiii. 31 to xvii. 26). It is evident from the words of Jesus as he entered the garden of Gethsemane (Mark xiv. 33, 34), as from those which had escaped him when the Greeks sought him the last day in the temple (John xii. 27), that his own heart was greatly troubled during the supper by the apparent defeat which was now close at hand. His quietness and self-possession during the

supper, particularly when tenderly reproving his disciples for petty ambition, or when solemnly dismissing the traitor, or warning Peter of his denials, must not blind us to the depth of the emotion which was stirring his own soul. It is only as we remember his trouble of heart that it is possible justly to value the ministry which in varied ways he rendered to his disciples that night. In the discourses reported by John he showed that he realized that the approaching separation would sorely try the faith of his followers, and he sought to strengthen them by showing his own calmness in view of it, and by promising them another who should abide with them spiritually as his representative, and continue for them the work which he had begun. He therefore urged them to maintain their devotion to him, still to seek and find the source of their life and secret of their strength in fellowship with him â present, though unseen among them. He sought to convince them that his departure was to be for their advantage, that fellowship with him spiritually would be far more real and efficacious than the intercourse they had already enjoyed. Pie whose own heart was " exceeding sorrowful even unto death " bade his disciples not to let their hearts be troubled nor afraid. How long the conversation continued, of when the company left the upper chamber, cannot be told. At some time before the arrival at Gethsemane

Jesus turned to God in prayer for the disciples whom he was about to leave to the severe trial of their faith, asking for them that realization of eternal life which he had enjoyed and exemplified in his own intimate life with his Father. With this his ministry to them closed for the time, and, crossing the Kidron, he entered the garden of Gethsemane weighed down by the sorrow of his own soul.

196. OF the garden of Gethsemane it is only known that it was across the Kidron, on the slope of the Mount of Olives. Tradition has long pointed to an enclosure some fifty yards beyond the bridge that crosses the ravine on the road leading eastward from St. Stephen's gate. Most students feel that this is too near the city and the highway for the place of retreat chosen by Jesus. Archaeologically and sentimentally the identification of places connected with the life of Jesus is of great interest. Practically, however, it is easy to over-emphasize the importance of such an identification. Granted the fact that in some olive grove on the mountain-side, where an oil-press gave a name to the place (Gethsemane), Jesus withdrew with his disciples on that last night, and all that is important is known. It is of far higher importance to see rightly the relation of what took place in that garden to the things which preceded and followed it in the life of Jesus. At that time Jesus saw pressed to his lips the "cup" from the bitterness of which his whole soul shrank. It was not an unlooked-for trial; some time earlier he had sought to cool the ardor of the ambition of James and John by telling them that they should drink of his cup, and declared that even the Son of Man came not to be ministered unto but to minister, and to give his life a ransom for many. The fourth gospel, whose representation omits the agony of Gethsemane and only reports its victory, tells how Jesus rebuked the violent impulse of Peter with the word, "The cup which my Father hath given me to drink shall I not drink it?" (John xviii. ll b); and all the gospels exhibit the marvellous quietness of spirit and dignity of self-surrender which characterized Jesus throughout his trial and execution. In Gethsemane, however, we see the struggle in which that calmness and self-mastery were won.

197. It is unbecoming to consider that scene with any vulgar curiosity to know what it was that made Jesus so drawback from the drinking of his "cup." It is not unfitting, however, to recognize that in his cry, "Abba, Father, all things are possible unto thee; remove this cup from me" (Mark xiv. 36), an in-fense longing of his own soul's life had expression. There was something in the fate which he saw before him from which his whole being shrank. But stronger than this was his fixed desire to do his Father's will. Here was supremely illustrated the truth that " he came down from heaven, not to do his own will, bat the will of him that sent him" (John vi. 38). The fullest allowance for the shrinking of the most delicately constituted nature from pain and death completely fails to account for this dread of Jesus. He was no coward, drawmg back from sufferings which for simple physical pain were over and again more than matched by many of the martyrs to truth who preceded and followed him. He himself declared to the sons of Zebedee that they should share a cup in kind like unto his, suffering for the kingdom of God, for the ' salvation of the world. Yet therefiortkffetelice!" evident between what others have had to bear and the cup from which Jesus shrank. The death which now stood before him in the path of obedience had in it a bitterness quite unexplained by the pain and disappointment it entailed. That excess of bitterness can probably never be understood by us. A hint of its nature may be found in the " shame of the cross" which the author of Hebrews (xii. 2; xiii. 13) emphasizes, and in the " curse " of the cross which made it a stumbling block to Paul and his Jewish brethren (Gal. iii. 13; I. Cor. i. 23). Jesus came from the garden ready to endure the cross in obedience to his Father's will; but it was a costly obedience, a complete emptying of himself (Phil. ii. 7, 8).

198. The loneliness of Jesus in his struggle is emphasized in the gospels of Mark and Matthew. In search of sympathy he had confessed to the disciples his trouble of heart, and had taken his three intimates with him when he withdrew from the others for prayer, asking them to watch with him. They were too heavy of heart and weary of body to stand by in his bitter hour, and instead of being in readiness to warn him of the approach of the hostile band, he had to awake them to their danger. The fourth gospel reports that after the struggle Jesus bore marks of majesty which astonished and overawed his foes when he calmly told them that he was the one they were seeking. Their fear was overcome, however, when Judas gave the appointed sign by kissing his Master (Mark xiv. 45). The thought for the disciples' safety which John records (xviii. 8) is another proof that the fight had been won, and Jesus had fully resumed the self-emptying ministry appointed to him by his Father.

199. The band that arrested Jesus was accompanied by a Roman cohort from the garrison of the city, but it was not needed, for the disciples offered no appreciable resistance; on the contrary, "they all forsook him and fled" (Mark xiv. 50). Having arrested Jesus, the band took him to Annas, the actual leader of Jewish affairs, though not at the time the official high-priest. He had held that office some time before, but had been deposed by the Roman governor of Syria after being in power for nine years. His influence continued, however, for although he was never reinstated, he seems to have been able to secure the appointment for members of his own family during a period of many years. Caiaphas, the legal high-priest, was his son-in-law. Annas, as the leader of aristocratic opinion in Jerusalem, had doubtless been foremost in the secret

counsels which led to the decision to get rid of Jesus, hence the captive was, as a matter of course, taken first to his house. The trial by the Jewish authorities was irregular. There seems to have been an informal examination of Jesus and various witnesses, first before Annas, and then before Caiaphas and a group of members of the sanhedrin, the outcome of which was complete failure to secure evidence against Jesus from their false witnesses, and the formulation of a charge of blasphemy in consequence of his answer to the high-priest acknowledging himself to be the Messiah (Mark xiv. 61-64). The early hours before the day were given over to mockery and ill-usage of the captive Jesus. When morning was come, the sanhedrin was convened, and he was condemned to death on the charge of blasphemy (Mark xv. 1; Luke xxii. 66-71), and then was led in bonds to the Roman governor for execution, since the Romans had taken from the sanhedrin the authority to execute a death sentence (John xviii. 31). Before Pilate the Jews had to name an offence recognized by Roman law; his accusers therefore falsified his claim and made him out a political Messiah, hostile to Roman rule (Luke xxiii. 1, 2). Pilate soon saw that the charge was trumped up, and sought in every way, while keeping the good-will of the people, to escape the responsibility of giving sentence against Jesus. His first effort was a simple declaration that he found no fault in the prisoner (Luke xxiii. 4); then, having heard that he was a Galilean, he tried to transfer the case to Herod, who happened to be in the city at the time (Luke xxiii. 5-12); he then sought to compromise by agreeing to chastise Jesus and then release him (Luke xxiii. 13-16); next he offered the people their choice between the innocent Jesus and Barabbas, a convicted insurrectionist (Mark xv. 6-15; Luke xxiii. 16-24), and the people, instructed by the priests, chose Barabbas, caring nothing for a Messiah who would allow himself to be arrested without resistance; the fourth gospel tells of Pilate's still further effort, by appealing to the people's sympathy, to escape giving sentence, even after he had delivered Jesus to the soldiers for the preliminary scourging. Finding the Jews ready to urge, at length, a religious charge, Pilate's superstitious fear was roused (John xix. 7-12), and he sought again to release him, but was finally cowed by thei threat of an accusation against him at Rome, and, mocking the people by sitting in judgment to condemn Jesus as their king, he gave sentence against the man whom he knew to be innocent (John xix. 12-16).

200. Some of Jesus' disciples and friends were witnesses of the early stages of the informal trial, in particular, John (John xviii. 15) and Peter. It was during the progress of the early examination that Peter was drawn into his denials by the comments made by the bystanders on his connection with the accused. It has been suggested that the house of the high-priest where Jesus was tried was built, like other Oriental houses, about a court so that the room where Jesus was examined was open to view from the court. In this case it is easy to see how Jesus could overhear his disciple's strenuous denials of any acquaintance with him, and could turn and give him that look which sent him out to weep bitterly (Luke xxii. 61, 62). If it be further assumed that Annas and Caiaphas occupied different sides of the same high-priestly palace, the double examination reported by John would still be within hearing from the one court in which the faithless disciple was a fascinated witness of his Master's trial.

201. Humanly speaking, it may be said that the fate of Jesus was sealed when the Sadducean leaders came to look on him seriously as a danger to the State (John xi.

47-50, note the mention of chief priests). The religious opposition was serious, and might have brought trouble, in some such way as it seems to have done to John the Baptist (see Matt. xvii. 10-13; Luke xiii. 31, 32); but it is doubtful whether the governor would have given much attention to a charge not urged by the men of influence in Jerusalem. The notable thing in connection with the last days of Jesus' life is the joint opposition of Sadducean priests and Pharisaic scribes. That the populace easily changed their cry from "hosanna" to "crucify him" is not surprising. Their hosannas were due to a complete misconception of Jesus' aim and purpose; disappointed in him, they would be the earliest to cry out against him, especially when the choice lay between him and a genuine insurrectionist.

202. Each fresh study of the trial of Jesus gives a fresh impression of his greatness. He who but a few hours before was pouring out his soul in prayer that his cup might pass, stands forth as the one calm and undisturbed actor among all those who took part in the tragic doings of that day. His judges and foes were all swayed by passion and self-interest and were ready to make travesty of justice, from the leaders of the sanhedrin who condemned him on one charge and accused him to the governor on another, to the governor himself, who appeared determined to release him if he could do it without risk of personal popularity, and who yet, in order to avoid accusation at Rome, gave sentence according to the people's will. The fickle populace crying "crucify him," the disciples who forsook him, the rock-apostle who denied even so much as knowledge of the man, show how all the currents of life about him were stirred and full of tumult. In all this, of which he was the occasion and centre, he stands the supreme example of dignity, self-mastery, and quietness. This is seen in his silence in the presence of Annas and Caiaphas, and later before

Pilate; in his frank avowal of his Messianic claim in reply to the high-priest's challenge, and of his kingly rank in answer to the governor's question; and in the look of reproof which he turned upon Peter. Not that he was without feeling. There is strong sense of outrage in his words, "If I have spoken evil, bear witness of the evil, but if well, why smitest thou me? " It was not the quietness of stoic indifference, but of perfect self-devotion to the Father's will. He maintained it from the time of his arrest to the last cry of trust with which he committed his spirit to his Father.

203. The scourging over, the mock homage of the soldiers done, he was led out beyond the city wall to be crucified. The exact place of the crucifixion can be determined as little as that of Gethsemane, though there is a tradition from the fourth century, and in addition there are many conjectures. Jesus was led, apparently, to the ordinary place of criminal execution, and with two others, probably insurrectionary robbers like those with whom Barabbas had been associated, he was crucified. Two episodes in the journey to the place of crucifixion are recorded, â the help which Simon of Gyrene was compelled to give to Jesus in carrying his cross (Mark xv. 21), and the word of Jesus to those who, following him, bewailed his fate (Luke xxiii. 27-31).

204. Of the cruelty and torture of crucifixion much has been written and often. It would be difficult to exaggerate it. The death by the cross was a death by hunger and exhaustion in ordinary cases; it was thus torture prolonged for many hours. It is noticeable, however, that it is not the suffering but the disgrace and shame of the cross that occupied the thought of the apostolic days. Indeed, were physical suffering

chiefly to be considered, it would have to be owned that the fact that Jesus died within a few hours released him from the most excruciating pains incident to this barbarous form of execution. The later ascetic thought loved, and still loves, to dwell on the physical torments of the Lord's death. They were severe enough to give us awe; but the biblical writers show a much healthier mind, and their thought does not invite comparison between the pains endured by the Master and those which some of his martyred followers bore with great fortitude. The disgrace of the cross was the uttermost; for the Romans it was the death of a slave, for the Jews it was patent proof of the curse of God (Deut. xxi. 23). The obedience of Jesus was unlimited when he submitted to death (Phil. ii. 8). It is on the shame of the cross, and on the sacrifice of himself for the life of the world when in obedience to his Father's will he "despised the shame," that the thought of the apostolic day laid emphasis. In this experience Jesus found himself in truth numbered with the transgressors; he was the object of scorn for all them that passed by, they mocked at him, at his works, and at his confident trust in God. In this last extremity the darkness of Geth-semane again swept over Jesus' soul, when he cried out "My God, my God," recalling the words of one of the saints of old in his hour of distress (Ps. xxii.). Yet, like him, Jesus kept hold on the certainty of deliverance; the darkness passed at length.

205. The evangelists preserve several sayings of Jesus from the cross, the records of the different gospels being remarkably diverse. Mark and Matr thew record the exclamation, "My God, my God (Eloi, Eloi), why hast thou forsaken me," which the bystander misconstrued as a call for Elijah, thinking this pseudo-Messiah was reproaching Elijah for failing to come to his help. The same gospels tell of the loud cry with which Jesus died. Luke omits the call Eloi, and gives in place of the last expiring cry the prayer of trust, "Father, into thy hands I commend my spirit" (xxiii. 46). Earlier, however, this gospel tells of Jesus' word to the penitent robher, "To-day shalt thou be with me in Paradise " (xxiii. 43) and of the prayer for his foes, that is, for the Jewish people who blindly condemned him (xxiii. 34). The oldest manuscripts cause some doubt whether this last saying was originally a part of the Gospel of Luke. If it was not it would belong in the same class with the story of the sinful woman which we now find in John, both being authentic records of the life of Jesus, though from some other source than that in which we now find them. The fourth gospel gives quite an independent group of sayings. It interprets the dying cry as, "It is finished" (xix. 30), and preceding this it gives the cry, "I thirst" (xix. 28), which led to the offering of the vinegar of which the first two gospels speak. Earlier it tells of the committal of Mary to the care of the beloved disciple (xix. 26, 27). Of these seven sayings, "Eloi," "I thirst," "Father, into thy hand I commend my spirit," and "It is finished" belong to the last hours of the life of the crucified one, after the darkness of which the first three gospels speak had overshadowed the land. Of the cause of that darkness they give no hint, for Luke's expression cannot mean an eclipse, since an eclipse at Passover time, that is, at full moon, is an impossibility. The conjecture that dense clouds hid the sun is common, and is as suitable as any other. Whatever the cause, the evangelists saw in it a token of nature's awe at the death of the Son of God. During the hours of the darkness the waves swept over his soul, as the cry "my God" shows to our reverent thought. But the last word of trust proves that the dying Jesus was not forsaken,

and that Calvary, like Gethsemane, was a battle won. The earlier sayings all express Jesus' continued spirit of ministry, showing even in his bitter pain his accustomed thoughtfulness for others' need. 206. It is futile to speculate on the cause of Jesus' early death. He certainly suffered a much shorter time than was ordinarily the case, as appears in the fact that at sunset it was necessary to break the legs of the robbers so as to hasten death, Jesus having already been some time dead. There is something attractive in the theory of Dr. Stroud (The Physical Cause of Christ's Death) that Jesus died of rupture of the heart. It may have been true, but the evidences on which he based his argument are insufficient for proof. To the Jews the death of their victim did not give all the satisfaction they desired. In the first place, Pilate insisted on mocking them by posting over the head of Jesus the placard, "The King of the Jews " (see John xix. 19-22); moreover, their haste had brought the crime into close proximity to the feast which they were eager to keep from defilement; so that they had still to beg of Pilate that he would hasten the death of the victims, that their bodies might not remain to desecrate the following Sabbath sanctity (John xix. 31-37); while for those who witnessed it the death of Jesus deepened the impression that a hideous crime had been committed in the slaughter of an innocent man (Mark xv. 39).

207. Among the bystanders few of the disciples of Jesus were to be found â they were hiding in fear. Yet some faithful women, and two courageous councillors of Jerusalem, were bold enough to make their loyalty known. These two men, Joseph of Arimathea and Nicodemus, were members of the sanhedrin, but they had had no part in the condemnation of Jesus; and after knowing that he was dead, Joseph begged of Pilate the body, and he and Nicodemus took Jesus down from the cross and laid him in a tomb which Joseph owned near the place of crucifixion, rendering such tender ministries as were possible in the closing hours of the day. The women who had witnessed his end meanwhile were arranging also to anoint the body. They took notice where the two friends had laid him, and then went away to rest on the Sabbath day, according to the commandment.

208. To the Jews it was a high day, the first Sabbath in the eight days of their holy feast (John xix. 31). They had eagerly guarded their conduct that no ceremonial defilement might prevent their sharing in the paschal feast. They believed that they had rid their nation of a dangerous disturber of its peace, and men whose conscience shrank not from making God's house a house of merchandise, who would punish one who ventured to cure a mortal disease if it chanced to cross their Sabbath traditions, who had condemned to death the holiest man and godliest teacher the world had ever seen because he did not square with their heartless formalism, â such men hardly had conscience enough to feel repentance or remorse for the cowardly injustice and crime with which of their own choice they had reddened their hands (Matt, xxvii. 25). They doubtless kept their feast with satisfaction. Not a few hearts, however, were heavy with grief and disappointed hope. They had believed that Jesus " was he that should redeem Israel " (Luke xxiv. 21). Stunned, they could not throw away the faith which he had kindled in their hearts. Yet he was dead, and only faintly, if at all, did they recall his prediction of suffering and his certainty of triumph through it all (John xx. 9). What remained for them was the last tender ministry to their dead Lord.

The day of the resurrection â Sunday. The visit of the women to the tomb â Matt, xxviii. 1-8; Mark xvi. 1-8; Luke xxiv.

1-12; John xx. 1-10. Jesus' first appearance; to Mary â Matt, xxviii. 9 10; Mark xvi. 9-11; John xx. 11-18. The report of the watch â Matt, xxviii. 11-15. The appearance to Simon Peter â I. Cor. xv. 5. The walk to Emmaus â Mark xvi. 12, 13; Luke xxiv. 13-35. The appearance to the ten in the evening â Mark xvi. 14; Luke xxiv. 36-43; John xx. 19-25; I. Cor. xv. 5. One week laterâ Sunday. The appearance to the eleven, with

Thomas â John xx. 26-29. Later appearances. To seven disciples by the sea of Galilee â

John xxi. 1-24. To a company of disciples in Galilee â Matt, xxviii. 16-20; Mark xvi. 15-18; I. Cor. xv. 6. The appearance to James â I. Cor. xv. 7. To the disciples in Jerusalem, followed by the ascension â Mark xvi. 19, 20; Luke xxiv. 44-53; Acts i. 1-12; I. Cor. xv. 7.

THE EESUEKECTION 209. CHEISTIANITY as a historic religious movement starts from the resurrection of Jesus from the dead. This is very clear in the preaching and writings of Paul. The first distinctively Christian feature in his address at Athens is his statement that God had designated Jesus to be the judge of men by having " raised him from the dead " (Acts xvii. 31), and for him the resurrection was the demonstration of the divinity of Christ (Rom. i. 4), and the confirmation of the Christian hope (I. Cor. xv.). With him the prime qualification for an apostle was that he should have seen the risen Lord (I. Cor. ix. 1). The early preaching as recorded in Acts shows the same feature, for after repeated testimony to the fact that God had raised up Jesus, Peter summed up his address with the declaration, "Let all the house of Israel therefore know assuredly, that God hath made him both Lord and Christ, this Jesus whom ye crucified " (Acts ii. 36). In fact the buoyancy of hope and confidence of faith which gave to the despised followers of the Nazarene their strength resulted directly from the experiences of the days which followed the deep gloom that settled over the disciples when Jesus died.

210. It can but seem strange to us that after Jesus had so often foretold his death and the resurrection which should follow it, his disciples were thrown into despair by the cross. Joseph of Arimathea and Nico-demus when they embalmed his body may not have known of these teachings which Jesus gave to the nearer circle of his followers, but it is difficult to believe that the women who prepared their spices to anoint his body (Mark xvi. 1) had heard nothing of these predictions, and it is certain that the apostles who received with incredulity the first news of the resurrection were the men whom Jesus had sought to prepare for this glorious victory. The disciples do not seem to have finished "questioning among themselves what the rising again from the dead should mean" (Mark ix. 10, compare Luke xviii. 34) until Jesus himself explained it by his return to them after his crucifixion. It was formerly common to conclude from the scepticism of the disciples that Jesus could not have told them, as he is reported to have done, that he would rise again the third day. It is now widely conceded, however, that if he foresaw and foretold his death, he surely coupled with it a promise of resurrection, otherwise he must have surrendered his own conviction that he was Messiah; for a Messiah taken and held captive by death was apparently

as foreign to Jesus' thought as it was unthinkable for the men of his generation. The inability of the disciples to adjust their Messianic ideas to the death of their Master was not removed by the rebuke Jesus administered to Peter at Csesarea Philippi; their objections were only silenced. It would seem that even when they saw his death to be inevitable, they were simply dumb with hope that in some way he would come off victor; the cross and the tomb crushed out that hope â at least from most of them. If one disciple, his closest friend, recalled and believed his words when he saw the empty tomb (John xx. 8), others were cast into still deeper sorrow by the report, and could only say, "But we hoped that it was he which should redeem Israel" (Luke xxiv. 21).

211. The light which banished the gloom from the hearts of Jesus' followers dawned suddenly. There was no time for gradual readjustment of ideas and the springing of hope from a faith which would not die. The uniform early tradition is that Jesus showed himself alive to his disciples " on the third day," that is, a little over thirty-six hours from the time of his death. Not only the gospels, but Paul, who wrote many years before our evangelists, testify to this (I. Cor. xv. 4), as does the very early observance of the first day of the week as " the Lord's day," and the substitution of " the third day " for " after three days " in the gospels which made use of our Gospel of Mark (compare parallels with Mark viii. 81; ix. 31; x. 34, and see Holtzmann, Ntth I. 309). Of the events which occurred on that third day and after, our earliest account is that of Paul. He gives a simple catalogue of the appearances of the risen Lord, referring to them as well known, in fact as the familiar subject matter of his earliest teaching (I. Cor. xv. 4-8). He gives definite date to none of these appearances, indicating only their sequence. He tells of six different manifestations, beginning with an appearance to Cephas on the third day, then to the twelve, then to a large company of disciples, â above five hundred, â then to James, then to all the apostles. The sixth in the list'is his own experience, which he puts in the same class with the appearances of the first Easter morning. Two of these instances are found only in Paul's account, the appearance to James and to the five hundred brethren, though this last may probably be the same as is referred to in the Gospel of Matthew (xxviii. 16-20).

212. The gospel records are much fuller, but they differ from each other even more than they do from Paul. Mark is unhappily incomplete, for the last twelve verses in that gospel, as we have it, are lacking in the oldest manuscripts, and were probably written by a second-century Christian named Aristion, as a substitute for the proper end of the gospel which seems by some acci- dent to have been lost. These twelve verses are clearly compiled from our other gospels. They have value as indicating the currency of the complete tradition in the early second century, but they contribute nothing to our knowledge of the resurrection. All, then, that Mark tells is that the women who came early on the first day of the week to anoint the body of Jesus found the tomb open and empty, and saw an angel who bade them tell the disciples that the Lord had risen. How the record originally continued no one knows, for Matthew and Luke use the same general testimony up to the point where Mark breaks off, and then go quite different ways. Of the two Matthew is closer to Mark than is Luke. The first gospel adds to the record of the second an account of an appearance of Jesus to the women as they went to report to the disciples, and then tells of the meeting of Jesus

with the disciples on a mountain in Galilee, and his parting commission to them. It gives no account of the ascension. Luke agrees with Mark in general concerning the visit of the women to the tomb, the angelic vision, and the report to the disciples. He says nothing of an appearance of Jesus to the women on their flight from the tomb, but, if xxiv. 12 is genuine (see R. V. margin), he, like John, tells of Peter's visit to the sepulchre.

213. Luke further reports the appearances of Jesus to two on their way to Emmaus, to Simon, and to the eleven in Jerusalem, â this last being blended consciously or unconsciously with the final meeting of Jesus with the disciples before his ascension. The genuine text of the gospel (xxiv. 50) says nothing of the ascension itself, but clearly implies it. In contrast with Matthew it is noticeable that Luke shows no knowledge of any appearance of Jesus to his disciples in Galilee. John is quite independent of Mark, as well as of Matthew and Luke. He mentions only Mary Magdalene in connection with the early visit to the tomb, though perhaps he implies the presence of others with her (" we " in xx. 2). He tells of a visit of Peter and John to the tomb, of an appearance of Jesus to Mary Magdalene, of an appearance to ten of the disciples in the evening, and a week later to the eleven, including Thomas. So far this gospel makes no reference to appearances in Galilee; but in the appendix (chapter xxi.) there is added a manifestation to seven disciples as they were fishing on the Sea of Galilee.

214. Criticism which seeks to discredit the gospels, for instance most recently Reville in his " Je sus de Nazareth," discovers two separate and mutually exclusive lines of tradition, â one telling of appearances in Galilee, represented by Mark and the last chapter in John, the other telling of appearances in or near Jerusalem, and found in Luke and the twentieth chapter of John. It is said that the gospels have sought to blend the two cycles, as when Matthew tells of an appearance to the women in Jerusalem on their way from the tomb, and when the last chapter of John adds to the original gospel a Galilean appearance. Luke, however, who makes no reference at all to Galilean manifestations, is taken to prove that originally the one cycle knew nothing of the other. This theory falls, however, before the uniform tradition of appearances on the third day, which must have been in Jerusalem, and the very early testimony of Paul to an appearance to above five hundred brethren at once, which could not have been in Judea. It need not surprise us that there should have been two cycles of tradition, not however mutually exclusive, if Jesus did appear both in Jerusalem and in Galilee. The same kind of local interest which is supposed to explain the one-sidedness of the synoptic story of the public ministry would easily account for one line of tradition which reported Galilean appearances, and another which reported those in Jerusalem. Luke may have had access to information which furnished him only the Jerusalem story. John and Peter, however, must have known the wider facts. The very divergences and seeming contradictions of the gospels, troublesome as they are, indicate how completely certainty regarding the fact of the resurrection removed from the thought of the apostolic day nice carefulness concerning the testimony to individual manifestations of the risen Lord. Doubtless the first preaching rested, as in the case of Paul, on a simple " I have seen the Lord." When later the detailed testimony was wanted for written gospels, it had suffered the lot common to orally transmitted

records, and divergences had sprung up which it is no longer possible for us to resolve. They do not, however, challenge the fact which lies behind all the varied testimony.

215. A general view of the events of that third day and those which followed can be constructed from our gospels and Paul. Early on the first day of the week certain women, including Mary Magdalene, Mary the mother of James and Joses, Salome, Joanna, and others, came to anoint the body of Jesus. On their arrival they found that the stone had been rolled back from the tomb. Mary Magdalene saw that the grave was empty and ran to tell Peter and John. The others saw also a vision of angels which said that Jesus was alive and would see his disciples in Galilee, and ran to report this to the disciples. Meanwhile Mary Magdalene returned, following Peter and John who ran to see the tomb, and found it empty as she had said. She lingered after they left, and Jesus appeared to her, she mistaking him at first for the gardener. She then went to tell the disciples that she had seen the Lord. These events evidently occurred in the early morning. The next incident reported is that of the walk of two disciples, not of the twelve, to Emmaus, and the appearance of Jesus to them. At first they did not recognize him, not even when he taught them out of the scriptures the necessity that the Messiah should die. He was made known when at evening he sat down with them to a familiar meal. Either before or after this event he had shown himself to Peter. This is the first manifestation reported by Paul. If Luke xxiv. 12 is genuine (see R. V. margin), he also tells that when the two again reached Jerusalem the apostles received them with the news that Peter had seen the Lord. That same evening Jesus appeared suddenly among the disciples in their well-guarded upper room. His coming was such that he had to convince the disciples that he was not simply a disembodied spirit. Luke says that he did this by bidding them handle him, and by eating part of a fish before them. According to John, Thomas was not with the others at this first meeting with the disciples. A week later, presumably in Jerusalem, Jesus again manifested himself to the little company, Thomas being with them, and dispelled the doubt of that disciple who loved too deeply to indulge a hope which might only disappoint. He had but to see in order to believe, and make supreme confession of his faith. The next appearance was probably that to the seven disciples by the Sea oÂ- Galilaej when Peter, who denied thrice, was thrice tested concerning his love for his Lord. Then apparently followed the meeting on the mountain reported in Matthew, which was probably the same as the appearance to the five hundred breth-r n; then, probably still in Galilee, Jesus appeared to his brother James, who from that time on was a leader among the disciples. The next manifestation of which record is preserved was the final one in Jerusalem, after which Jesus led his disciples out as far as Bethany and was separated from them, henceforth to be thought of by them as seated at the right hand of God.

216. This construction of the story as given in the New Testament does violence to the accounts in one particular. It holds that Matthew's report of the meeting of Jesus with the women on their way from the tomb on Easter morning is to be identified with his meeting with Mary Magdalene. This can be done only if it is supposed that in the transmission of the tradition the commission given the women by the angel (Mark xvi. 6 f.) became blended with the message given to Mary by the Lord (John xx. 17), the result being virtually the same for the religious interest of the first Christians, while

for the historic interest of our days it constitutes a discrepancy. The difficulty is less on this supposition than on any other. It is highly significant that the account of the most indubitable fact in the view of the early Christians is the most difficult portion of the gospels for the exact harmonist to deal with. This is not of serious moment for the historical student. It is rather a warning against theoretical ideas of inspiration.

217. The universal acknowledgment that the early Christians firmly believed in the resurrection of their Lord has made the origin of that firm conviction a question of primary importance. The simple facts as set forth in the New Testament serve abundantly to account for the faith of the early church, but they not only involve a large recognition of the miraculous, they also contain perplexities for those who do not stumble at the supernatural; hence there have been many attempts to find other solutions of the problem. Some of the explanations offered may be dismissed with a word: for instance, those which, in one form or other, renew the old charge found in the first gospel, that the disciples stole the body of Jesus, and then declared that he had risen; and those which assume that the death of Jesus was apparent only, that he fainted on the cross, and then the chill of the night air and of the sepulchre served to revive him, so that in the morning he was able to leave the tomb and appear to his disciples as one risen from the dead. This apparent-death theory involves Jesus in an ugly deception, while the theory that, the disciples or any group of them removed the body of Jesus and then gave currency to the notion that he had risen, builds the greatest ethical and religious movement known to history on a lie. A slightly different explanation which was very early suggested was that the Jews themselves, or perhaps the gardener, had the body removed, and that when Mary found the tomb empty she let her faith conclude that his absence must be due to his resurrection.

218. This last explanation has in recent times been revived in connection with the so-called vision-hypothesis by Renan and Reille. Mary found the tomb empty, and being herself of a highly strung nervous nature â she had been cured by Jesus of seven devils â by thinking about the empty tomb she soon worked herself into an ecstasy in which her eyes seemed to behold what her heart desired to see. She communicated her vision to the others, and by a sort of nervous contagion, they, too, fell to seeing visions, and it is the report of these that we have in the gospels. The vision-hypothesis takes with some, Strauss for instance, a different form. These deny that the tomb was found empty at all, and regard this story as a contribution of the later legend-making spirit. They hold that the disciples fled from Jerusalem as soon as the death of Jesus was an assured fact, and not until after they found themselves amid the familiar scenes of Galilee, did their faith recover from the shock it had received in Jerusalem. In Galilee the experiences of their life with Jesus were lived over again, and the old confidence in him as Messiah revived. Thus thinking about the Lord, their hearts would say, "He cannot have died," and after a while their faith rose to the conviction which declared, "He is not dead;" then they passed into an ecstatic mood and visions followed which are the germ out of which the gospel stories have grown.

219. These different forms of the vision-hypothesis have been subjected to most searching criticism by Keim, who is all the more severe because his own thought has so much that is akin to them. There are two objections which refute the hypothesis. The first is that the uniform tradition which connects the resurrection and the first

appearances with the " third day " after the crucifixion leaves far too short a time for the recovery of faith and the growth of ecstatic feeling which are requisite for these visions, even supposing that the disciples' faith had such recuperative powers. The second is that once such an ecstatic mood was acquired it would be according to experience in analogous cases for the visions to continue, if not to increase, as the thought of the risen Lord grew more clear and familiar; yet the tradition is uniform that the appearances of the risen Christ ceased after, at most, a few weeks. The only later one was that which led to the conversion of Paul; and though Paul was a man somewhat given to ecstatic experiences (see II. Cor. xii.), he carefully distinguishes in his own thought his seeing of the Lord and his heavenly visions. In a word, the disciples of Jesus never showed a more healthy, normal life than that which gave them strength to found a church of believers in the resurrection in the face of persecution and scorn.

220. Keim seeks to avoid the difficulties which his own acute criticism disclosed in the ordinary vision-theory, by another which rejects the gospel stories as legendary, yet frankly acknowledges that the faith of the apostles in the resurrection was based on a miracle Their certainty was so unshakable, so uniform, so abiding, that it can be accounted for only by acknowledging that they did actually see the Lord. This seeing, however, was not with the eyes of sense, but with the spiritual vision, which properly perceives what pertains to the spirit world into which the glorified

Lord had withdrawn when he died. In his spiritual estate he manifested himself to his disciples, by a series of divinely caused and therefore essentially objective visions, in which he proved to them abundantly that he was alive, was victor over death, and had been exalted by God to his right hand. This theory is not in itself offensive to faith. It concedes that the belief of the disciples rested on actual disclosures of himself to them by the glorified Lord. The difficulty with the theory is that it relegates the empty tomb to the limbo of legend, though it is a feature of the tradition which is found in all the gospels and clearly implied in Paul (I. Cor. xv. 4; compare Rom. vi. 4); it also fails to show how this glorified Christ came to be thought of by the disciples as risen, rather than simply glorified in spirit. This criticism brings us back to the necessity of recognizing a resurrection which was in some real sense corporeal, difficult as that conception is for us. The gospels assert this with great simplicity and delicate reserve. They represent Jesus as returning to his disciples with a body which was superior to the limitations which hedge our lives about. It may be well described by Paul's words, "It is sown a natural body; it is raised a spiritual body." Yet the records indicate that when he willed Jesus could offer himself to the perception of other senses than sight and hearing â " handle me and see" is not an invitation that we expect from a spiritual presence. If, however, we have to confess an unsolved mystery here, and still more in the record of his eating in the presence of the disciples (Luke xxiv. 41-43), it is permitted us to own that our knowledge of the possible conditions of the fully perfected life are not such as to warrant great dogmatism in criticising the account The empty tomb, the objective presence of the risen Jesus, the renewed faith of his followers, and their new power are established data for our thought. With these, many of the details may be left in mystery, because we have not yet light sufficient to reveal to us all that we should like to know.

221. The ascension of the risen Christ to his Father is the presupposition of all the New Testament teaching. The Acts, the Epistles, and the Apocalypse join in the representation that he is now at the right hand of God. In fact it may be said that such a view is involved in the doctrine of the resurrection, for the very idea of that victory was that death had no more dominion over him. It is a fact, however, that none of our gospels in their correct text (see Luke xxiv. 51, R. V. margin) tell of the ascension. Luke clearly implies it, and John says that Jesus told Mary to tell the disciples that he was about to ascend to his Father and their Father. In Luke's later book, however (Acts i. 1-11), he gives a full acount of a last meeting of Jesus with the disciples, and of his ascension to heaven before their eyes. This withdrawal in the cloud must be understood as an acted parable; for, in reality, there is no reason for thinking that the clouds which hung over Olivet that day were any nearer God's presence than the ground on which the disciples stood. For them, however, such a disappearance would signify vividly the cessation of their earthly intercourse with their Lord, and his return to his home with the Father. The word of Jesus to Mary (John xx. 17) may fairly be interpreted to mean that Jesus had ascended to the Father on the day of the resurrection, and that each of his subsequent manifestations of himself were like that which later he granted to Paul near Damascus. In fact it is easier to view the matter in this way than to conceive of Jesus as sojourning in some hidden place for forty days after his resurrection. What the disciples witnessed ten days before Pentecost was a withdrawal similar to those which had separated him from them frequently during the recent weeks, only now set before their eyes in such a way as to tell them that these manifestations had reached an end; they must henceforth wait for the other representative of God and Christ, the Spirit, given to them at Pentecost.

222. The faith with which the disciples waited for the promised spirit was a very different faith from that which Peter confessed for his fellows at Caesarea Philippi. It had the same supreme attachment to a personal friend who had proved to be God's Anointed; the same readiness to let him lead whithersoever he would; the same firm expectation of a restitution of all things, in which God should set up his kingdom visibly, with Jesus as the King of men. Now, however, their trust was much fuller than before, and they looked for a still more glorious kingdom when their friend and Lord should come from heaven to assume his reign. They expected Christ to return soon in glory, yet his death and victory made them ready to endure any persecution for him, certain that, like the sufferings which he endured, it would lead to victory. These disciples had no idea that in preaching a religion of personal attachment to their Master, in filling all men's thoughts with his name, in building all hope on his return, and guiding all life by his teaching and spirit, they were cutting their moorings from the religion of their fathers. They remained loyal to the law, they were constant in the worship; but they had poured new wine into the bottles, and in time it proved the inadequacy of the old forms and revolutionized the world's religious life.

223. IN nothing does the contrast between Jesus and John the Baptist appear more clearly than in their attitude towards common social life. John had his training and did his work apart from the homes of men. The wilderness was his chosen and fit scene of labor. From this solitude he sent forth his summons and warning to his people. They who sought him for fuller teaching went after him and found him where

he was. They then returned to their homes and their work, leaving the prophet with his few disciples in their seclusion. With Jesus it was otherwise. His first act, after attaching to himself a few followers, was to go into Galilee to the town of Cana, and there with them to partake in the festivities of a wedding. While it is true that most of his teaching was by the wayside, among the hills, or by the sea, it is still a surprise to discover how often his ministry found its occasion as he was sitting at table in the house of some friend, real or feigned. The genuine friendships of Jesus as they appear in the gospels are among the most characteristic features of his life â witness the home at Bethany, the women who followed him even to the cross, and ministered to him of their substance, and the "beloved disciple." Jesus calls attention to this contrast between himself and John, reminding the people how some of the scornful pointed the finger at himself as " a gluttonous man and a wine-bibber, a friend of publicans and sinners." He received his training as a carpenter while John was in his wilderness solitude. Men who would probably have stood with admiration before John had he visited their synagogue, found Jesus too much one of themselves, and would none of him as a prophet (Mark vi. 2, 3).

224. A like contrast sets Jesus apart from the scribes of his day. These were revered by the people, in part perhaps because they held the common folk in such contempt. Their attitude was frank â "this multitude which knoweth not the law is accursed" (John vii. 49). The popular enthusiasm for Jesus filled them with scorn, until it began to give them alarm. They were glad to be reverenced by the people, to interpret the law for them " binding heavy burdens and grievous to be borne; " but showed little genuine interest in them. Jesus, on the other hand, not only had the reverence of the multitudes, but welcomed them. First his words and his works drew them, then he himself enchained their hearts. Outcasts, rich and poor, crowded into his company, and found him not only a teacher, a prophet of righteousness rebuking their sins and calling to repentance, but a friend, who was not ashamed to be seen in their homes, to have them among his closest attendants, and to be known as their champion. It was when such as these were pressing upon him to hear him that Jesus replied to the criticism of the scribes in the three parables of recovered treasure which stand among the rarest gems of the Master's teaching (Luke xv.).

225. One class only in the community failed of his sympathy, â the self-righteous hypocrites, who thought that godliness consisted in scrupulous regard for pious cere-monies, and that zeal was most laudable when lirected to the removal of motes from their brothers' dyes. For these Jesus had words of rebuke and burning scorn. It has been common with some to emphasize his friendship for the poor as if he chose them for their poverty, and the unlettered for their ignorance. Yet Jesus had no faster friends than the women who followed from Galilee and ministered to him of their substance, and the two sanhedrists, Joseph whose new tomb received his body, and Nicodemus whose liberality provided the spices which embalmed him; for these, and not the Galilean fishermen, were faithful to the last at the cross and at the grave. In no home did Jesus find a fuller or more welcome friendship than in Bethany, where all that is told us of its conditions suggests the opposite of poverty. The rich young ruler, who showed his too great devotion to his possessions, would hardly have sought out Jesus with his question, if he was known as the champion of poverty as in itself essential

to godliness. The demand made of him surprised him, and was suited to his special case. Jesus saw clearly the difficulties which wealth puts in the way of faith, but he recognized the power of God to overcome them, and when Zaccheus turned disciple, the demand for complete surrender of possessions was not repeated. On the contrary Jesus taught his disciples that even " the unrighteous mammon " should be used to win friends (Luke xvi. 9), so ministering unto some of " the least of these my brethren " (Matt. xxv. 40). The beatitude in Luke's report of the sermon on the mount (Luke vi. 20) was not for the poor as poor simply, but for those poor folk lightly esteemed who had spiritual sense enough to follow Jesus, while the well-to-do as a class were content with the " consolation" already in hand. Jesus' interest was in character, wherever it was manifest, whether in the repentance of a chief of the publicans, or in the widow woman's gift of " all her living;" whether it appeared in the hunger for truth shown by Nicodemus, a teacher of Israel, or in the woman that was a sinner who washed his feet with her tears. He was the great revealer of the worth of simple humanity, in man, woman, or child. Our world has' never seen another who so surely penetrated all masks or disguising circumstances and found the man himself, and having found him loved him.

226. This sympathy for simple manhood was manifested in a genuine interest in the common life of men in business, pleasure, or trouble. It is significant that the first exercise of his miraculous power should have been to relieve the embarrassment of his host at a wedding feast. Doubtless we are to understand that the miracle had a deeper purpose than simply supplying the needed wine (John ii. 11); but the significant thing is that Jesus should choose to manifest his glory in this way. It shows a genuine appreciation of social life quite impossible to an ascetic like the Baptist. The same appears in the way Jesus allowed his publican apostle to introduce him to his former associates, to the great scandal of the Pharisees; for a feast at which Jesus and a number of publicans were the chief guests accorded not with religion as they understood it. Jesus, however, seems to have found it a welcome opportunity to seek some of his lost sheep. The illustrations which he used in his teaching were often his best introduction to the common heart, for they were drawn from the occupations of the people who came to listen; while the aid Jesus gave to his disciples in their fishing showed not only his power, but also his respect for their work, a respect further proved when he called them to be fishers of men.

227. Beyond this interest in life's joy and its occupations was that unfailing sympathy with its troubles which drew the multitudes to him. He was far more than a healer; he studied to rid the people of the idea that he was a mere miracle-monger. He healed them because he loved them, and he asked of those who sought his help that they too should feel the personal relation into which his power had brought them. This seems to be in part the significance of his uniform demand for faith. Doubtless Mary, out of whom he had cast seven devils, and Simon the leper, who seems to have experienced his power to heal, are only single instances of many who found in him far more than at first they sought. No further record remains of the paralytic who carried off his bed, but left the burden of his sins behind, nor of the woman who loved much because she had been forgiven much, nor of the Samaritan whose life he uncovered that he might be able to give her the living water. Some who had his help for body

or heart may have gone away forgetful, after the fashion of men, but in the company of those who were bold to bear his name after his resurrection there must have been many who could not forget.

228. Jesus' interest in common life was genuine, and he entered into it with his heart. The incident of the anointing of his feet as he sat a guest in a Pharisee's house shows that he was keenly sensitive to the treatment he received at the hands of men. He had nothing to say of the slights his host had shown him, until that host began mentally to criticise the woman who was ministering to him in her love and penitence. Then with quiet dignity Jesus mentioned the several omissions of courtesy which he had noticed since he came in, contrasting the woman's attention with Simon's neglect (Luke vii. 36-50). One of the saddest things about Gethsemane was Jesus' vain pleading with his disciples for sympathy in his awful hour. They were too much dazed with awe and fear to lend him their hearts' support. He recognized indeed that it was only a weakness of the flesh; yet he craved their friendship's help, and repeatedly asked them to watch with him, for his soul was exceeding sorrowful. In contrast with this disappointment stands the joy with which Jesus heard from Peter the confession which proved that the falling off of popular enthusiasm had not shaken the loyalty of his chosen companions, â "Blessed art thou, Simon Bar-Jonah: for flesh and blood have not revealed it unto thee, but my Father which is in heaven" (Matt. xvi. 17). There is the sorrow of loneliness as well as rebuke in his complaint, "O faithless generation, how long shall I be with you? how long shall I bear with you?" (Mark ix. 19), and the lamentation over Jerusalem comes from a longing heart (Luke xiii. 34).

229. The independence of human sympathy which Jesus often showed is all the more glorious for the evidence the gospels give of his longing for it. When he put the question to the twelve, "Would ye also go away?" (John vi. 67), there is no hint in his manner that their defection with the rest would turn him at all from faithfully fulfilling the task appointed to him by his Father. In fact only now and then did he allow his own hunger to appear. Ordinarily he showed himself as the friend longing to help, but not seeking ministry from others; he rather sought to win his disciples to unselfishness by showing as well as saying that he came not to be ministered unto but to minister. He washed the feet of his disciples to rebuke their petty jealousies, but we have no hint that he showed that he felt personal neglect. His own heart was full of " sorrow even unto death," but his word was, "Let not your heart be troubled; " he asked in vain for the sympathy of his nearest friends in Gethsemane, yet when the band came to arrest him he pleaded, "Let these, the disciples, go their way."

THE TEACHER WITH AUTHORITY 230. To his contemporaries Jesus was primarily a teacher. The name by which he is oftenest named in the gospels is Teacher, â translated Master in the English versions and the equivalent of Rabbi in the language used by Jesus (John i. 38). People thought of him as a rabbi approved of God by his power to work miracles (John iii. 2), but it was not the miracles that most impressed them. The popular comment was, "He taught them as one having authority, and not as the scribes" (Matt. vii. 29). Two leading characteristics of the scribes were their pride of learning, and their bondage to tradition. In fact the learning of which they were proud was knowledge of the body of tradition on whose sanctity they insisted; their teaching was scholastic and pedantic, an endless citing of precedents and discussion of trifles. To all this Jesus presented a refreshing contrast. In commending truth to the people, he was content with a simple " verily," and in denning duty he rested on his unsupported " I say unto you," even when his dictum stood opposed to that which had been said to them of old time.

231. In this freedom from the bondage of tradition Jesus was not alone. John the Baptist's message had been as simple and unsupported by appeal to the elders.

Jesus and John both revived the method of the older prophets, and it is in large measure due to this that the people distinguished them clearly from their ordinary teachers, and held them both to be prophets. One thing involved in this authoritative method was a frank appeal to the conscience of men. So completely had the scribes substituted memory of tradition for appeal to the simple sense of right, that they were utterly dazed when Jesus undertook to settle questions of Sabbath observance and ceremonial cleanliness by asking his hearers to use their religious common sense, and consider whether a man is not much better than a sheep, or whether a man is not denied rather by what comes out of his mouth than by what enters into it (Matt. xii. 12; Mark vii. 15). Jesus was for his generation the great discoverer of the conscience, and for all time the champion of its dignity against finespun theory and traditional practice. All his teaching has this quality in greater or less degree. It appears when by means of the parable of the Good Samaritan he makes the lawyer answer his own question (Luke x. 25-37), when he bids the multitude in Jerusalem "judge not according to the appearance, but judge righteous judgment " (John vii. 24), when he asks his inquisitors in the temple whose image and superscription the coin they used in common business bears (Mark xii. 16). His whole work in Galilee was proof of his confidence that in earnest souls the conscience would be his ally, and that he could impress himself on them far more indelibly than any sign from heaven could enforce his claim.

232. Jesus was not only independent of the traditions of the scribes, he was also very free at times with the letter of the Old Testament. When by a word he " made all meats clean" (Mark vii. 19), he set himself against the permanent validity of the Levitical ritual. When the Pharisees pleaded Moses for their authority in the matter of divorce, Jesus referred them back of Moses to the original constitution of mankind (Matt. xix. 3-9). His general attitude to the Sabbath was not only opposed to the traditions of the scribes, it also disregarded the Old Testament conception of the Sabbath as an institution. Yet Jesus took pains to declare that he came not to set aside the old but to fulfil it (Matt. v. 17). The contrasts which he draws between things said to them of old and his new teachings (Matt. v. 21-48) look at first much like a doing away of the old. Jesus did not so conceive them. He rather thought of them as fresh statements of the idea which underlay the old; they fulfilled the old by realizing more fully that which it had set before an earlier generation. He was the most radical teacher the men of his day could conceive, but his work was clearing rubbish away from the roots of venerable truth that it might bear fruit, rather than rooting up the old to put something else in its place.

233. The Old Testament was for Jesus a holy book. His mind was filled with its stories and its language. In the teachings which have been preserved for us he has made use of writings from all parts of the Jewish scriptures. â Law, Prophets, and Psalms. The Old Testament furnished him the weapons for his own soul's struggle with

temptation (Matt. iv. 4, 7, 10), it gave him arguments for use against his opponents (Mark xii. 24-27; ii. 25-27), and it was for him an inexhaustible storehouse of illustration in his teaching. When inquirers sought the way of life he pointed them to the scriptures (Mark x. 19; see also John v. 39), and declared that the rising of one from the dead would not avail for the warning of those who were unmoved by Moses and the prophets (Luke xvi. 31). When Jesus' personal attitude to the Old Testament is considered it is noticeable that while his quotations and allusions cover a wide range, and show very general familiarity with the whole book, there appears a decided predominance of Deuteronomy, the last part of Isaiah, and the Psalms. It is not difficult to see that these books are closer in spirit to his own thought than much else in the old writings; his use of the scripture shows that some parts appealed to him more than others.

234. Jesus as a teacher was popular and practical rather than systematic and theoretical. The freshness of his ideas is proof that he was not lacking in thorough and orderly thinking, for his complete departure from current conceptions of the kingdom of God indicates perfect mastery of ethical and theological truth. It is all the more remarkable, therefore, that so much of his profoundest teaching seems to have been almost accidental. The most formal discourse preserved to us is the sermon on the mount, in which human conduct is regulated by the thought of God as Father and Searcher of hearts. For the rest the great ideas of Jesus have utterance in response to specific conditions presented to him in his ministry. His most radical sayings concerning the Sabbath followed a criticism of his disciples for plucking ears of grain as they passed through the fields on the Sabbath day (Mark ii. 23-28); his authority to forgive sins was announced when a paralytic was brought to him for healing (Mark ii. 1-12); so far as the gospels indicate, we should have missed Jesus' clearest statement of the significance of his own death but for the ambitious request of James and John (Mark x. 35-45). Examples of the occasional character of his teaching might be greatly multiplied. He did not seek to be the founder of a school; important as his teachings were, they take a place in his work second to his personal influence on his followers. He desired to win disciples whose faith in him would withstand all shocks, rather than to train experts who would pass on his ideas to others. His disciples did become experts, for we owe to them the vivid presentation we have of the exalted and unique teaching of their Master; but they were thus skilful because they surrendered themselves to his personal mastery, and learned to know the springs of his own life and thought.

235. Nothing in the teaching of Jesus is more remarkable than his confidence that men who believed in him would adequately represent him and his message to the world. The parable of the Leaven seems to have set forth his own method. We owe our gospels to no injunction given by him to write down what he said and did. He impressed himself on his followers, filled them with a love to himself which made them sensitive to his ideas as a photographic plate is to light, teaching them his truth in forms that did not at first show any effect on their thought, but were developed into strength and clearness by the experiences of the passing years. Christian ethics and theology are far more than an orderly presentation of the teaching of Jesus; in so far as they are purely Christian they are the systematic setting forth of truth involved, though

not expressed, in what he said and did in his ministry among men. His ideas were radical and thoroughly revolutionary. His method, however, had in it all the patience of God's working in nature, and the hidden noiseless power of an evolution is its char acteristic. Hence it was that he chose to teach some things exclusively in figure. So great and unfamiliar a truth as the gradual development of God's kingdom was unwelcome to the thought of his time. He made it, therefore, the theme of many of his parables; and although the disciples did not understand what he meant, the picture remained with them, and in after years they grew up to his idea.

236. Jesus' use of illustration is one of the most marked features of his teaching. In one sense this simply proves him to be a genuine Oriental, for to contemplate and present abstract truths in concrete form is characteristic of the Semitic mind. In the case of Jesus, however, it proves more: the variety and homeliness of his illustrations show how completely conversant he was alike with common life and with spiritual truth. There is a freedom and ease about his use of figurative language which suggests, as nothing else could, his own clear certainty concerning the things of which he spoke. The fact, too, that his mind dealt so naturally with the highest thoughts has made his illustrations unique for profound truth and simple beauty. Nearly the whole range of figurative speech is represented in his recorded words, including forms like irony and hyperbole, often held to be unnatural to such serious speech as his.

237. Another figure has become almost identified with the name of Jesus, â such abundant and incom- parable use did he make of it. Parable was, however, no invention of his, for the rabbis of his own and later times, as well as the sages and prophets who went before them, made use of it. As distinguished from other forms of illustration, the parable is a picture true to actual human life, used to enforce a religious truth. The picture may be drawn in detail, as in the story of the Lost Son (Luke xv. 11-32), or it may be the con-cisest narration possible, as in the parable of the Leaven (Matt. xiii. 33); but it always retains its character as a narrative true to human experience. It is this that gives parable the peculiar value it has for religious teaching, since it brings unfamiliar truth close home to every-day life. Like all the illustrations used by Jesus, the parable was ordinarily chosen as a means of making clear the spiritual truth which he was presenting. Illustration never finds place as mere ornament in his addresses. His parables, however, were sometimes used to baffle the unteachable and critical. Such was the case on the occasion in Jesus' life when attention is first called in the gospels to this mode of teaching (Mark iv. 1-34). The parable of the Sower would mean little to hearers who held the crude and material ideas of the kingdom which prevailed among Jesus' contemporaries. It was used as an invitation to consider a great truth, and for teachable disciples was full of suggestion and meaning; while for the critical curiosity of unfriendly hearers it was only a pointless story, â a means adopted by Jesus to save his pearls from being trampled under foot, and perhaps also to prevent too early a decision against him on the part of his opponents.

238. In nothing is Jesus' ease in handling deepest truth more apparent than in his use of irony and hyperbole in his illustrations. In his reference to the Pharisees as " ninety and nine just persons which need no repentance" (Luke xv. 7), and in his question, "Many good works have I shewed you from the Father, for which of these works do you stone me? " (John x. 32), the irony is plain, but not any plainer than

the rhetorical exaggeration of his accusation against the scribes, "You strain out a gnat and swallow a camel" (Matt, xxiii. 24), or his declaration that ' it is easier for a camel to go through a needle's eye than for a rich man to enter into the kingdom of God " (Mark x. 25), or his charge, "If a man cometh unto me and hateth not his own father and mother. he cannot be my disciple" (Luke xiv. 26). The force of these statements is in their hyperbole. Only to an interpretation which regards the letter above the spirit can they cause difficulty. In so far as they remove Jesus utterly from the pedantic carefulness for words which marked the scribes they are among the rare treasures of his teachings. The simple spirit will not busy itself about finding something that may be called a needle's eye through which a camel can pass by squeezing, nor will it seek a camel which could conceivably be swallowed, nor will it stumble at a seeming command to hate those for whom God's law, as emphasized indeed by Jesus (Mark vii. 6-13), demands peculiar love and honor. The childlike spirit which is heir of God's kingdom readily understands this warning against the snare of riches, this rebuke of the hypocritical life, and this demand for a love for the Master which shall take the first place in the heart. 239. Jesus sometimes used object lessons as well as illustrations, and for the same purpose, â to make his thought transparently clear to his hearers. The demand for a childlike faith in order to enter the kingdom of God was enforced by the presence of a little child whom Jesus set in the midst of the circle to whom he was talking (Mark ix. 35-37). The unworthy ambitions of the disciples were rebuked by Jesus' taking himself the menial place and washing their feet (John xiii. 1-15).

240. The simplicity and homeliness of Jesus' teaching are not more remarkable than the alertness of mind which he showed on all occasions. The comment of the fourth gospel, " he needed not that any one should bear witness concerning man, for he himself knew what was in man" (ii. 25), doubtless refers to his supernatural insight, but it also tells of his quick perception of what was involved in each situation in which he found himself. Whether it was Nicodemus coming to him by night, or the lawyer asking, "Who is my neighbor? " or a dissatisfied heir demanding that his brother divide the inheritance with him, or a group of Pharisees seeking to undermine his power by attributing his cures to the devil, or trying to entrap him by a question about tribute, Jesus was never caught unawares. His absorption in heavenly truth was not accompanied by any blindness to earthly facts. He knew what the men of his day were thinking about, what they hoped for, to what follies they gave their hearts, and what sins hid God from them. He was eminently a man of the people, thoroughly acquainted with all that interested his fellows, and in the most natural, human way. Whatever of the supernatural there was in his knowledge did not make it unnatural.

As he was socially at ease with the best and most cultivated of his day, so he was intellectually the master of every situation. This appears nowhere more strikingly than in his dealing with his pharisaic critics. When they were shocked by his forgiveness of sins, or offended by his indifference to the Sabbath tradition, or goaded into blasphemy by his growing influence over the people, or troubled by his disciples' disregard of the traditional washings, or when later they conspired to entrap him in his speech, â from first to last he was so manifestly superior to his opponents that they withdrew discomfited, until at length they in madness killed, without reason, him against whom they could find no adequate charge. His lack of "learning" (John vii. 15) was simply his innocence of rabbinic training; he had no diploma from their schools. In keenness of argument, however, and invincibleness of reasoning, as well as in the clearness of his insight, he was ever their unapproachable superior. His reply to the charge of league with Beelzebub is as merciless an exposure of feeble malice as can be found in human literature. He was as worthy to be Master of his disciples' thinking as he was to be Lord of their hearts.

241. In the teaching of Jesus two topics have the leading place, â the Kingdom of God, and Himself. His thought about himself calls for separate consideration, but it may be remarked here that as his ministry progressed he spoke with increasing frankness about his own claims. It became more and more apparent that he sought to be Lord rather than Teacher simply, and to impress men with himself rather than with his ideas. Yet his ideas were constantly urged on his disciples, and they were summed up in his conception of the kingdom of God, or the kingdom of heaven. This was the topic, directly or indirectly, of far the greater part of his teaching. The phrase was as familiar to his contemporaries as it is common in his words; but his understanding of it was radically different from theirs. He and they took it to mean the realization on earth of heavenly conditions (kingdom of heaven), or of God's actual sovereignty over the world (kingdom of God); but of the God whose will was thus to be realized they conceived quite differently. Strictly speaking there is nothing novel in the idea of God as Father which abounds in the teaching of Jesus. He never offers it as novel, but takes it for granted that his hearers are familiar with the name. It appears in some earlier writers both in and out of the Old Testament. Yet no one of them uses it as constantly, as naturally, and as confidently as did Jesus. With him it was the simple equivalent of his idea of God, and it was central for his personal religious life as well as for his teaching. " My Father " always lies back of references in his teaching to " your Father." This is the key to what is novel in Jesus' idea of the kingdom of God. His contemporaries thought of God as the covenant king of Israel who would in his own time make good his promises, rid his people of their foes, set them on high among the nations, establish his law in their hearts, and rule over them as their king. The whole conception, while in a real sense religious, was concerned more with the nation than with individuals, and looked rather for temporal blessings than for spiritual good. With Jesus the kingdom is the realization of God's fatherly sway over the hearts of his children. It begins when men come to own God as their Father, and seek to do his will for the love they bear him. It shows development towards its full manifestation when men as children of God look on each other as brothers, and govern conduct by love which will no more limit itself to friends than God shuts off his sunlight from sinners. From this love to God and men it will grow into a new order of things in which God's will shall be done as it is in heaven, even as from the little leaven the whole lump is leavened. Jesus did not set aside the idea of a judgment, but while his fellows commonly made it the inauguration, he made it the consummation of the kingdom; they thought of it as the day of confusion for apostates and Gentiles, he taught that it would be the day of condemnation of all unbrotherliness (Matt. xxv. 31-46). This central ideaâ a new order of life in which men have come to love and obey God as their Father, and to love and live for men as their brothers â attaches to itself naturally all the various phases of the teaching of Jesus, including his emphasis

on himself; for he made that emphasis in order that, as the Way, the Truth, and the Life, he might lead men unto the Father.

JESUS' KNOWLEDGE OF TRUTH 242. THE note of authority in the teaching of Jesus is evidence of his own clear knowledge of the things of which he spoke. As if by swift intuition, his mind penetrated to the heart of things. In the scriptures he saw the underlying truth which should stand till heaven and earth shall pass (Matt. v. 18); in the ceremonies of his people's religion he saw so clearly the spiritual significance that he did not hesitate to sacrifice the passing form (Mark vii. 14-23); such a theological development as the pharisaic doctrine of the resurrection he unhesitatingly adopted because he saw that it was based on the ultimate significance of the soul's fellowship with God (Mark xiii. 24-27); he reduced religion and ethics to simplicity by summing up all commandments in one, â Thou shalt love (Matt. xxii. 37-40); and at the same time insisted as no other prophet had done on the finality of conduct and the necessity of obedience (Matt. vii. 21-27). His penetration to the heart of an idea was nowhere more clear than in his doctrine of the kingdom of God as realized in the filial soul, and as involving a judgment which should take cognizance only of brotherliness of conduct. It would not be difficult to show that all these different aspects of his teaching grew naturally out of his knowledge of God as his Father and the Father of all men; they were the fruit, therefore, of personal certainty of ultimate and all-dominating truth.

243. If the knowledge of Jesus had been shown ttfily in matters of spiritual truth, it would still have marked him as one apart from ordinary men. There were other directions, however, in which he surpassed the common mind. The fourth gospel declares that "he knew what was in man" (ii. 25), and all the evangelists give evidence of such knowledge. Not only the designation of Judas as the traitor, and of Peter as the one who should deny him, before their weakness and sin had shown themselves, but also Jesus' quick reading of the heart of the paralytic who was brought to him for healing, and of the woman who washed his feet with her tears (Mark ii. 5; Luke vii. 47), and his knowledge of the character of Simon and Nathanael (John i. 42, 47,) as well as his sure perception of the intent of the various questioners whom he met, indicate that he had powers of insight unshared by his fellow men.

244. Furthermore, the gospels state explicitly that Jesus predicted his own death from a time at least six months before the end (Matt. xvi. 21), and they indicate that the idea was not new to him when he first communicated it to his disciples (Matt. xvi. 23; Mark ii. 20). He viewed his approaching death, moreover, as a necessity (Mark viii. 31-33), yet he was no fatalist concerning it. He could still in Gethsemane plead with his Father, to whom all things are possible, to open to him some other way of accomplishing his work (Mark xiv. 36). The old Testament picture of the suffering and dying servant of Jehovah (Isa. liii.) was doubtless familiar to Jesus. Although it was not interpreted Messianically by the scribes, Jesus probably applied it to himself when thinking of his death; yet the predictions of the prophets always provided for a non-fulfilment in case Israel should turn unto the Lord in truth (see Ezek. xxxiii. 10-20). Moreover, the contradiction which Jesus felt between his ideas and those cherished by the leaders of his people, whether priests or scribes, was so radical that his death might well seem inevitable; yet it was possible that his people might repent,

and Jerusalem consent to accept him as God's anointed. Neither prophecy, nor the actual conditions of his life, therefore, would give Jesus any fatalistic certainty of his coming death. In Gethsemane his heart pleaded against it, while his will bowed still to God in perfect loyalty. It is not for us to explain his prediction of death by appealing to the connection which the apostolic thought established between the death of Christ and the salvation of men, for we are not competent to say that God could not have effected redemption in some other way if the repentance of the Jews had, humanly speaking, removed from Jesus the necessity of death. All that can be said is that he knew the prophetic picture, knew also the hardness of heart which had taken possession of the Jews, and knew that he must not swerve from his course of obedience to what he saw to be God's will for him. Since that obedience brought him into fatal opposition to human prejudice and passion, he saw that he must die, and that such a death was one of the steps in his establishment of God's kingdom among men. So he went on his way ready " not to be ministered unto but to minister, and to give his life a ransom for many" (Mark x. 45).

245. With his prediction of his death the gospels usually associate a prophecy of his speedy resurrection. As has been already remarked (sect. 210), it is being generally recognized that if Jesus believed that he was the Messiah, he must have associated with the thought of death that of victory over death, which for all Jewish minds meant a resurrection from the dead. Jesus certainly taught that his death was part of his Messianic work, it could not therefore be his end. The prediction of the resurrection is the necessary corollary of his expectation of death; and it may reverently be believed that his knowledge of it was intimately involved with his certainty that it was as Messiah that he was to die.

246. From the time when he began to tell his disciples that he must die, Jesus began also to teach that his earthly ministry was not to finish his work, but that he should return in glory from heaven to realize fully all that was involved in the idea of God's kingdom. His predictions resemble in form the representations found in the Book of Daniel and the Book of Enoch; and the understanding of them is involved in difficulties like those which beset such apocalyptic writings. In general, apocalypses were written in times of great distress for God's people, and represented the deliverance which should usher in God's kingdom as near at hand. One feature of them is a complete lack of perspective in the picture of the future. It may be that this fact will in part account for one great perplexity in the apocalyptic sayings of Jesus. In the chief of these (Mark xiii. and parallels), predictions of the destruction of Jerusalem are so mingled with promises of his own second coming and the end of all things that many have sought to resolve the difficulty by separating the discourse into two different ones, â one a short Jewish apocalypse predicting the destruction of Jerusalem and the coming of the Son of Man within the life of that generation; the other, Jesus' own prediction of the end of all things, concerning which he warns his disciples that they be not deceived, but watch diligently and patiently for God's full salvation. The difficulties of this discourse as it stands are so great that any solution which accounts for all the facts must be welcomed. So far as this analysis seeks to remove from the account of Jesus' own words the references to a fulfilment of the predictions within the life of that generation, it is confronted by other sayings of Jesus

(Mark ix. 1) and by the problem of the uniform belief of the apostolic age that he would speedily return. That belief must have had some ground. What more natural than that words of Jesus, rightly or wrongly understood, led to the common Christian expectation? Some such analysis may yet establish itself as the true solution of the difficulties; it may be, however, that in adopting the apocalyptic form of discourse, Jesus also adopted its lack of perspective, and spoke coincidently of future events in the progress of the kingdom, which, in their complete realization at least, were widely separated in time. In such a case it would not be strange if the disciples looked for the fulfilment of all of the predictions within the limit assigned for the accomplishment of some of them.

247. Whatever the explanation of these difficulties, the gospels clearly represent Jesus as predicting his own return in glory to establish his kingdom, â a crowning evidence of his claim to supernatural knowledge. It is all the more significant, therefore, that it is in connection with his prediction of his future coming that he made the most definite declaration of his own ignorance: " Of that day or that hour knoweth no one, not even the angels in heaven, neither the Son, but the Father " (Mark xiii. 32). This confession of the limitation of his knowledge is conclusive. Yet it is not isolated. With his undoubted power to read " what was in man," he was not independent of ordinary ways of learning facts. When the woman was healed who touched the hem of his garment, Jesus knew that his power had been exercised, but he discovered the object of his healing by asking, "Who touched me? " and calling the woman out from the crowd to acknowledge her blessing (Mark v. 30-34); when the centurion urged Jesus to heal his boy without taking the trouble to come to his house, Jesus " marvelled " at his faith (Matt. viii. 10); when he came to Bethany, assured of his Father's answer to his prayer for the raising of Lazarus, he asked as simply as any other one in the company, "Where have ye laid him?" (John xi. 34). It should not be forgotten that his knowledge of approaching death, resurrection, and return in glory did not prevent the earnest pleading in Gethsemane, and it may be that his reply to the ambition of James and John, it " is not mine to give" (Mark x. 40), is a confession of ignorance as well as subordination to his Father.

248. The supernatural knowledge of Jesus, so far as its exercise is apparent in the gospels, was concerned with the truths intimately related to his reli- gious teaching or his Messianic work. There is no evidence that it occupied itself at all with facts of nature or of history discovered by others at a later day. When he says of God that " he maketh his sun to rise on the evil and the good " (Matt. v. 45), there is no evidence that he thought of the earth and its relation to the sun differently from his contemporaries; it is probable that his thought anticipated Galileo's discovery no more than do his words. Much the same may be said with reference to the purely literary or historical questions of Old Testament criticism, now so much discussed. If it is proved by just interpretation of all the facts that the Pentateuch is only in an ideal sense to be attributed to Moses, and that many of the psalms inscribed with his name cannot have been written by David, the propriety of Jesus' references to what " Moses said" (Mark vii. 10), and the validity of his argument for the relative unimportance of the Davidic descent of the Messiah, will not suffer. Had Jesus had in mind the ultimate facts concerning the literary structure of the Pentateuch, he could not have hoped to

hold the attention of his hearers upon the religious teaching he was seeking to enforce, unless he referred to the early books of the Old Testament as written by Moses. Jesus did repeatedly go back of Moses to more primitive origins (Mark x. 5, 6; John vii. 22); yet there is no likelihood that the literary question was ever present in his thinking. This phase of his intellectual life, like that which concerned his knowledge of the natural universe, was in all probability one of the points in which he was made like unto his brethren, sharing, as matter of course, their views on questions that were indifferent for the spiritual mission he came to fulfil. If this was the case, his argument from the one hundred and tenth Psalm (Mark xii. 35-37) would simply give evidence that he accepted the views of his time concerning the Psalm, and proceeded to use it to correct other views of his time concerning what was of most importance in the doctrine of the Messiah. The last of these was of vital importance for his teaching; the first was for this teaching quite as indifferent a matter as the relations of the earth and the sun in the solar system.

249. A more perplexing difficulty arises from his handling of the cases of so-called demoniac possession. He certainly treated these invalids as if they were actually under the control of demons: he rebuked, banished, gave commands to the demons, and in this way wrought his cures upon the possessed. It has already been remarked that the symptoms shown in the cases cured by Jesus can be duplicated from cases of hysteria, epilepsy, or insanity, which have come under modern medical examination. Three questions then arise concerning his treatment of the possessed. 1. Did he unquestioningly share the interpretation which his contemporaries put upon the symptoms, and simply bring relief by his miraculous power? 2. Did he know that those whom he healed were not afflicted by evil spirits, and accommodate himself in his cures to their notions? 3. Does he prove by his treatment that the unfortunates actually were being tormented by diabolical agencies, which he banished by his word? The last of these possibilities should not be held to be impossible until much more is known than we now know about the mysterious phenomena of abnormal psychical states. If this is the explanation of the maladies for Jesus day, however, it should be accepted also as the explanation of similar abnormal symptoms when they appear in our modern life, for the old hypothesis of a special activity of evil spirits at the time of the incarnation is inadequate to account for the fact that in some quarters similar maladies have been similarly explained from the earliest times until the present day. If, however, he knew his people to be in error in ascribing these afflictions to diabolical influence, he need have felt no call to correct it. If the disease had been the direct effect of such a delusion, Jesus would have encouraged the error by accommodating himself to the popular notion. The idea of possession, however, was only an attempt to explain very real distress. Jesus desired to cure, not to inform his patients. The notion in no way interfered with his turning the thought of those he healed towards God, the centre of help and of health. He is not open, therefore, to the charge of having failed to free men from the thraldom of superstition if he accommodated himself to their belief concerning demoniac possession. His cure, and his infusion of true thoughts of God into the heart, furnished an antidote to superstition more efficacious than any amount of discussion of the truth or falseness of the current explanation of the disease. On the other hand, if we are not ready to conclude that the action of Jesus has demonstrated

the validity of the ancient explanation, we may acknowledge that it would do no violence to his power, or dignity, or integrity, if it should be held that he did not concern himself with an inquiry into the cause of the disease which presented itself to him for help, but adopted unquestioningly the explanation held by all his contemporaries, even as he used their language, dress, manner of life, and in one particular, at least, their representation of the life after death (Luke xvi. 22 â Abraham's bosom). His own confession of ignorance of a large item of religious knowledge (Mark xiii. 32) leaves open the possibility that in so minor a matter as the explanation of a common disease he simply shared the ideas of his time. In this case, when one so afflicted came under his treatment, he applied his supernatural power, even as in cases of leprosy or fever, and cured the trouble, needing no scientific knowledge of its cause. If accommodation or ignorance led Jesus to treat these sick folk as possessed, it does not challenge his integrity nor his trustworthiness in all the matters which belong properly to his own peculiar work.

250. There is one incident in the gospels which favors the conclusion that Jesus definitely adopted the current idea, â the permission granted by him to the demons to go from the Gadarene into the herd of swine, and the consequent drowning of the herd (Mark v. 11-13). On any theory this incident is full of difficulty. Bernhard Weiss (LXt II. 226 ff.) holds that Jesus accommodated himself to current views, and that the man, having received for the possessing demons permission to go into the swine, was at once seized by a final paroxysm, and rushed among the swine, stampeding them so that they ran down the hillside into the sea.

251. In recent years the view has been somewhat widely advocated that his power over demoniacs was to Jesus himself one of the chief proofs of his Messiah-ship. His words are quoted: " If I, by the Spirit of God, cast out demons, then is the kingdom of God come upon you " (Matt. xii. 28); and " I beheld Satan falling as lightning from heaven " (Luke x. 18). The first of these is in the midst of an ad hominem reply of Jesus to the charge that he owed his power to a league with the devil (Matt. xii. 28); and the second was his remark when the seventy reported with joy that the demons were subject unto them (Luke x. 18). The gospels, however, trace his certainty of his Messiahship to quite other causes, primarily to his knowledge of himself as God's child, then to the Voice which, coming at the baptism, summoned him as God's beloved Son to do the work of the Messiah. Throughout his ministry Jesus exhibits a certainty of his mission quite independent of external evidences, â " Even if I bear witness of myself, my witness is true; for I know whence I came and whither I go " (John viii. 14).

252. WHEN Jesus called forth the confession of Peter at Csesarea Philippi he brought into prominence the question which during the earlier stages of the Galilean ministry he had studiously kept in the background. This is no indication, however, that he was late in reaching a conclusion for himself concerning his relation to the kingdom which he was preaching. From the time of his baptism and temptation every manifestation of the inner facts of his life shows unhesitating confidence in the reality of his call and in his understanding of his mission. This is the case whether the fourth gospel or the first three be appealed to for evidence. It is generally felt that the Gospel of John presents its sharpest contrast to the synoptic gospels in respect of

the development of Jesus' self-disclosures. A careful consideration of the first three gospels, however, shows that the difference is not in Jesus' thought about himself.

253. The first thing which impressed the people during the ministry in Galilee was Jesus' assumption of authority, whether in teaching or in action (Mark i. 27; Matt. vii. 28, 29). His method of teaching distinguished him sharply from the scribes, who were constantly appealing to the opinion of the elders to establish the validity of their conclusions. Jesus taught with a simple "I say unto you." In this, however, he differed not only from the scribes, but also from the prophets, to whom in many ways he bore so strong a likeness. They proclaimed their messages with the sanction of a "Thus saith the Lord; " he did not hesitate to oppose the letter of scripture as well as the tradition of the elders with his unsupported word (Matt. v. 38, 39; Mark vii. 1-23). His teaching revealed his unhesitating certainty concerning spiritual truth, and although he reverenced deeply the Jewish scriptures, and knew that his work was the fulfilment of their promises, he used them always as one whose superiority to God's earlier messengers was as complete as his reverence for them. He was confident that what they suggested of truth he was able to declare clearly; he used them as a master does his tools.

254. More striking than Jesus' independence in his teaching is the calmness of his self-assertion when he was opposed by pharisaic criticism and hostility. He preferred to teach the truth of the kingdom, working his cures in such a way that men should think about God's goodness rather than their healer's significance. Yet coincidently with this method of his choice he did not hesitate to reply to pharisaic opposition with unqualified self-assertion and exalted personal claim. Even if the conflicts which Mark has gathered together at the opening of his gospel (ii. 1 to iii. 6) did not all occur as early as he has placed them, the nucleus of the group belongs to the early time. Since the people greatly reverenced his critics, he felt it unnecessary to guard against arousing undue enthusiasm by this frank avowal of his claims. He consequently asserted his authority to forgive sins, his special mission to the sick in soul whom the scribes shunned as defiling, his right to modify the conception of Sabbath observance; even as, later, he warned his critics of their fearful danger if they ascribed his good deeds to diabolical power (Mark iii. 28-30), and as, after the collapse of popularity, he rebuked them for making void the word of God by their tradition (Mark vii. 13). His attitude to the scribes in Galilee from the beginning discloses as definite Messianic claims as any ascribed by the fourth gospel to this early period.

255. These facts of the independence of Jesus in his teaching and his self-assertion in response to criticism confirm the impression that his answer to John the Baptist (Matt. xi. 2-6) gives the key to his method in Galilee. In John's inquiry the question of Jesus' personal relation to the kingdom was definitely asked. The answer, "Blessed is he whosoever shall find none occasion of stumbling in me," showed plainly that Jesus was in no doubt in the matter, although for the time he still preferred to let his ministry be the means of leading men to form their conclusions concerning him. What he brought into prominence at Csesarea Philippi, therefore, was that which had been the familiar subject of his own thinking from the time of his baptism.

256. In the ministry subsequent to the confession of Peter the self-disclosures of Jesus became more frequent and clear. His predictions of his approaching death were

at the time the greatest difficulty to his disciples; when considered in their significance for his own life, however, they prove that his conviction of his Messiahship was as independent of current and inherited ideas as was his teaching concerning the kingdom. When he came to see that death was the inevitable issue of his work, he at once discovered in it a divine necessity; it does not seem to have shaken in the least his certainty that he was the Messiah. Associated with this conception of his death is the conviction which appears in all the later teachings, that in rejecting him his people were pronouncing their own doom. Because she would not accept him as her deliverer, Jerusalem's "house was left unto her desolate " (Luke xiii. 35). His sense of his supreme significance appears most clearly in some of the later parables, such as The Marriage of the King's Son (Matt. xxii. 1-14) and The Wicked Husbandmen (Matt. xxi. 33-44), which definitely connect the condemnation of the chosen people with their rejection of God's Son. Two other sayings in the first three gospels express the personal claim of Jesus in the most exalted form, â his declaration on the return of the seventy: "All things have been delivered unto me of my Father, and no man knoweth who the Son is save the Father, and who the Father is save the Son, and he to whomsoever the Son willeth to reveal him" (Luke x. 22; Matt. xi. 27); and his confession of the limits of his own knowledge: "But of that day and hour knoweth no one, not even the angels in heaven, neither the Son, but the Father" (Mark xiii. 32). The confession of ignorance, by the position given to the Son in the climax which denied that any save the Father had a knowledge of the time of the end, is quite as extraordinary as the claim to sole qualification to reveal the Father.

257. The similarity of these last two sayings to the discourses in the fourth gospel has often been remarked; the likeness is particularly close between them and the claims of Jesus recorded in the fifth chapter of John. It is interesting to note that in the incident which introduces the discourse in that chapter Jesus shows that he preferred, after healing the man at the pool, to avoid the attention of the multitudes, precisely as in Galilee he sought to check too great popular excitement by withdrawing from Capernaum after his first ministry there (Mark i. 35-39), and enjoining silence on the leper who had been healed by him (Mark ii. 44). When, however, he found himself opposed by the criticism of the Pharisees he spoke with unhesitating self-assertion and exalted personal claim, even as he did in like situations in Galilee. During his earlier ministry in Judea he had not shown this reserve. The cleansing of the temple, although it was no more than any prophet sure of his divine commission would have done, was a bold challenge to the people to consider who he was who ventured thus to criticise the priestly administration of God's house. In his subsequent dealings with Nicodemus and the Samaritan woman Jesus manifested a like readiness to draw attention to himself. From the time of the feeding of the multitudes all four of the gospels represent him as asserting his claims, with this difference, however, that in John it is the rule rather than the exception to find sayings similar to the two in which the self-assertion in the other gospels reaches its highest expression. Although the method of Jesus varied at different times and in different localities, yet it is evident that he stood before the people from the first with the consciousness that he had the right to claim their allegiance as no one of the prophets who preceded him would have been bold to do.

258. During the course of his ministry Jesus used of himself, or suffered others to use with reference to him, many of the titles by which his people were accustomed to refer to the Messiah. Thus he was named "the Messiah" (Mark viii. 29; xiv. 61; John iv. 26); "the King of the Jews " (Mark xv. 2; John i. 49; xviii. 33, 36, 37); "the Son of David" (Mark x. 47, 48; Matt. xv. 22; xxi. 9, 15); "the Holy One of God" (John vi. 69; compare Mark i. 24); "the Prophet" (John vi. 14; vii. 40). It is evident that none of these titles was common; they represent, rather, the bold venture of more or less intelligent faith on the part of men who were impressed by him. There are two names, however, that are more significant of Jesus' thought about himself, â " the Son of God" and "the Son of Man."

259. The latter of these titles is unique in the use Jesus made of it. Excepting Stephen's speech (Acts vii. 56), it is found in the New Testament only in the sayings of Jesus, and its precise significance is still a subject of learned debate. The expression is found in the Old Testament as a poetical equivalent for Man, usually with emphasis on human frailty (Ps. viii. 4; Num. xxiii. 19; Isa. li. 12), though sometimes it signifies special dignity (Ps. lxxx. 17). Ezekiel was regularly addressed in his visions as Son of Man (Ezek. ii. 1 and often; see also Dan. viii. 17), probably in contrast with the divine majesty.

260. In one of Daniel's visions (vii. 1-14) the world-kingdoms which had oppressed God's people and were to be destroyed were symbolized by beasts that came up out of the sea, â a winged lion, a bear, a four-headed winged leopard, and a terrible ten-horned beast; in contrast with these the kingdom of the saints of the Most High was represented by " one like unto a son of man," who came with the clouds of heaven (vii. 13, 14). Here the language is obviously poetic, and is used to suggest the unapproachable superiority of the kingdom of heaven to the kingdoms of the world. The expression "one like unto a son of man" is equivalent, therefore, to "one resembling mankind." The vision in Daniel had great influence over the author of the so-called Similitudes of Enoch (Book of Enoch, chapters xxxvii. to lxxi.). He, however, personified the "one like unto a son of man," and gave the title " the Son of Man " to the heavenly man who will come at the end of all things, seated on God's throne, to judge the world. This author used also the titles "the Elect One" and "the Righteous One" (or "the Holy One of God"), but "the Son of Man " is the prevalent name for the Messiah in these Similitudes.

261. The facts thus stated do not account for Jesus' use of the expression. Many of his sayings undoubtedly suggest a development of the Daniel vision resembling that in the Similitudes. This does not prove that Jesus or his disciples had read these writings, though it does suggest the possibility that they knew them. It is probable, however, that the apocalypses gave formulated expression to thoughts that were more widely current than those writings ever came to be. The likeness between the language of Jesus and that found in the Similitudes may therefore prove no more than that the Daniel vision was more or less commonly interpreted of a personal Messiah in Jesus' day.

262. Much of the use of the title by Jesus, however, is completely foreign to the ideas suggested by Enoch and Daniel. Besides apocalyptic sayings like those in Enoch (Mark viii. 38 and often), the name occurs in predictions of his sufferings

and death (Mark viii. 31 and often), and in claims to extraordinary if not essentially divine authority (Mark ii. 10, 28 and parallels); it is also used sometimes simply as an emphatic " I" (Matt. xi. 19 and often). Whatever relation Jesus bore to the Enoch writings, therefore, the name " the Son of Man "as he used it was his own creation.

263. Students of Aramaic have in recent years asserted that it was not customary in the dialect which Jesus spoke to make distinction between "the son of man" and "man," since the expression commonly used for "man" would be literally translated "son of man." It is asserted, moreover, that if our gospels be read substituting "man" for "the Son of Man " wherever it appears, it will be found that many supposed Messianic claims become general statements of Jesus' conception of the high prerogatives of man, while in other places the name stands simply as an emphatic substitute for the personal pronoun. Thus, for instance, Jesus is found to assert that authority on earth to forgive sins belongs to man (Ma V ii. 10), and, toward the end of his course, to have oaught simply that he himself must meet with suffering (Mark viii. 31), and will come on the clouds to judge the world (Mark viii. 38). The proportion pf cases in which the general reference is possible is.

however, very small; and even if the equivalence of " man " and " son of man " should be established, most of the statements of Jesus in which our gospels use the latter expression exhibit a conception of himself which challenges attention, transcending that which would be tolerated in any other man. The debate concerning the usage in the language spoken by Jesus is not yet closed, however, and Dr. Gustaf Dalman (WJ I. 191-197) has recently argued that the equivalence of the two expressions holds only in poetic passages, precisely as it does in Hebrew, and that our gospels represent correctly a distinction observed by Jesus when they report him, for instance, as saying in one sentence, " the Sabbath was made for man " (Mark ii. 27), and in the next, " the Son of Man is lord even of the Sabbath." The antecedent probability is so great that the dialect of Jesus' time would be capable of expressing a distinction found in the Hebrew of the Old Testament and in the Syriac of the second-century version of the New Testament, that Dalman's opinion carries much weight.

264. Many of those who look for a distinct significance in the title "the Son of Man," find in it a claim by Jesus to be the ideal or typical man, in whom humanity has found its highest expression. It thus stands sharply in contrast with "the Son of God," which is held to express his claim to divinity. So understood, the titles represent truth early recognized by the church in its thought about its Lord. Yet it must be acknowledged that the conception " the ideal man" is too Hellenic to have been at home in the thought of those to whom Jesus addressed his teaching. If the phrase suggested anything more to his hearers than the human frailty or the human dignity of him who bore it, it probably had a Messianic meaning like that found in the Similitudes of Enoch. A hint of this understanding of the name appears in the perplexed question reported in John (xii. 34): " We have heard out of the law that the Messiah abideth forever; and how sayest thou, The Son of Man must be lifted up? who is this Son of Man?" Here the difficulty arose because the people identified the Son of Man with the Messiah, yet could not conceive how such a Messiah could die. In fact, if the conception of the Son of Man which is found in Enoch had obtained any general currency among the people, either from that book or independently of it, it was

so foreign to the earthly condition and manner of life of the Galilean prophet, that it would not have occurred to his hearers to treat his use of the title as a Messianic claim until after that claim had been published in some other and more definite form. Their Son of Man was to come with the clouds of heaven, seated on God's throne, to execute judgment on all sinners and apostates; the Nazarene fulfilled none of these conditions. The name, as used by Jesus, was probably always an enigma to the people, at least until he openly declared its Messianic significance in his reply to the high-priest's question at his trial (Mark xiv. 62), and gave the council the ground it desired for a charge of blasphemy against him.

265. What did this title signify to Jesus? His use of it alone can furnish answer, and in this the variety is so great that it causes perplexity. "The Son of Man came eating and drinking " is his description of his own life in contrast with John the Baptist (Matt. xi. 18, 19). " The Son of Man hath not where to lay his head " was his reply to one over-zealous follower (Matt. viii. 20). Unseemly rivalry among his disciples was rebuked by the reminder that " even the Son of Man came not to be ministered unto but to minister " (Mark x. 42-45). When it became needful to prepare the disciples for his approaching death he taught them that "the Son of Man must suffer many things. and be killed, and after three days rise again" (Mark viii. 31). On the other hand, the paralytic's cure was made to demonstrate that "the Son of Man hath authority upon the earth to forgive sins " (Mark ii. 10). Similarly it is the Son of Man who after his exaltation shall come " in the glory of his Father with the holy angels " (Mark viii. 38). In these typical cases the title expresses Jesus' consciousness of heavenly authority as well as self-sacrificing ministry, of coming exaltation as well as present lowliness; and the suffering and death which were the common lot of other sons of men were appointed for this Son of Man by a divine necessity. The name is, therefore, more than a substitute for the personal pronoun; it expresses Jesus' consciousness of a mission that set him apart from the rest of men.

266. We do not know how Jesus came to adopt this title. Its association with the predictions of his coming glory shows that he knew that in him the Daniel vision was to have fulfilment. The predictions of suffering and death, however, are completely foreign to that apocalyptic conception, being akin rather, as Professor Charles has suggested, to the prophecies of the suffering servant in the Book of Isaiah (Book of Enoch, p. 314-317). Moreover, it may not be fanci- ful to find in his claims to heavenly authority a hint of the thought of the eighth Psalm, "Thou madest him to have dominion over the works of thy hands; thou hast put all things under his feet" (see Dalman WJ I. 218). Although the name expresses a consciousness of dignity, vicarious ministry, and authority, similar to thoughts found in Daniel, Isaiah, and the Psalms, it was not deduced from these scriptures by any synthesis of diverse ideas. It rather indicates that Jesus in his own nature realized a synthesis which no amount of study of scripture would ever have suggested. He drew his conception of himself from his own self-knowledge, not from his Messianic meditations. On his lips, then, " the Son of Man " indicates that he knew himself to be the Man whom God had chosen to be Lord over all (compare Dalman as above). The lowly estate which contradicted the Daniel vision prevented Jesus' hearers from recognizing in the title a Messianic

claim; for him, however, it was the expression of the very heart of his Messianic consciousness.

267. If Jesus gave expression to his official consciousness when he used the name "the Son of Man," the title "the Son of God" may be said to express his more personal thought about himself. It is necessary to distinguish between the meaning of this title to the contemporaries of Jesus and his own conception of it. In the popular thought "the Son of God" was the designation of that man whom God would at length raise up and crown with dignity and power for the deliverance of his people. This meaning followed from the Messianic interpretation of the second Psalm, in which the theocratic king is called God's son (Ps.

ii. 7). In another psalm, which Jesus himself quotes (John x. 34), magistrates and judges are called " sons of the Most High " (Txxxii. 6). Another Old Testament use casts light on this, â the designation of Israel as God's son, his firstborn (Ex. iv. 22; Hos. i. 10), with which may be compared a remarkable expression in the so-called Psalms of Solomon (xviii. 4), "Thy chastisement was upon us that is, Israel as upon a son, firstborn, only begotten." In all these passages that which constitutes a man the son of God is God's choice of him for a special work, while Israel collectively bears the title to suggest God's fatherly love for the people he had taken for his own. The Messianic title, therefore, described not a metaphysical, but an official or ethical, relation to God. It is certainly in this sense that the high-priest asked Jesus " Art thou the Messiah the son of the Blessed?" (Mark xiv. 61), and that the crowd about the cross flung their taunts at him (Matt, xxvii. 43), and the demoniacs proclaimed their knowledge of him (Mark iii. 11; v. 7). The name must be interpreted in this sense also in the confession of Nathanael (John i. 49); moreover, it was not the coupling of the names "Messiah" and "son of the living God" in Peter's confession that gave it its great significance for Jesus. In all of these cases there is no evidence that there has been any advance over the theocratic significance which made the title "the Son of God" fitting for the man chosen by God for the fulfilment of his promises.

268. The case is different with the name by which Jesus was called at his baptism (Mark i. 11). The difference here, however, arises not from anything in the name as used on this occasion, but from that in

Jesus which acknowledged and accepted the title. With Jesus the consciousness that God was his Father preceded the knowledge that as "his Son" he was to undertake the work of the Messiah. The force of the call at the baptism is found in the response which his own soul gave to the word "Thou art my Son." The nature of that response is seen in his hahitual reference to God as in a peculiar sense his Father. The name " Father" for God was used by him in all his teaching, and there is no evidence that he or any of his hearers regarded it as a novelty. Psalm ciii. 13 and Isaiah Ixiii. 16 indicate that the conception was natural to Jewish thinking. The unique feature in Jesus' usage is his careful distinction between the general references to "your Father" and his constant personal allusions to "my Father." Witness the reply to his mother in the temple (Luke ii. 49); his word to Peter, "Flesh and blood hath not revealed it unto thee, but my Father which is in heaven" (Matt. xvi. 17), his solemn warning, "Not every one that saith unto me Lord, Lord, shall enter into the kingdom of heaven, but he that doeth the will of my Father which is in heaven " (Matt. vii. 21), and the promise, "Every one who shall confess me before men. him will I also confess before my Father" (Matt. x. 32). In the fourth gospel the same intimate reference is common: so, for example, the temple is "my Father's house" (ii. 16), the Sabbath cure is defended because "my Father worketh even until now " (v. 17), the cures are done "in My Father's name " (x. 25), "I am the vine, and my Father is the husbandman" (xv. 1). This mode of expression discloses a consciousness of unique filial relation to God which is independent of, even as it was antecedent to, the consciousness of official relation.

269. The full name "the Son of God" was seldom applied by Jesus to himself, the only recorded instances being found in the fourth gospel (v. 25; ix. 35?; x. 36; xi. 4). He frequently acquiesced in the use of the title by others in addressing him (for example, John i. 49; Matt. xvi. 16; xxvi. 63 f.; Mark xiv. 61 f.; Luke xxii. 70); but for himself he preferred the simpler phrase "the Son." This mode of expression occurs often in John, and is found also in the two passages, already noticed, in which the other gospels give clearest expression to the extraordinary self-assertion of Jesus (Matt. xi. 27; Luke x. 22; and Mark xiii. 32). In the first of them his claim to be the only one who can adequately reveal God is founded on the consciousness that the relation between himself and God is so intimate that God alone adequately knows him, whom men were so ready to set at nought, and he alone knows God. This relation, in which he and God stand together in contrast with all other men, is expressed by the unqualified names, "the Father" and "the Son." In the second passage Jesus confessed the limitation of his knowledge, but again in such a way as to set himself and God in contrast not only with men, but also with "the angels in heaven." Such assertions as these indicate that he who, knowing his full humanity, chose the title "the Son of Man " to express his consciousness that he had been appointed by God to be the Messiah, was yet aware in his inner heart that his relation to God was even closer than that in which he stood to men.

270. There is no word in John which goes beyond the two self-declarations of Jesus which crown the record of the other evangelists, yet in the fourth gospel the same claim to unique relation to God is more frequently and frankly avowed. The most unqualified assertion of intimacyâ " I and the Father are one " (x. 30) â states what is clearly implied throughout the gospel (so xiv. 6-11; xvi. 25; and particularly xvii. 21, "that they may be one, even as we are one "). It has often been said, and truly, that this claim to unity with the Father, taken by itself, signifies no more than perfect spiritual and ethical harmony with God. Yet when the words are considered in their connection, and more particularly when the two supreme self-declarations in the synoptic gospels are associated with them, they express a sense of relation to God so utterly unique, so strongly contrasting the Father and the Son with all others, that we cannot conceive of any other man, even the saintliest, taking like words upon his lips.

271. These titles in which Jesus gave expression to his official and his personal consciousness present clearly the problem which he offers to human thought. Jesus stands before us in the gospels as a man aware of completest kinship with his brethren, yet conscious at the same time of standing nearer to God than he does to men.

272. It is highly significant that the gospel which records most fully the claim of Jesus to be more closely related to God than he was to men, most fully records also his

definite acknowledgment of dependence on his Father, and of that Father's supremacy over him and all others. " The Son can do nothing of himself" (John v. 19), "I speak not from myself"

(xiv. 10), "my Father is greater than all" (x. 29), " the Father is greater than I" (xiv. 28), â these confessions join with the common reference to God as " him that sent me " (v. 30 and often) in giving voice to his own spirit of reverence. It appears as clearly in his habitual submission to his Father's will, â " My meat is to do the will of him that sent me, and to accomplish his work " (John iv. 34); "I am come down from heaven, not to do mine own will, but the will of him that sent me" (John vi. 38). This submission reached its fulness in the prayer of Gethsemane, recorded in the earlier gospels, â " Father, all things are possible unto thee; remove this cup from me: how-beit not what I will, but what thou wilt " (Mark xiv. 36). Jesus was a man of prayer; not only in Gethsemane, but also throughout his ministry he habitually sought his Father in that communion in which the soul of man finds its light and strength for life's duty. When he was baptized (Luke iii. 21), after the first flush of success in Capernaum (Mark i. 35), before choosing the twelve (Luke vi. 12), before the question at Csesarea Philippi (Luke ix. 18), at the transfiguration (Luke ix. 29), on the cross (Luke xxiii. 46), â at all the crises of his life he turned to God in prayer. Moreover, prayer was his habit, for it was after a night of prayer which has no connection with any crisis reported for us (Luke xi. 1), that he taught his disciples the Lord's prayer in response to their requests. The prayer beside the grave of Lazarus (John xi. 41, 42) suggests that his miracles were often, if not always (compare Mark ix. 29), preceded by definite prayer to God. His habit of prayer was the natural expression of his trust in God. From the resistance to the temptations in the wilderness to the last cry, "Father, into thy hands I commend my spirit," his life is an example of childlike faith in God.

273. Yet throughout his life of obedience and trust Jesus never gave one indication that he felt the need of penitence when he came before God. He perceived as no one else has ever done the searching inwardness of God's law, and demanded of men that they tolerate no lower ambition than to be like God, yet he never breathed a sigh of conscious failure, or gave sign that he blushed when the eternal light shone into his own soul. He was baptized, but without confession of sin. He challenged his enemies to convict him of sin (John viii. 46). Such a challenge might have rested on a man's certainty that his critics did not know his inner life; but hypocrisy has no place in the character of Jesus. The reply to the rich young ruler, "Why callest thou me good? " (Mark x. 18), even if it was a confession that freedom from past sin was still far less than that absolute goodness that God alone possesses, simply sets in stronger light his silence concerning personal failure, and his omission in all his praying to seek forgiveness. It is probable, however, that that reply deals not with the "good" as the "ethically perfect," but as the "supremely beneficent," so that Jesus simply reminded the seeker after life that God alone is the one to be approached as the Gracious and Merciful One by sinful men (see DalmanwJ I. 277). Thus the reply becomes a fresh expression of the reverence of Jesus, and still further emphasizes his failure to confess his sinfulness.

274. In all this thought about himself Jesus stands before us as a man, conscious of his close kinship with his fellows. Like them he hungered and thirsted and grew

weary, like them he longed for friendship and for sympathy, like them he trusted God and prayed to God and learned still to trust when his request was denied. He stands before us also as a man conscious of being anointed by God for the great work which all the prophets had foretold, and of being fully equipped with authority and power and the promise of unapproachable dignity. Of deep religious spirit and great reverence for the scriptures of his people, he yet used these scriptures as a master does his tools, to serve his work rather than to instruct him in it. He drew his knowledge from within and from above, and proclaimed his own fulfilment of the scriptures when he filled them with new meaning. A man always devout, always at prayer, he is never seen, like Isaiah, prostrate before the Most High, crying, "I am undone " (Isa. vi. 5). In his moments of greatest seriousness and most manifest communion with heaven he looked to God as his nearest of kin, and felt himself a stranger on the earth fulfilling his Father's will. He felt heaven to be his home not simply by God's gracious promise, but by the right of previous possession. His kinship with men was a condescension, his natural fellowship was with God.

275. The miracles with which the gospels have filled the record of Jesus' life have caused perplexity to many, and they belong with other mysterious things recorded for us in the story of the past or occurring under the incredulous observation of our scientific generation. They all pale, however, before the unaccountable exception presented to universal human experience by this Man of Nazareth. It confronts us when we think of the unschooled Jew who, in his thought of God, rose not only above all of his generation, but higher than all who had gone before him, or have come after, one who built on the foundation of the past a superstructure of religion new, and simple, and clearly heavenly. It confronts us when we think of this Man who believed that it was given to him to establish the kingdom that should fill the whole earth, and who had the boldness and the faith to ignore the opposition of all the world's wisdom and of all its enthroned power, and to fulfil his task as the woman does who hides her leaven in the meal, content to wait for years, or millenniums, until his truth shall conquer in the realization of God's will on earth even as it is done in heaven. It confronts us when we consider that the Man who has shown his brethren what obedience means, who has taught them to pray, who has been for all these centuries the Way, the Truth, the Life, by whom they come to God, habitually claimed without shadow of abashment or slightest hint of conscious presumption, a nature, a relation to God, a freedom from sin, that other men according to the measure of their godliness would shun as blasphemy. If the personal claim was true, and not the blind pretence of vanity, the Jesus of the gospels is the exception to the uniform fact of human nature, but he is no longer unaccountable; and if his claim was true, his knowledge of the absolute religion, and his choice of the irresistible propaganda, are no less extraordinary, but they are not unaccountable. Paul, whose life was transformed and his thinking revolutionized by his meeting with the risen Jesus, thought on these things and believed that " the name which, is above every name " was his by right of nature as well as by the reward of obedience (Phil. ii. 5-11). John, who leaned on Jesus' breast during his earthly life, and who meditated on the meaning of that life through a ministry of many decades, came to believe that he whom he had seen with his eyes, heard with his ears, handled with his hands, was, indeed, " the Word made flesh "

(John i. 14), through whom the very God revealed his love to men. Through all the perplexities of doubt, amidst all the obscurings of irrelevant speculations, the hearts of men to-day turn to this Jesus of Nazareth as their supreme revelation of God, and find in him "the Master of their thinking and the Lord of their lives."

"Lord, to whom shall we go? Thou hast the words of eternal life. And we have believed and know that thou art the Holy One of God."

1. A CONCISE account of the voluminous literature on this subject maybe found at the close of the article JESUS CHRIST by Zockler in Schajf-Herzog, Encyclopedia of Religious Knowledge. Of the earlier of the modern works it is well to mention David Friedrich Strauss, Das Leben Jesu (2 vols. 1835), in which he sought to reduce all the gospel miracles to myths. August Neander, Das Leben Jesu Christi, 1837, wrote in opposition to the attitude taken by Strauss. Both of these works have been translated into English. Ernst Kenan, Vie de Jesus (1863, 16th ed. 1879), translated, The Life of Jesus (1863), is a charming, though often superficial and patronizing, presentation of the subject. For vivid word pictures of scenes in the life of Jesus his book is unsurpassed. Re-nan's inability to appreciate the more serious aspects of the work of Christ appears constantly, while his effort to discover romance in the life of Jesus is offensive. More important than any of these is Theodor Keim, Geschichte Jesu von Nazara (1867-72, 3 vols.), translated, The History of Jesus of Nazara (1876-81, 6 vols.). The author rejects the fourth gospel and holds that Matthew is the most primitive of the synoptic gospels; he does not reject the supernatural as such, but reduces it as much as possible by recognizing a legendary element in the gospels. When the work is read with these peculiarities in mind, it is one of the most stimulating and spiritually illuminating treatments of the subject 2. Critically more trustworthy, and exegetically very valuable, is Bernhard Weiss, Das Leben Jesu (3d ed. 1889, 2 vols.), translated from the first ed., The Life of Christ (1883, 3 vols.). It is more helpful for correct understanding of details than for a complete view of the Life of Jesus. Rivalling Weiss in many ways, yet neither so exact nor so trustworthy, though more interesting, is Willibald Beyschlag, Das Leben Jesu (3d ed. 1893, 2 vols.). The most important discussion in English is Alfred Edersheiin, The Life and Times of Jesus the Messiah (1883 and later editions, 2 vols.). This is valuable for its illustration of conditions in Palestine in the time of Jesus by quotations from the rabbinic literature. The material used is enormous, but is not always treated with due criticism, and the book should be read with the fact in mind that most of the rabbinic writings date from several centuries after Christ. Schiirer (see below) should be used wherever possible as a counter-balance. Dr. Edersheim follows the gospel story in detail; his book is, therefore, a commentary as well as a biography.

3. Albert Reville, Jesus de Nazareth (1897, 2 vols.), aims to bring the work of Kenan up to date, and to supply some of the lacks which are felt in the earlier treatise. The book is pretentious and learned. In some parts, as in the treatment of the youth of Jesus, and of the sermon on the mount, it is helpfully suggestive. The Jesus whom the author admires, however, is the Jesus of Galilee. The journey to Jerusalem was a sad mistake, and the assumption of the Messianic role a fall from the high ideal maintained in the teaching in Galilee. In criticism M. Reville accepts the two document synoptic

theory, and assigns the fourth gospel to about 140 A. D. He rejects the supernatural, explaining many of the miracles as legendary embellishments of actual events.

4. The most important treatment of the subject is the article JESUS CHRIST by William Sanday in the Hastings Bible Dictionary (1899). It is of the highest value, discussing the subject topically with great clearness and with a rare combination of learning and common sense. S. T. Andrews, The Life of Our Lord (2d ed. 1892), is a thorough and very useful study of the gospels, considering minutely all questions of chronology, harmony, and geography. It presents the different views with fairness, and offers conservative conclusions. G. H. Gilbert, The Student's Life of Jesus (1896), is complete in plan and careful in treatment, while being very concise. Dr. Gilbert faces the problems of the subject frankly, and his treatment is scholarly and reverent. James Stalker, The Life of Jesus Christ (1880), is a short work whose value lies in the good conception which it gives of the ministry of Jesus viewed as a whole. In simplicity, insight, and clearness the book is a classic, though now somewhat out of date. Studies in the Life of Christ, by A. M. Fairbairn (1882), is of great value for the topics considered. The title indicates that the treatment is fragmentary. The long treatises of Farrar (1875, 2 vols.) and Geikie (1877, 2 vols.) are useful as commentaries on the words and works of Jesus. Farrar often interprets most helpfully the essence of an incident, and Geikie furnishes a mass of illustrative material from rabbinic sources, though with less criticism than even Edersheim has used. Neither of these works, however, deals with the fundamental problems of the composition of the gospels, nor are they satisfactory on other perplexing questions, for example, the miraculous birth.

5. The most important accessory for the study of the life of Jesus is Emil Schürer, Geschichte des Judischen Volkes im Zeitalter Jesu Christi (2d ed. 1886, 1890, 2 vols. A 3d ed. of 2d part in 2 vols., 1898), translated, A History of the Jewish People in the Time of Jesus Christ (1885-6, 5 vols.). The political history of the Jews from 175 B. C. to 135 A. D., and the intellectual and religious life of the times in which Jesus lived, with the Jewish literature of Palestine and the dispersion, are all treated with thoroughness and masterful learning. W. Baldensperger, Das Selbstbewusstsein Jesu im Lichte der messianischen

Hoffnungen seiner Zeit (2d ed. 1892), furnishes in the first part a survey of the Messianic hopes of the Jews which is in many respects the most satisfactory account that is accessible. The second part discusses the problem of Jesus' conception of himself in a reverent and learned way. George Adam Smith, The Historical Geography of the Holy Land (1894), is indispensable for the study of the physical features of the land as they bear on its history, and on the work of Jesus. The maps are the best that have yet appeared.

6. Discussions of the Teaching of Jesus in works on Biblical Theology have much that is important for the study of Jesus' life. The most significant is H. H. Wendt, Die Lehre Jesu (1886, 2vols.). The second volume has been translated The Teaching of Jesus (1892, 2 vols.); the first volume of the original work is an elaborate discussion of the sources, and has not been done into English. Reference may be made especially to H. J. Holtz-mann, Lehrbuch der Neutestamentlichen Theologie (1897, 2 vols.), and also to G. H. Gilbert, The Revelation of Jesus (1899). Gustaf Dalinan, Die Worte

Jesu (1898), of which the first volume only has appeared, is a study of the meaning of the most significant expressions used in the gospel records of the teaching of Jesus, made with the aid of thorough knowledge of Aramaic usage and of the language of post-canonical Jewish literature.

7. A good synopsis or Harmony of the gospels is most useful. The best Harmony is that of Stevens and Burton (1894), which exhibits the divergencies of the parallel accounts in the gospels as faithfully as the agreements. A good synopsis of the Greek text of the first three gospels is Huck, 77102956(1892). Robinson's Greek Harmony of the Gospels, edited by M. B. Riddle, using Tischen-dorf s text, has also valuable notes discussing questions of harmony.

ABBREVIATIONS

AndlOL. Andrews, The Life of Our Lord, 2ded., 1892.

BaldsJ. Baldensperger, Das Selbstbewusstsein Jesu, 2ded., 1892.

BeyslJ. Beyschlag, Das Leben Jesu, 3d ed., 2 vols., 1893.

BovonnTTh. Bovon, Th ologie du Nouveau Testament, 1892.

DalmanwJ. Dalman, Die Worte Jesu, I, 1898.

EderslJM. Edersheim, The Life and Times of Jesus the Messiah, 2 vols., 1883.

FairbsLX. Fairbairn, Studies in the Life of Christ, 1882.

GilbertlJ. Gilbert, The Student's Life of Jesus, 1896.

GilbertrJ. Gilbert, The Revelation of Jesus, 1899.

Holtzntth. Holtzmann, Neutestamentliche Theologie, 2 vols., 1897.

KeimjN. Keim, The History of Jesus of Nazara, 6 vols., 1876-81.

RevillejN. Rdville, Je"sus de Nazareth, 2 vols., 1897.

SandayhastbD. Sanday, the article JESUS CHRIST in the Hastings Bible Dictionary, 1899.

SchlirerjPTX. Schiirer, The History of the Jewish People in the Time of Jesus Christ, 1885-86. Division I. vols. i. and ii.; Division II. vols. i., ii., and iii.

SmithhGHL. Smith, Historical Geography of the Holy Land, 1894.

SB Stevens and Burton, Harmony of the Gospels, 1894.

WeisslX. Weiss, The Life of Christ, 3 vols., 1883.

WendtlJ. Wendt, Die Lehre Jesu, 2 vols., 1886.

WendttJ. Wendt, The Teaching of Jesus, 2 vols., 1892.

Enbib. Encyclopedia Biblica, 1899.

HastbD. Hastings' Dictionary of the Bible, 1898.

SBD 2. Smith's Dictionary of the Bible, revision of the first volume of the original English edition, 1893.

8. Read Sanday HastbD II. 604-609. On the Land, its physical characteristics, its political divisions, its climate, its roads, and its varying civilization, SmithhGHL is unsurpassed. Its identifications of disputed localities are cautious. Robinson, Biblical Researches in Palestine, and Thomson, The Land and the Book, give fuller detail concerning particular localities, but no such general view as Smith.

9. On Political conditions, SchiirerjPTX I. i. and ii. is the fullest and most trustworthy treatise. More concise essays are Oscar Holtzmann, Nt. Zeitgeschichte (1895), 57-118; S. Mathews, History of NT Times in Palestine (1899), 1-158; Riggs, Maccabean and Roman Periods of Jewish History (1900), especially Â Â 206-234,

257-267, 276-282. On the Religious Life and Parties in Palestine, SchiirerjPTX II. i. and ii.; 0. Holtzmann, Ntzcitg, 136-177; Mathews, NT Times, see index; Riggs, Mac. and Rom. Periods, Â Â 235-256; Muirhead, The Times of Christ (1898), 69-150. In addition Wellhausen, Die Pharisder und die Sadducaer (1874); on the Essenes, Conybeare in HastbD I. 767-772, also Lightfoot, Colos-sians, 80-98, 347-419; Wellhausen, Isr. u. jiid. Ge-schichte 8 (1897), 258-262; on the Samaritans, A. Cowley, in Expos. V. i. 161-174; Jew. Quar. Rev. VIII. (1896) 662-575.

10. On the Messianic hope, SchtlrerjPTX IT. ii. 126-187; BaldsJ 3-122; Muirhead, Times of Xt., 112-150; Briggs, Messiah of the Gospels (1894), 1-40; WendttJ I. 33-84; Mathews, NT Times, 159-169; Biggs, Mac. and Rom. Periods, Â Â 251-256.

11. On the language of Palestine see Arnold Meyer, Jesu Muttersprache (1896); DalmanwJ I. 1-57; Schtirer JPTX II. i. 8-10, 47-51; Neubauer, Studia Biblica, I. 39-74.

12. On Jewish literature dating near the times of Jesus see Schtirer JPTX II. iii.; BaldsJ. 3-122; EderslJM I. 31-39; Deane, Pseudepigrapha (1891); Thomson, Books which influenced our Lord, etc. (1891); and special editions, such as Alexandre, Sibylline Oracles (1869); Deane, The Wisdom of Solomon (1881); Charles, The Book of Enoch (1893), The Apocalypse of Baruch (1896), The Assumption of Moses (1897), and The Book of Jubilees (1895); Charles and Morfill, The Secrets of Enoch (1896); Ryle and James, The Psalms of the Pharisees Psalms of Solomon (1891); Bensly and James, Fourth Esdras (1895); Charles, Enbib I. 213-250; HastbD I. 109 f.; Porter, HastbD I. 110-123; James, Enbib I. 249-261.

THE SOURCES 13. On the sources outside the gospels see Anthony, Introduction to the Life of Jesus, 19-108; KeimjN 1.12-59; BeyslJ I. 59-72; GilbertlJ 74-78; Knowling, Witness of the Epistles; Stevens, Pauline Tieol. 204-208; Sabatier, Apostle Paul, 76-85. On Josephus as a source see also SchurerjPTX I. ii. 143-149; Keville JN I. 272-280. On the individual gospels see Burton, The Purpose and Plan of the Four Gospels (Univ. Chic. Press, 1900); Bruce, With Open Face, 1-61; Weiss, Introduction to N. T., II. 239-386; Julicher, Einleitung i. d. NT, 189-207. On Matthew, Burton Bib. Wld. I. 1898, 37-44, 91-101 j on Mark, Swete, Comm. on Mark, ix-lxxxix; on Luke, Plummer, Comm. on Luke, xi-lxx; Mathews, Bib. Wld. 1895, 1.336-342, 448-455; on John, Burton, Bib. Wld. 1899, I. 16-41, 102-105; Westcott, Comm. on John, v-lxxvii; Rhees in Abbott's The Bible as Literature, 281-297. On the synoptic question see Saiiday SBD, 2 1217-1243, and Expositor, Feb.-June, 1891; Woods, Studio, Biblica, II. 59-104; Salmon, Introduction? 99-151, 570-581; Stanton in HastbD II. 234-243; Jillicher, Mini. 207-227. A. Wright, Composition of the Four Gospels (1890) and Some NT Problems (1898), defends the oral tradition theory in a modified form. On possible dislocations in John see Spitta, Urchris-tentum, I. 157-204; Bacon, Jour. Bib. Lit. 1894, 64-76; Burton, Bib. Wld. 1899, I. 27-35. For the history of opinion see specially H. J. Holtzmann, Einl? 340-375. On the Johannine question see Sanday, Expositor, Nov. 1891-May 1892; Schiirer, Cont. Rev. Sept. 1891; Watkins SBD 2 1739-1764; Burton, Bib. Wld. 1899,1,16-41; Reynolds in HastbD II. 694-722; Zahn, Einl. II. 445-564 (defends Johannine authorship); Julicher, Einl. 238-250 (rejects Johaunine authorship). For the history of opinion see Watkins, Bampton Lecture for 1890; Holtzmann, Einl. 433-438. P. Ewald, Hauptproblem der evang. Frage, argues the authenticity of the fourth gospel from the one-sidedness of the synoptic story. See also Jour. Bib. Lit. 1898, I. 87-102.

14. Reville proposes to reconstruct Jos. Ant. xviii. 3. 3 thus: " ' At that time appeared Jesus, a wise man, who did astonishing things. That is why a good number of Jews and also of Greeks attached themselves to him Then follows some phrase probably signifying that these adherents had committed the error of proclaiming him Christ, and then ' denounced by the leading men of the nation, this Jesus was condemned by Pilate to die on the cross. But those who had loved him before persevered in their sentiment, and still to-day there exists a class of people who take from him their name Christians.""

15. On the testimony of Papias (Euseb. Ch. Hist. iii. 39. 4) see Lightfoot, Cont. Rev. 1875, II. 379 ff., and Mcgiffert's notes in his Eusebius, 170 ff.

16. For a collection of probably genuine Agrapha see Kopes, Diespruche Jesu, 154-161, and Amer. Jour. Theol. 1897, 758-776; Eesch, Agrapha, gives a much longer list. He is criticised by Eopes. On lost and uncanonical gospels see Salmon, Intrj 173-190, 580-591; Kriiger, Early Christian Literature, 50-57. For the recently discovered Gospel of Peter see Swete, The Gospel of Peter; and on the so-called Sayings of Jesus found in Egypt in 1896 see Harnack, Expositor, V. vi. 321-340, 401-416, and essay by Sanday and Lock. Apocryphal Gospels are most conveniently found in Ante-nicene Fathers, VIII. 361-476.

THE HARMONY OF THE GOSPELS 17. The Diatessaron of Tatian is translated with notes by Hill, The Earliest Life of Christ. See also Ante-nic. Fathers, IX. 35-138.

18. For the extreme position concerning Doublets see Holtzmann, Hand-commentar zum NT I. passim. E. Haupt, Studien u. Kritiken, 1884, 25, remarks that Jesus must often have repeated his teaching in essentially the same form.

CHRONOLOGY 19. For data and discussion of the various problems see Wieseler, Chronological Synopsis; Lewin, Fasti Sacra; KeimjN II. 379-402; AndlOL 1-52; SchilrerjPTX I. ii. 30-32, 105-143; 0. Holtzmann, Ntzeitg, 118-124, 125-127, 131-132; Turner HastbD I. 403-415;

Ramsay, Was Christ born at Bethlehem; and von Soden in Enbib. I. 799-812. For patristic opinion concerning the length of Jesus' ministry, see HastbD I. 410. For the argument for a one-year ministry, see KeimjN II. 398; 0. Holtzmann, Ntzeitg, 131 f. For two years, see Wieseler, Chron. Synop. 204-220; WeisslX

I. 389-392; Turner in HastbD. For three years, see AndlOL 189-198; note by Eobertson in Broadus, Harmony of the Gospels, 241-244. Compare RevillejN

II. 227-231 j Zahn, Einl. II. 516 f.

THE EAKLY YEARS 20. On the problem of the Virgin birth see GilbertlJ 79-89; WeisslX I. 211-233; Swete, Apos. Creed, 42-55; Bruce, Apologetics, 407-413; Ropes, Andover Rev. 1893, 695-712; FairbsLX 30-45; Godet, Comm. on Luke, Rem. on chaps. I. and II.; BovonnTTh I. 198-217. These maintain historicity. The other side: BeyslJ I. 148-174; Meyer, Comm. on Matt., Rem. on 1.18; KeimjN II. 38-101; Reville, New World, 1892, 695-723, and JN I. 361-408; Holtzmannntth I. 409-415. On the early years of Jesus see EderslJM I. 217-254; WeisslX I. 275-293; Hughes, Manliness of Xt, 35-60; WendttJ I. 90-96; Stapfer, Jesus Christ before Us Ministry; FairbsLX 46-63; BeyslJ II. 44-65; Reville JK I. 409-438.

21. For some of the early legends concerning the birth and childhood of Jesus, see the so-called Protevangelium of James, the Gospel of Pseudo-Matthew, and the Gospel of Thomas, Ante-nic. Fathers, VIII. 361-383, 395-398. For Jewish calumnies see Laible, J. X. im Thalmud, 9-39.

22. On the two genealogies see AndlOL 62-68; WeisslX I. 211-221; Godet on Luke, iii. 23-38. These refer Luke's genealogy to Mary. Hervey SBD 2 1145-1148, Plummer on Luke, iii. 23, EderslJM I. 149, Gil- bertlJ 81 f., with the early fathers (see Plummer), refer both to Joseph. For the view that they are unauthentic see Holtzmann, Hand-comm. I. 39-41; Bacon in HastbD II. 137-141.

23. On the " brethren " of Jesus see Mayor, HastbD I. 320-326; AndrewslOL 111-123. These make the brethren sons of Joseph and Mary. Lightfoot, Galatiansâ 252-291, regards them as sons of Joseph by a former marriage.

JOHN THE BAPTIST 24. On the character and work of John the Baptist see KeimjN II. 201-266 and references in the index under John the Baptist. Keim's is much the most satisfactory treatment; it is, moreover, Keim at his best. See also Ewald, Hist, of Israel, VI. 160-200; WeisslX I. 307-316; FairbsLX 64-79; W. A. Stevens, Homil. Kev. 1891, II. 163 fif.; Bebb in HastbD II. 677-680; Wellhausen Isr. u. judische Geschichte, 342 f.; Feather, Last of the Prophets. Eeynolds, John the Baptist, obscures its excellencies by a vast amount of irrelevant discussion.

25. On the existence of a separate company of disciples of John see Mk. ii. 18, Mt. ix. 14, Lk. v. 33; Mk. vi. 29, Mt. xiv. 12; Mt. xi. 2 f., Lk. vii. 18 f.; Lk. xi. 1; Jn. i. 35 f.; iii. 25; Ac. xix. 1-3. Consult Lightfoot, Colossians, 400 ff.; Baldensperger, Der Prolog des vierten Evangeli-ums, 93-152.

THE MESSIANIC CALL 26. On the baptism of Jesus see WendttJ I. 96-101; EderslJM I. 278-287; BaldsJ 219-229. WeisslX I. 316-336 says that the baptism meant for Jesus, already conscious of his Messiahship, " the close of his former life and the opening of one perfectly new" (322); KeimjN II. 290-299 makes it an act of consecration, but eliminates the Voice and Dove; BeyslJ I. 215-231 thinks that Jesus, conscious of no sin, yet not aware of his Messiahship, sought the baptism carrying " the sins and guilt of his people on his heart, as if they were his own " (229). Against Beyschlag see E. Haupt in Studien u. Kritiken, 1887, 381. Baldensperger shows clearly that the Messianic call was a revelation to Jesus, not a conclusion from a course of reasoning.

27. On the temptation see WendttJ I. 101-105; WeisslX I. 337-354; EderslJM I. 299-307; Fair-bairnsLX 80-98; BaldsJ 230-236; BeyslJ I. 231-237; KeimjN II. 317-329. All these see in temptation the necessary result of the Messianic call at the baptism.

28. The locality of the baptism of Jesus cannot be determined. Tradition has fixed on one of the fords of the Jordan near Jericho, see SmithhGHL 496, note 1. On the probable location of Bethany (Bethabarah) (Jn. i. 28) see discussion in AndlOL 146-151; Enbib 548; and especially Smith's note as above.

29. On the anointing of Jesus with the Holy Spirit see WeisslX I. 323-336; BeyslJ I. 230 f. For the influence of the Spirit in the later life of Jesus see Mk. i. 12; Mt. iv. 1; Lk. iv. 1; iv. 14, 18, 21; Mk. iii. 29, 30; Mt. xii. 28; Jn. iii. 34; compare Ac. i. 2; x. 38. Clearly these refer not to the ethical and religious indwelling of the Divine

Spirit (comp. Rom. i. 4), but to the special equipment for official duty. This is the OT sense, see Ex. xxxi. 2-5; Jud. iii. 10; I. Sam. xi. 6; Isa. xi. If.; xlii. 1; Ixi. 1; and consult Schultz, Old Test. Theol. II. 202 f. Jesus seems to have needed a like divine equipment, notwithstanding his divine nature. See Gilbertl J 121 f.

30. How this Messianic anointing is to be related to the doctrine of Jesus' essential divine nature cannot be determined with certainty. It must not be forgotten, however, that it is a datum for Christology, and that it cannot be explained away. It indicates one of the particulars in which Jesus was made like unto his brethren. What was involved when the Son of God " emptied himself and was made in the likeness of men" (Phil. ii. 7) we can only vaguely conceive. Two views of early heretical sects seem rightly to have been rejected. The Docetic view, held by some Gnostics of the 2d cent., dates the incarnation from the baptism, but distinguishes Christ from the human Jesus, who only served as a vehicle for the manifestation of the Son of God; the Christ descended on Jesus at the baptism, ascending again to heaven from the cross, compare Mt. iii. 16 and xxvii. 50 in the Greek; see Schaff Hist, of Xn Church? II. 455 f. The recently discovered Gospel of Peter presents this view, Gosp. Pet. Â 5. The Nestorian view represents that the baptism was, in a sense, Jesus' " birth from above " (Jn. iii. 3, 5); thus the incarnation was first complete at the baptism though the Logos had been associated with Jesus from the beginning. See Schaff, Hist, of Xn Church, 2 III. 717ff.; Conybeare, History of Xmas, Amer. Jour. Theol. 1899, 1-21.

31. The traditional locality of the temptation is a mountain near Jericho called Quarantana, see And. LOL 155; the tradition seems to date no further back than the crusades. It is, however, probable that the " wilderness " (Mt. iv. 1, Mk. i. 12, Lk. iv. 1) is the same wilderness mentioned in connection with John's earlier life and work (Mt. iii. 1, Mk. i. 4), the region W and NW of the Dead Sea, see SmithhGHL 317. Others (Stanley, Sinai and Palestine, 308; EderslJM I. 300, 339 notes) hold that the temptation took place in the desert regions SE of the sea of Galilee; this is possibly correct, though the record in the gospels suggests the wilderness of Judea. On the source of the temptation story see WeisslX I. 339 ff.; BeyslJ I, 234; Bacon, Bib. Wld. 1900,1.18-25, 32. SandayhastbD II. 612 f.; GilbertlJ 144-157; WeisslX I. 355-387; AndlOL 155-165; Edersl JM I. 336-363; BeyslJ II. 129-148 (assigns here a considerable part of the synoptic account of work in Capernaum).

33. The early confessions. On the genuineness of the Baptist's testimony to " the Lamb of God " see M. Dods in Expos. Gk. Test. 1.695 f.; Westcott, Comm. on John, 20; EderslJM I. 342 ff.; WeisslX I. 362 f. (thinks the evangelist added " who taketh away the sin of the world "); Holtzmann, Hand-comm. IV. 38 f. holds that the evangelist has put in the mouth of the Baptist a conception which was first current after the death of Jesus. On the confessions of Nathanael and the others, see Jour. Bib. Lit. 1898, 21-30.

34. Cana is probably the modern Khirbet Kana, eight miles N of Nazareth. A rival site is Kefr Kenna, three and one-half miles NE from Nazareth. See Enbib and HastbD, also AndlOL 162-164.

35. The miracles of Jesus are challenged by modern thought. It is customary in reading other documents than the N. T. instantly to relegate the miraculous to the domain of legend. Miracles, however, are integral parts of the story of Jesus' life,

and those who attempt to write that life eliminating the supernatural are constrained to recognize that he had marvellous power as an exorcist and healer of some forms of nervous disease. So E. A. Abbott, The Spirit on the Waters, 169-201. Our knowledge of nature does not warrant a dogmatic definition of the limits of the possible; see James, The Will to Believe, vii.-xiii., 299-327. The question is confessedly one of adequate evidence. The evidence for the supreme miracle â the transcendent character of Jesus â is clear, see Part III. chap. iv. j and the miracu- lous element in the story of his life must be considered in view of this supreme miracle. In association with him his miracles gain in credibility. In estimating the evidence for them their dignity and worthiness is important. What the devout imagination would do in embellishing the story of Jesus is exhibited in the apocryphal gospels; the miracles of the canonical gospels are of an entirely different type, which commends them as authentic. By definition a miracle is an event not explicable in terms of ordinary human experience. It is therefore futile to attempt to picture the miracles of Jesus in their occurrence, for the imagination has no material except that furnished by ordinary experience. For our day the miracles are of importance chiefly for the exhibition they give of the character of Jesus; they can be studied with this in view without regard to the curious question how they happened. Eead SandayhastbD II. 624-628; and see Fisher, Grounds of Christian and Theistic Belief, chaps, iv.â vi., Supernatural Origin of Christianity chap, xi.; Bruce, Miraculous Element in the Gospels; Apologetics, 409 ff.; Illingworth, Divine Immanence; Rainy, Orr, and Dods, The Supernatural in Christianity.

PART II. â THE MINISTRY I

GENERAL SURVEY 36. SandayhastbD II. 6091; GilbertlJ 136-143; AndlOL 125-137; BeyslJ I. 256-295.

THE EARLY MINISTRY IN JUDEA 37. SandayhastbD II. 612 b-613 b; WeisslX II. 3-53; EderslJM I. 364-429; BeyslJ II. 147-168; GilbertlJ 158-179.

38. On the chronological significance of John iv. 35 see AndlOL 183; WeisslX II. 40; Wieseler, Synop. 212 ff., who find indication that the journey was in December. EderslJM I. 419 f.; Turner in HastbD I. 408, find indication of early summer. Some treat iv. 35 as a proverb with no chronological significance; so Alford, Comm. on John.

39. Geographical notes. Aenon near Salim has not been identified. Most favor a site in Samaria, seven miles from a place named Salim, which lay four miles E of Shechem, see Conder, Tent Work in Palestine, 11.57, 58; Stevens, Jour. Bib. Lit. 1883,128-141. But can John have been baptizing in Samaria? WeisslX II. 28 says "it is perfectly impossible that he John can have taken up his station in Samaria." Other suggestions are: some place in the Jordan valley (but then why remark on the abundance of water, Jn. iii. 23?); near Jerusalem; and in the south of Judea. See AndlOL 173-175. Sychar is the modern 'Askar, about a mile and three-quarters from Nablus (Shechem), and half a mile N of Jacob's well. See SmithhGHL 367-375.

40. General questions. Was the temple twice cleansed? (see sect. 116). Probably not. The two reports (Jn. ii. 13-22; Mk. xi. 15-18 s) are similar in respect of Jesus 7 indignation, its cause, its expression, its result, and a consequent challenge of his authority. They differ in the time of the event (John assigns to first Passover, synoptics to the last) and in a possibly greater sternness in the synoptic account. These

differences are no greater than appear in other records of identical events (compare Mt. viii. 5-13 with Lk. vii. 2-10), while the repetition of such an act would probably have been met by serious opposition. If the temple was cleansed but once, John indicates the true time. At the beginning of the ministry it was a demand that the people follow the new leader in the purification of God's house and the establishment of a truer worship. At the end it could have had only a vindictive significance, since the people had already signified to the clear insight of Jesus that they would not accept his leadership. For two distinct cleansings see the discussion in AndlOL 169 f., 437; EderslJM I. 373; Pluramer on Luke xix. 45 f. For one cleansing at the end see KeimjN V. 113-131. For one cleansing at the beginning see WeisslX II. 6 ff.; BeyslJ II. 149 ff.; GilbertlJ159ff.

41. The journey to Galilee. Do John (iv. 1-4, 43-45) and Mark (i. 14 = Mt. iv. 12; Lk. iv. 14) report the same journey? Both are journeys from the south introducing work in Galilee; yet the reasons given for the journey are different (compare Jn. iv. 1-3 with Mk. i. 14). If the Pharisees had a hand in John's "delivering up" (Mk. i. 14; comp. Jos. Ant. xviii. 5. 2), the same hostile movement may have impelled Jesus to leave Judea. He may not have heard of John's imprisonment until after his departure, or some time before he opened his new ministry in Galilee. See GilbertlJ 173 f. AndlOL 176-182 argues against the identification.

42. The nobleman's son (Jn. iv. 46-54). Is this a doublet of Mt. viii. 5-13; Lk. vii. 2-10? John differs from synoptics in the time, the place, the disease, the suppliant, his plea, and Jesus' attitude. Matthew and Mark differ from each other concerning the bearers of the centurion's messages to Jesus. John's account is similar to synoptic superficially, but is probably not a doublet. Compare Syro-Phcsnician's daughter (Mk. vii. 29 f.). See GilbertlJ 202; Meyer on John iv. 51-54; Plummer on Luke vii. 10. WeisslX II. 45-51 identifies. Read SandayhastbD II. 613.

THE MINISTRY IN GALILEE 43. Read SandayhastbD II. 613-630; GilbertlJ 180-283. Consult WeisslX II. 44 to III. 153; EderslJM I. 472 to II. 125; BeyslJ II. 140-147,168-294. See AndlOL 209-363 for discussion of details, and KeimjN III. 10 to IV. 346 for an illuminating, though not unprejudiced, topical treatment.

44. Geographical notes. Capernaum. The site is not clearly identified, two ruins on the NW of Sea of Galilee are rival claimants, â Tell Hum and Khan Minyeh. Tell Hum is advocated by Thomson, Land and Book, Central Pal. and Phoenicia (1882), 416-420; Khan Minyeh, by SmithhGHL 456, Enbib I. 696 ff. Latter is probably correct. See AndlOL 224-237.

Bethsaida. The full name is Bethsaida Julias, located at entrance of Jordan into the Sea of Galilee. Smithenbib I. 565 f., HGHL 457 f., shows that there is no need of the hypothesis of a second Bethsaida to meet the statement in Mk. vi. 45, or that in Jn. i. 44. See also AndlOL 230-236. Ewing HastbD 1.282 f. renews the argument for two Bethsaidas.

Chorazin was probably the modern Kerazeh, about one mile N of Tell Hum, and back from the lake. See Smithenbib I. 751; HGHL 456; AndlOL 237 f.

45. The mountain of the sermon on the mount (Mt. v. 1; Lk. vi. 12) probably refers to the Galilean highlands as distinct from the shore of the lake. More definite location is not possible. See AndlOL 268f.; EderslJM I. 524. The traditional site, the

Horns of Hattin, is a hill lying about seven miles SW from Khan Minyeh, which has near the top a level place (Lk. vi. 17) flanked by two low peaks or "horns."

46. The country of the Gerasenes, Gadarenes, or Ger-gesenes. Gadarenes is the best attested reading in Mt. viii. 28, Gerasenes in Mk. v. 1 and Lk. viii. 26; Ger-gesenes has only secondary attestation. Gadara is identified with Um Keis on the Yarmuk, some six miles SE of the Sea of Galilee. This cannot have been the site of the miracle, though it is possible that Gadara may have controlled the country round about, including the shores of the sea. Gerasa is the name of a city in the highlands of Gilead, twenty miles E of Jordan, and thirty-five SE of the Sea of Galilee, and it clearly cannot have been the scene of the miracle. Near the E shore of the sea Thomson discovered the ruins of a village which now bears the name Khersa. The formation of the land in the neighborhood closely suits the narrative of the gospels. This is now accepted as the true identification. See Thomson Land and Book, Central Palestine, 353-355; SBD 2 1097-1100; HastbD II. 159 f.; AndlOL 296-300. The name " Gadarenes " may indicate that Gadara had jurisdiction over the region of Khersa; the names " Gerasenes " and " Gergesenes " may be derived directly and independently from Khersa, or may be corruptions due to the obscurity of Khersa.

47. The feeding of the five thousand took place on the E of the sea, in a desert region, abundant in grass, and mountainous, and located in the neighborhood of a place named Bethsaida. Near the ruins of Bethsaida Julias is a plain called now Butaiha, " a smooth, grassy place near the sea and the mountains," which meets the requirements of the narrative. See AndlOL 322 f.

48. The return of Jesus from the regions of Tyre " through Sidon " (Mk. vii. 31) avoided Galilee, crossing N of Galilee to the territory of Philip and "the Decap-olis." This latter name applies to a group of free Greek cities, situated for the most part E of the Jordan. Most of the cities of the group were farther S than the Sea of Galilee; some, however, were E and NE of that sea, hence Jesus' approach from Csesarea Philippi or Damascus could be described as " through Decapolis." See SmithhGHL 593-608; Enbib I. 1051 if.; Sc. hurerjPTX II. i. 94-121.

49. Of Magadan (Mt. xv. 39) or Dalmanutha (Mk. viii. 10) all that is known is that they must have been on the W coast of the Sea of Galilee. They have never been identified, though there are many conjectures. See SBD, 2 HastbD, and Enbib.

50. Ccesarea Philippi was situated at the easternmost and most important of the sources of the Jordan, it is called Panias by Jos. Ant. xv. 10. 3, now Banias. Probably a sanctuary of the god Pan. Here Herod the Great built a temple which he dedicated to Caesar; Philip the Tetrarch enlarged the town and called it Csesarea Philippi. See SBD; 2 HastbD; Enbib.

51. The mountain of the transfiguration. The traditional site, since the fourth century, is Tabor in Galilee. Most recent opinion has favored one of the shoulders of Hermon, owing to the supposed connection of the event with the sojourn near Caesarea Philippi. WeisslX III. 98 points out that there is no evidence that Jesus lingered for "six days" (Mk. ix. 2) near that town, and that therefore the effort to locate the transfiguration is futile. GilbertlJ 274 thinks that Mk. ix. 30 is decisive in favor of a place outside Galilee; he therefore holds to the common view that Hermon is the true locality. See AndlOL 357 f.

52. General questions. Was Jesus twice rejected at Nazareth? (comp. Lk. iv. 16-30 with Mk. vi. 1-6 a; Mt. xiii. 54-58). Here are two accounts tliat read like independent traditions of the same event; they agree concerning the place, the teaching in the synagogue on the Sabbath, the astonishment of the Nazarenes, their scornful question, and Jesus' rejoinder. Luke makes no reference to the disciples (Mk. vi. 1) nor to the working of miracles (Mk. vi. 5) j Matthew and Mark, on the other hand, say nothing of an attempt at violence. These differences are no more serious, however, than appear in the two accounts of the appeal of the centurion to Jesus (Mt. viii. 5-8; Lk. vii. 3-7). Moreover, Lk. iv. 23 indicates a time after the ministry in Capernaum had won renown, which agrees with the place given the rejection in Mark. The general statement (Lk. iv. 14 f.) suggests that the visit to Nazareth is given at the beginning as an instance of "preaching in their synagogues." The three accounts probably refer to one event reported independently. For identification see WeisslX III. 34 j Plummer on Luke iv. 30; GilbertlJ 254 f. For two rejections see Godet's supplementary note on Lk. iv. 16-30; Meyer on Mt. xiii. 53-58; EderslJM L 457, note 1; Wieseler, Synopsis, 278. BeyslJ I. 270 identifies but prefers Luke's date.

53. Were there two miraculous draughts of fish? Lk. v. 1-11 is sometimes identified with Jn. xxi. 3-13. So WendtlJ I. 211 f., WeisslX II. 57 f., and Meyer on Luke v. 1-11. Against the identification see Alford, Godet, and Plummer on the passage in Luke. The two are alike in scene, the night of bootless toil, the great catch at Jesus' word. They differ in personnel, antecedent relations of the fishermen with Jesus, the effect of the miracle on Peter, and the subsequent teaching of Jesus, as well as in time. These differences make identification difficult.

54. Where in the synoptic story should the journey to the feast in Jerusalem (Jn. v.) be placed? There is nothing in John's narrative to identify the feast, although it is his custom to name the festivals to which he refers (Passover, ii. 13, 23; vi. 4 j xi. 55; xii. 1; Tabernacles, vii. 2; Dedication, x. 22). Even if John wrote " the feast' rather than "a feast" (the MSS. vary, A B D and seven other uncials omit the article), it would be impossible to decide between Passover and Tabernacles. The omission of the article suggests either that the feast was of minor importance, or that its identification was of no significance for the understanding of the following discourse. Since a year and four months probably elapsed between the journey into Galilee (Jn. iv. 35) and the next Passover mentioned in John (vi. 4), v. 1 may refer to any one of the feasts of the Jewish year. The commonest interpretation prefers Purim, a festival of a secular and somewhat hilarious type, which occurred on the 14th and 15th of Adar, a month before the Passover. It is difficult to believe that this feast would have called Jesus to Jerusalem. See WeisslX II. 391; GilbertlJ 137-139, 142, 234-235. Against this interpretation see EderslJM II. 765. Edersheim advocates the feast of

Wood Gathering on the 15th of Ab â about our August. On this day all the people were permitted to offer wood for the use of the altar in the temple, while during the rest of the year the privilege was reserved for special families. See LJM II 765 f.; Westcott, Comm. on John, add. note on v. 1, argues for the feast of Trumpets, or the new moon of the month Tisri, â about our September, â which was celebrated as the beginning of the civil year. Others have suggested Pentecost, fifty days after the Passover; the day of Atonement â but this was a fast, not a feast; and Tabernacles.

The majority of those who do not favor Purim prefer the Passover, notwithstanding the difficulty of thinking that John would refer to this feast simply as "a feast of the Jews." Read AndIOL 193-198, remembering that the question must be considered independently of the question of the length of Jesus' ministry. The impossibility of determining the feast renders the adjustment of this visit to the synoptic story very uncertain. It may be that there was some connection between the Sabbath controversy in Galilee (Mk. ii. 23-28) and the criticism Jesus aroused in Jerusalem (Jn. v.). If so, one of the spring feasts, Passover or Pentecost, would best suit the circumstances; but this arrangement is quite uncertain.

55. Do the five conflicts of Mk. ii. 1 to Hi. 6 belong at the early place in the ministry of Jesus to which that gospel assigns them? It is commonly held that they do not, and the argument for a two-year ministry rests on this assumption (see SandayhastbD II. 613). Holtz-mann, Hand-commentar I. 9 f., remarks that at least for the cure of the paralytic and for the call and feast of Levi (Mk. ii. 1, 13, 15) the evangelist was confident that he was following the actual order of events; note the call of the fifth disciple, Mk. ii. 13, between the call of the four, Mk. i. 16-20, and that of the twelve, iii. 16-19. The question about fasting may owe its place (Mk. ii. 18-22) to association with the criticism of Jesus for eating with publicans (Mk. ii. 16). In like manner the second Sabbath conflict (Mk. iii. 1-6) may be attached to the first (ii. 23-28) as a result of the identity of subject, for it is noteworthy that Mark records only these two Sabbath conflicts; moreover, the plot of Herodians and Pharisees to kill Jesus strongly suggests a later time for the actual occurrence of this criticism. The first Sabbath question, however, may belong early, as Mark has placed it. Weiss, Markusevangelium, 76, LX II. 232 ff., places these conflicts late. Edersheim, LJM II. 51 ff., discusses the Sabbath controversies after the feeding of the multitudes. EevillejN II. 229 places the first of them early.

56. The sermon on the mount. Luke (vi. 12-19 = Mk. iii. 13-19 a) indicates the place in the Galilean ministry; Matthew has therefore anticipated in assigning it to the beginning. The identity of the two sermons (Mt. v. 1 to-vii. 27; Lk. vi. 20-49) is shown by the fact that each begins with beatitudes, each closes with the parables of the wise and foolish builders, each is followed by the cure of a centurion's servant in Capernaum (Mt. viii. 5-13; Lk. vii. 1-10), and the teachings which are found in each account are given in the same order. Matthew is much fuller than Luke, many teachings given in the sermon in Matthew being found in later contexts in Luke. Much of the sermon in Matthew, however, evidently belonged to the original discourse, and was omitted by Luke, perhaps because of less interest to Gentile than to Jewish Christians. The following sections are found elsewhere in Luke, and were probably associated with the sermon by the first evangelist: Mt. v. 25, 26; Lk. xii. 58, 59; Mt. vi. 9-13; Lk. xi. 2-4; Mt. vi. 19-34; Lk. xii. 21-34; xi. 34-36; xvi. 13; Mt. vii. 7-11; Lk. xi. 9-13; Mt. vii. 13, 14; Lk. xiii. 24. The first evangelist's habit of grouping may explain also the presence in his sermon of teachings which he himself has duplicated later, thus: Mt. v. 29, 30 = xviii. 8, 9; v. 32 = xix. 9, com p. Mk. x. 11, ix. 43-47, Lk. xvi. 18; Mt. vi. 14,15 = Mk. xi. 25. Matthew vii. 22, 23 has the character of the teachings which follow the confession at Caesarea Philippi, and is quite unlike the other early teachings. It may belong to the later time,

for it was natural for the early Christians to associate together teachings which the Lord uttered on widely separated occasions. The sermon as originally given may be analyzed as follows: The privileges of the heirs of the kingdom of God, Mt. v. 3-12; Lk. vi. 20-26; their responsibilities, Mt. v. 13-16; the relation of the new to the old, Mt. v. 17-19; the text of the discourse, Mt. v. 20; the new conception of morality, Mt. v. 21-48; Lk. vi. 27-36; the new practice of religion, Mt. vi. 1-8, 16-18; warning against a censorious spirit, Mt. vii. 1-6; Lk. vi. 37-42; the tree judged by its fruits, Mt. vii. 16-20; Lk. vi. 43-46; the wise and foolish builders, Mt. vii. 24-27 j Lk. vi. 47-49.

57. The discourse in parables. Matthew gives seven parables at this point (xiii.), Mark (iv. 1-34) has three, one of them not given in Matthew, Luke (viii. 4-18) gives in this connection but one, â the Sower. Many think that the Tares of Matthew (xiii. 24-30, 36-43) is a doublet of Mark's Seed growing secretly (iv. 26-29); so Weiss LX II. 209 note, against which view see WendtlJ I. 178 f., and Bruce, Parabolic Teaching ofxt, 119. Matthew has probably made here a group of parables, as in chapters v. to vii. he has made a group of other teachings. The interpretation of the Tares, and of the Draw-net (xiii. 40-43, 49, 50), may indicate that these parables were spoken after Jesus began to teach plainly concerning the end of the world (Mk. viii. 31 to ix. 1), Luke gives the Mustard Seed and Leaven in another connection (xiii. 18-21), and it may be that Matthew has taken them out of their true context to associate them with the other parables of his group; yet in popular teaching it must be recognized that illustrations are most likely to be repeated in different situations. On the parables see Goebel, The Parables of Jesus (1890), Bruce, The Parabolic Teaching of Christ, 3d ed. (1886), Julicher,

Die Gleichnissreden Jesu (2 vols. 1899), and the commentaries on the gospels.

58. The instructions to the twelve. Mt. ix. 36 to xi. 1. x. 1, 5-14 corresponds in general with Mk. vi. 7-11; Lk. ix. 1-5. The similarity is closer, however, between x. 7-15 and Lk. x. 3-12 â the instructions to the seventy (see sect. A 68). The rest of Mt. x. (16-42) is paralleled by teachings found in the closing discourses in the synoptic gospels, and in teachings preserved in the section peculiar to Luke (ix. 51 to xviii. 14. See SB sects. 88-92, footnotes). It is probable that here the first evangelist has made a group of instructions to disciples gathered from all parts of the Lord's teachings; such a collection was of great practical value in the early time of persecution.

59. Did Jesus twice feed the multitudes? All the gospels record the feeding of the five thousand (Mt. xiv. 13-23; Mk. vi. 30-46; Lk. ix. 10-17; Jn. vi. 1-15), Matthew (xv. 32-38) and Mark (viii. 1-9) give also the feeding of the four thousand. The similarities are so great that the two accounts would be regarded as doublets if they occurred in different gospels. The difficulty with such an identification is chiefly the reference which in both Matthew (xvi. 9, 10) and Mark (viii. 19, 20) Jesus is said to have made to the two feedings. The evangelists clearly distinguished the two. In view of this fact the differences between the accounts become important. These concern the occasion of the two miracles, the number fed, the nationality of the multitudes (compare Jn. vi. 31 and Mk. vii. 31), the number of loaves and of baskets of broken pieces (the name for basket is different in the two cases, and is preserved consistently in Mk. viii. 19, 20; Mt. xvi. 9, 10). See GilbertlJ 259-262, Gould, and Swete, on

Mk. viii. 1-9; Meyer, Alford, on Mt. xv. 32-38. WeisslX II. 376 f., BeyslJ I. 279 f., WendtlJ I. 42, Holtzmann Hand-comm. 1.186 ff., identify the accounts. See also SandayhastbD II. 629.

60. Did Peter twice confess faith in Jesus as Messiah? Synoptics give his confession at Caesarea Philippi (Mk. viii. 27-30; Mt xvi. 13-20; Lk. ix. 18-21). John, however, gives a confession earlier at Capernaum (vi. 66-71). WeisslX III. 53 identifies the two, placing that in John at Ceesarea Philippi, since there is no evidence that all of the long discourse of Jn. vi. was spoken in Capernaum the day after the feeding of the five thousand. This may be correct, yet the marked recognition which Jesus gave to the confession at Caesarea Philippi does not demand that he first at that time received a confession of his disciples' faith. The confession in Jn. vi. 68, 69 declared that the twelve were not shaken in their faith by the recent defection of many disciples. At Csesarea Philippi the confession was made after the revulsion of popular feeling had been made fully evident, and after the twelve had had time for reaction of enthusiasm consequent upon the growing coldness of the multitudes and active opposition of the leaders. The confession of Caesarea Philippi holds its unique significance, whether or not Jn. vi. 68 is identified with it.

61. The journey to Tabernacles (Jn. vii.). Where in the synoptic story should it be placed? Lk. ix. 51 ffÂ records the final departure from Galilee. The journey of Jn. vii. is the last journey from Galilee given in John. Yet the two are very different. In John, Jesus went in haste, unpremeditatedly, in secret, and unaccompanied, and confronted the people with himself unexpectedly during the feast. In Luke (Mk. x. 1 and Mt. xix. 1 are so general that they give no aid) he advanced deliberately, with careful plans, announcing his coining in advance, accompanied by many disciples, with whom he went from place to place, arriving in Jerusalem long after he had set out. The two journeys cannot be identified. John seems to keep Jesus in the south after the Tabernacles, but his account does not forbid a return to Galilee between Tabernacles and Dedication (x. 22). After the hurried visit to Tabernacles, Jesus probably went back to Galilee, and gathered his disciples again for the final journey towards his cross â for the visit to Jerusalem had given fresh evidence of the kind of treatment he must expect in the capital (Jn. vii. 32, 45-52; viii. 59). See AndlOL 369-379. Andrews suggests that the feast occurred before the withdrawal to Caesarea Philippi (376); this is possible, but it seems more natural to place it during the sojourn in Capernaum after the return from the north (Mk. ix. 33-50). See SB, sects. 82-85.

62. On the phenomena and interpretation of Demoniac Possession see J. L. Nevius, Demon Possession and allied Themes; Conybeare, Jew. Quar. Eev. VIII. (1896) 576-608, IX. (1896-7) 59-114, 444-470, 581-603; J. Weiss in Realencyklopadie, Hauck-Herzog, IV. 408-419; Binet, Alterations of Personality, 325-356; James, Psychology, I. 373-400; and the articles on DEMONS in Enbib and HastbD.

THE JOURNEY THROUGH PEREA TO JERUSALEM 63. Kead SandayhastbD II. 630-632; see GilbertlJ 298-310; WeisslX III. 157-223; KeimjN V. 1-64; BeyslJ I. 287-294. II. 333-419; AndlOL 365-420; EderslJM II. 126-360.

64. This journey began sometime between Tabernacles and Dedication (October and December) of the last year of Jesus' life, and continued until the arrival in Bethany six days before the last Passover.

65. Geographical notes. Perea â a part of the domain of Antipas â was the Jewish territory E of the Jordan. Its northern limit seems to have been marked by Pella (Jos. Wars, iii. 3. 3) or Gadara (Wars, iv. 7. 3), and its E boundary was marked by Philadelphia (Ant. xx. 1. 1); it extended S to the domain of Aretas, king of Arabia. The population was mixed, though predoini- natiugly Jewish. Cities of the Decapolis, however, lay within the limits of Perea, and introduced Greek life and ideas to the people. On the highlands back from the Jordan it was a fertile and well populated land. See SmithhGHL 5391; SchurerjPTX II. i. 2-4.

66. On Bethany and Jericho see BDs and, for the latter, SmithhGHL 266 ff.

67. Ephraim (John xi. 54) is generally identified with the Ephron of II. Chron. xiii. 19 (Jos. Wars, iv. 9. 9). Robinson located it at et Taiyibeh, 4 m. NE of Bethel, and 14 from Jerusalem. See HastbD I. 728; SBD 3 975.

68. General questions. The mission of the seventy. Luke records two missions, that of the twelve (ix. 1-6), and that of the seventy (x. 1-24). Many regard these as doublets, similar to the two feedings in Mark. So WeisslX II. 307 ff., BeyslJ I. 275, WendtlJ I. 84 f. In favor of this conclusion emphasis is given to the fact that in Jewish thought seventy symbolized the nations of the world as twelve symbolized Israel. It is suggested that in his search for full records Luke came upon an account of the mission of disciples which had already been modified in the interests of Gentile Christianity, and failing to recognize its identity with the account of the mission furnished by Mark, he added it in his peculiar section. The similarity of the instructions given follows from the nature of the case. A second sending out of disciples is suitable in view of the entrance into a region hitherto unvisited. As Dr. Sanday has remarked, the sayings connected by Luke with this mission bear witness to the authenticity of the account. There is therefore no need to identify the two missions. See particularly Sanday HastbD II. 614, also Gil-bertlJ 226-230, Plummer's Comm. on laike, 269 ff. Luke probably gives the correct place for the thanksgiving, self-declaration, and invitation of Jesus, in which the synop-tists approach most nearly to the thought of John (Lk. x. 21, 22 j Mt. xi. 25-30). The return of the seventy (Lk. x.

17-20) followed the woes addressed to the unbelieving cities (Lk. x. 13-16; Mt. xi. 20-24).

69. The destination of the seventy. It is customary to think of them as sent to the various cities of Perea (see AndlOL 381-383). Were it not for the words " whither he himself was about to come" (Lk. x. 1), it would be natural to conclude that they were sent E to Gerasa and Philadelphia, and S to the regions of the Dead Sea. If John's account is accepted, Jesus spent not a little time of the interval between his departure from Galilee and his final arrival in Bethany in and near Jerusalem. It may be that after the withdrawal from the Dedication he went far into the Pereau districts. But John x. 40 is against it. The question must be left unanswered. The messengers may have visited places in all parts of Palestine.

THE CONTROVERSIES OF THE LAST WEEK 70. See GilbertlJ 311-335; WeisslX III. 224-270; AndlOL 421-450; KeimjN V. 65-275; BeyslJ II. 422-434; EderslJM II. 363-478; SandayhastbD II 632 f.

71. The supper at Bethany. John is definite, "six days before the passover" (xii. 1). Synoptists place it after the day of controversy, on the Wednesday preceding the

Passover (Mk. xiv. 1, 3-9; Mt. xxvi. 2, 6-13). John is probably correct. The rebuke of Judas (Jn. xii. 4-8) was probably associated in the thought of the disciples witli his later treachery; consequently the synop-tists report the plot of Judas and this supper in close connection.

72. The Messianic entry into Jerusalem is regarded by Beville as a surrender by Jesus of his lofty Messianic ideal in response to the temptation to seek a popular following. Keim with finer insight says, "Even if it had certainly been his wish to bring the kingdom of heaven near in Jerusalem quietly and gradually, and with a healthy mental progress, as in Galilee, yet. in the face of the irritability of his opponents, in the face of the powerful means at their disposal of crushing him. there remained but one chance, â reckless publicity, the conquest of the partially prepared nation by means, not of force, but of idea. He came staking his life upon the venture, but also believing that God must finish his work through life or death " (JN V. 100 f.).

73. The question about the resurrection was probably a familiar Sadducean problem with which they made merry at the expense of the scribes. On the resurrection in Jewish thought see Charles, Escliatology, Hebrew, Jewish, and Christian, by index. For the scepticism of the Sadducees see also Ac. xxiii. 8; Jos. Wars, ii. 8. 14.

74. On the "great commandment" see EderslJM II. 403 ff.

75. The eschatological discourse presents serious exe-getical difficulties. Many cut the knot by assuming that Mk. xiii. and s contain a little Jewish apocalypse written shortly before the destruction of Jerusalem, which has been blended with genuine predictions of Jesus concerning his second coming. See Charles, Eschatology, 323-329; WendtlJ I. 9-21; HoltzmannnttH I. 325'ff.; and Bruce's criticism in Expos. Gk. Test. I. 287 f., also San-day's note in HastbD II. 635 f.

76. On the relation of proselytes to Judaism see Schurer JPTX II. ii. 291-327. The synagogue in heathen lands drew to itself by its monotheism and its pure ethics the finest spirits of paganism. But few of them, however, submitted to circumcision, and became thus proselytes. Most of them constituted the class of " them that fear God" to whom Paul constantly appealed in his apostolic mission. The Greeks of Jn. xii. 20 ff. were probably circumcised proselytes.

77. On Judas see Plummer in HistbD II. 796ff.; EderslJM II. 471-478; WeisslX III. 285-289; AndlOL by index. De Quincey's essay on Judas Iscariot is an elaborate defence.

THE LAST SUPPER 78. GilbertlJ 335-354; WeisslX III. 273-318; Ed-erslJM II. 479-532; AndlOL 450-497; KeimjN V. 275-343; BeyslJ II. 434-448; SandayhastbD II. 633-638.

79. The day of the last supper. John seems clearly to place it on the day before the Passover â 13 Nisan. See xiii. 1, 29; xviii. 28; xix. 14, 31, 42. Synoptists as clearly declare that the supper was prepared on the " first day of unleavened bread, when they sacrificed the Passover" (Mk. xiv. 12; see also Lk. xxii. 15); this is confirmed by the similarity between the Passover ritual as tradition has preserved it, and the course of events at the supper. Unless interpretation can remove the contradiction, John must have the preference. WeisslX III. 273-282, BeyslJ II. 390-399, accept John and correct the synoptists by him; thus the supper anticipated the Passover. Some hold that John can be interpreted harmoniously with synoptists, and be shown to indicate

that the supper was on the 14th Nisan. So EderslJM II. 508, 5661,6121; AndlOL 452-481; GilbertlJ 335-339. Others believe that a true interpretation of synoptists shows that in calling the last supper a Passover they correctly represent the character, but misapprehend the time, of the meal. For this argument see Muirhead, Times of Xt, 163-169, and read SandayhastbD II. 633-636 and his references. The debate is still on, but the advantage seems to be with those who assign the supper to the 13th and the crucifixion to the 14th Nisan.

80. Did Jesus institute a memorial sacrament? Head SandayhastbB II, 636-638, and Thayer, in Jour. Bib.

Lit. 1899, 110-131; see also Mcgiffert, Apostolic Age, 68 ff. note; Holtzmannntth I. 296-304.

81. The Passover ritual. The order according to the rabbis was the following: the first cup of wine and water was taken by the leader, who gave thanks over it, and then it was shared by all (compare Lk. xxii. 17); then the head of the company washed his hands â Dr. Eders-heim connects with this the washing of the disciples' feet, which changed the ceremony from an act of distinction into one of humble service; after this the dishes were brought on the table, then the leader dipped some of the bitter herbs into salt water or vinegar, spoke a blessing, and partook of them, then handed them to each of the company; then one of the loaves of unleavened bread was broken; after this a second cup was filled, and before it was drunk the significance of the Passover was explained by the leader in reply to a question by the youngest of the company, after which the first part of the Hallel (Ps. cxiii., cxiv.) was sung, and then the cup was drunk; then followed the supper itself beginning with " the sop, " â a piece of the paschal lamb, a piece of unleavened bread, and bitter herbs, wrapped together and dipped in the vinegar, â which was passed around the company (compare the sop which Jesus gave to Judas); after the supper came a third cup, known as " the cup of blessing " (see I. Cor. x. 16); then followed grace after meat; then a fourth cup, in connection with which the remainder of the Hallel was sung (Ps. cxv. to cxviii.), followed by certain other songs and prayers. See EderslJM II. 496-512; AndlOL 488-494.

82. The washing of the disciples' feet. John (xiii. 1-11) says this occurred "during supper" (v. 2), and before the designation of the traitor. Luke (xxii. 23-30) tells of a dispute about greatness among the disciples. This dispute may have arisen over the assignment of places at table (compare Lk. xiv. 7 ff.; Mk. x. 33-45); if so, the reason for the lesson in humility is apparent. See AndlOL 482-484; EderslJM II. 492-503.

83. Did Jesus twice predict Peter's denials? Mark (xiv. 26-31) and Matthew (xxvi. 30-35) place the prediction after the departure for Gethsemane; Luke (xxii. 31-34) and John (xiii. 36-38), during the supper. AndlOL 494 ff. thinks Peter was warned twice, EderslJM. II. 535-537 holds to one warning on the way to Gethsemane. Antecedent probability favors this view.

84. Where in John should the institution of the sacrament be placed? Probably after the departure of Judas (Mark xiv. 21 f.; Matt. xxvi. 26), thus not before xiii. 30. The most likely place is between verses 32 and 33. There is no break at this point, and it remains a mystery why John's account of the passion omitted this central feature of early Christian belief and practice. The omission argues for rather than against

apostolic authorship, as a forger would not have ventured to disregard the leading service of the church in an account of the life of its Lord. See Westcott, Comm. on John, 188.

85. On the possible disarrangement of the last discourses (xiii. 31 to xvi. 33) in our text of John see Spitta, Urchristentum, I. 168-193; Bacon, Jour. Bib. Lit. 1894, 64-76; Burton, Bib. Wld. 1899 I. 32.

VIII

THE SHADOW OF THE CROSS 86. SeegilbertlJ354-384; AndlOL497-588; WeisslX III. 319-381; BeyslJ I. 390-432, II. 448-473; EderslJM II. 533-620; KeimjN VI. 1-274; SandayhastbD II. 632 f.

87. On the location of Gethsemane and Golgotha see AndlOL 499 f., 575-588; and HastbD II. 164, 226 f.

88. On the progress of Jesus' trial by the Jewish authorities, see AndlOL 505-516; GilbertlJ 359-363. The legality of the trial has been carefully discussed by A. T. Innes, The Trial of Jesus Christ.

89. On the form and sequence of Peter's denials, see Westcott, Comm. on John, 263-266; AndlOL 516-621.

90. The Words from the Cross. Matthew (xxvii. 46) and Mark (xv. 34) report one; Luke (xxiii. 34?, 43, 46) adds three, omitting the one found in Matthew and Mark; John adds three more (xix. 26 f., 28, 30). Luke xxiii. 34 is bracketed by Westcott and Hort because omitted by a very important group of MSS. (fr a BD) and some early versions. The saying is almost certainly authentic, though it may have been added to Luke by some early copyist. See Westcott and Hort, N. T. in Greek, II. Appendix, 68; and Plummer, Comm. on Luke, 544 f.

THE RESURRECTION AND ASCENSION 91. Read SandayhastbD II. 638-643; see KeimjN VI. 274-383, for a still valid criticism of the position of RevillejN II. 428-478; see also WeisslX III. 382-409; BeyslJ I. 433-481, II. 474-493; BovonnTTh I. 350-375; GilbertlJ 385-405; Loofs, Die Auferstehungsberichte und ihr Wert; EderslJM II. 621-652; AndlOL 589-639.

92. The last twelve verses of Mark (xvi. 9-20) are omitted by the oldest MSS (KB) and by the recently discovered Sinaitic Syriac, as well as by other versions and fathers. An Armenian MS. has been found ascribing the section to one Ariston, or Aristion, a second century elder, and this explanation of the origin of the verses is widely accepted. The gospel cannot have ended with the words 11 for they were afraid," but no satisfactory explanation of the condition of its text has been found. For a recent hypothesis see Bohrbach, Der Schluss des Markusevangeli-ums; on Aristion as the author, see Conybeare in Expos. IV. viii. (1893) 241, IV. x. 219, V. ii. 401; see also San-day HastbD II. 6381, Bruce, Expos. Gk. Test. I. 454 f.

discussion of textual evidence see Westcott and Hort,

NT in Greek, II. Appendix, 28-51, and Burgon, The last twelve verses of St. Mark (a passionate defence).

Luke xxiv. 51 is omitted by N D and several old Latin MSS. See Pluinmer and Bruce on the passage.

93. "After three days" This formula, which appears often in Mark, is altered in parallels in Matthew and Luke to " on the third day " (see Concordance). Jesus died

on Friday, lay in the tomb over Saturday, and rose very early Sunday morning. Thus he spent a part of Friday, and a part of Sunday, and all of Saturday in the grave. According to Jewish reckoning this was counted three days.

94. Emmaus. A village about 60 furlongs from Jerusalem. Cannot have been the Emmaus in the Shephelah, 20 m. from Jerusalem. May have been el Kubeibeh, 63 furlongs distant on the road from Jerusalem to Lydda. See AndlOL 617-619; but also HastbD I. 700.

PART III. â THE MINISTER I

THE FRIEND OF MEN 95. Bead Mathews, The Social Teachings of Jesus, especially 132-174; see also Kobinson, The Saviour in the Newer Light, 343 ff.

THE TEACHER WITH AUTHORITY 96. See WendttJ I. 106-151; Stevens, Theol. of the N. T. 1-16; Beyschlag, N. T. Theology, I. 31-34. In particular on the Parables see references in sect. A 56. On the content of Jesus' teaching see WendttJ 2 vols. â,

Dalman, Die Worte Jesu; Stevens, Theol. of the N. T. 17-244; Beyschlag, N. T. Theol. I. 27-299; Mathews, Social Teaching of Jesus; Gilbert, The Revelation of Jesus; Bruce, The Kingdom of God.

JESUS KNOWLEDGE OF TRUTH 97. Adamson, The Mind in Christ; GilbertrJ 169 f., 240-242; Schwartzkopf, The Prophecies of Jesus Christ.

JESUS CONCEPTION OP HIMSELF 98. BaldsJ 125-282; Stalker, Christology of Jesus f Holtzmannntth I. 234-304; WendttJ II. 122-183; GilbertkJ 167-228; Stevens, Theol. of the N. T. 41-64, 199-212. On the title " Son of Man" see particularly DalmanwJ I. 191-219; Charles, Eschatology, 214 f. note; against, A. Meyer, Jesu Muttersprache, 91-101, and others. See also Holtzmannntth I. 246-264. On the name "Son of God," see DalmanwJ I. 219-237; Holtzmann Ntth I. 265-278; Stalker, Christology, 86-123; Gilbert, as above. On the personal religion of Jesus see Burton, Bib. Wld. 1899, II. 394-403. For the total impression of the character of Jesus, read Bushnell, The Character of Jesus.

UNIVERSITY OF TORONTO LIBRARY

Acme Library Card Pocket

Under Pat. "Ret. Index File." Made by LIBRAEY BUEEAU

Lightning Source UK Ltd.
Milton Keynes UK
UKOW04f1641280116

267316UK00002B/428/P